FOUR EMPERORS AND AN ARCHITECT

How Robert Adam rediscovered the Tetrarchy

Alicia Salter

With a Foreword by
John Julius Norwich

Lexicon Publishing

FRONT COVER, CLOCKWISE FROM LEFT:
The sculpture of the Tetrarchs in Venice.
Portrait of Robert Adam attributed to George
Willison (by permission of the National Portrait
Gallery). Detail of Plate XLIX from the *Ruins
of Spalatro* by Robert Adam (by permission
of the National Library of Scotland).

Printed in Exeter by Short Run Press Limited

Published by Lexicon Publishing 2013
Copyright © Alicia Salter
ISBN: 978-0-9575719-0-7

To Ray for his limitless patience and to
Guy, Emma Louise and Nicholas
for all their input and encouragement

CONTENTS

FOREWORD

IN THE FIRST CENTURY AD, soon after the birth of Christ, a very curious thing happened. The whole focus of the civilised world shifted to the East. Its centre was no longer Rome, which had become little more than a backwater. Read the Acts of the Apostles or the Epistles of St Paul, and the fact stares you in the face. Both Paul's great missionary journeys were confined to the Eastern, Greek-speaking Mediterranean. Only one of his epistles – that to the Romans – was directed to anywhere in Italy.

This was in no way a religious phenomenon, except insofar as Rome continued to stand for the old classical beliefs – in Jupiter, Minerva, Venus and the rest – which nobody seriously accepted any more. The modern thinkers and scientists, astronomers and mathematicians, were all Greeks – the Greek world extending from Sicily to Asia Minor. Moreover, with Persia now the Empire's principal enemy, the lines of communication from Rome would have been prohibitively long. The Emperor Diocletian – one of the two heroes of this book – seeing how unwieldy his Empire had become, had had the idea of turning it into a tetrarchy, to be ruled jointly by two senior and two junior Emperors; but it is worth noting that none of the four resided in Rome.

Frankly, it wasn't a very good idea in the first place. A ship can't have four captains; the whole experiment ended in tears; and a sorely disillusioned Emperor did what no Emperor had ever done before – he abdicated, retiring to a magnificent palace he had built himself on the Dalmatian coast where, he said, he would grow cabbages. The remaining Tetrarchs had to fight it out between themselves. In 306 one of them, Constantius Chlorus, died in York, and his son Constantine was acclaimed Emperor on the spot; he it was who ultimately succeeded in gathering all the power once more into a single pair of hands – his own – before Christianising the Empire and, in AD 330, giving it its new capital on the shores of the Bosphorus.

There now pass rather more than 14 centuries, until a brilliant and obviously fascinating young Scotsman – a star of the Edinburgh Enlightenment – decided, as part of his Grand Tour, to study the remains of Diocletian's palace, which in his day embraced the town he called Spalatro. (The Italians called it Spalato, and we know it today by the somewhat less euphonious Croatian name of Split.) It was only with considerable difficulty that he was given permission to go, and I was greatly surprised to learn that he was allowed to remain for only five weeks; the monumental volume which resulted, lavishly illustrated by his friend, the artist and antiquary Charles-Louis Clérisseau, suggests that he was there for years.

The book which you now hold in your hands will tell you all about Diocletian and his palace, and about Robert Adam and his astonishing achievement. But it will tell you far more: about the Balkans, about the three other Tetrarchs, and about Adam's subsequent career, not only in his great country houses – Syon and Kedleston to name but two – but also in what was perhaps his most extraordinary enterprise, the Adelphi in London.

Alicia Salter has done a superb job, and deserves our congratulations as well as our thanks. I am certainly grateful to her; she has taught me a lot.

John Julius Norwich

PROLOGUE

LIKE ROBERT ADAM, I made Diocletian's acquaintance in both Rome and Split ('Spalatro' as Adam calls it) and, like him, I was amazed at what I found. Two hundred and fifty years after his visit to Split in 1756, the palace Adam planned to research continues to fascinate visitors. Both Diocletian's Mausoleum and his Temple of Aesculapius survive complete with even their vaults intact. In addition, the entire substructure of the palace remains and is one of the finest examples of Roman construction in the world. Few ancient buildings anywhere have been as fortunate.

Unlike Adam, perhaps, I became intrigued by the other three Tetrarchs – Maximian, Galerius and Constantius Chlorus – and set out to discover more about Diocletian's colleagues. I found a fascinating story. Four men, all of Illyrian stock (and therefore *not* native Romans), had ruled as colleagues and Emperors for 12 years. They remained loyal to each other, willingly sharing titles and openly acknowledging the debt each owed the other. Yet, at the same time, they retained their independence, maintaining separate courts and building extravagant palaces within their individual capitals. These capitals – Nicomedia, Thessalonica, Milan and Trier – spanned the Roman world.

Not only did they build four magnificent urban palaces, but two of the Emperors, Diocletian and Galerius, also built country homes: Diocletian chose today's Split and Galerius picked Felix Romuliana in today's Serbia. This fascination with architecture was to continue into the next generation with Maximian's son, Maxentius. The basilica he commissioned for the Roman Forum broke new ground, winning him a reputation that outshone those of his predecessors. Described as 'one of the great architectural achievements of classical antiquity',[1] the Basilica of Maxentius was to prove enormously influential to subsequent generations.

Between them, the four Tetrarchs controlled the Roman Empire during one of its most difficult periods. While under Diocletian's direction they could successfully bury their differences, but after Diocletian's abdication and departure for Split everything fell apart, leaving a power vacuum which Constantine the Great (Constantius Chlorus's son) was ultimately to fill.

I have had the opportunity of learning about the Tetrarchs in far greater detail than Adam ever had. We both wanted to explore their buildings in Rome and Split, but I was able to research other fragments further afield – something I have enjoyed enormously. In an attempt to get under the skin of these extraordinary men, I have visited Belgrade, Niš in eastern Serbia, Thessalonica in Greece and Trier in Germany as well as Luxor in Egypt and Palmyra in Syria. I have included sections of historical background where I thought it appropriate and where I felt it contributed to a greater understanding of their achievements.

The interpretation of the Tetrarchic period has proved highly tendentious: written sources are few and those that do exist take extreme positions dependent on their viewpoint. This makes it a minefield for someone like myself who wishes to write an accessible history for the non-specialist. Therefore, although aware of the considerable controversy that the period evokes among contemporary historians, I have chosen to limit myself to the narrative of the period and leave the interpretation to others. My version largely reflects the image projected by the Tetrarchs themselves and those who wrote about them shortly afterwards.

All four Emperors grew up in the Balkans, which by then had been under Roman control for many years. This area has an unusual topography, the geographical characteristics of which separate it from the rest of south-eastern Europe. As a result the lifestyle which developed there was very different from that across the Adriatic in Italy and was instrumental in forming a hardy, self-reliant breed of men. The Tetrarchs are little known in the West outside academic circles; in part this is because political events of the last four hundred years have meant that travel to

---

J. Ward-Perkins, *Roman Imperial Architecture* (1981).

8

the area has been at best risky and at worst downright dangerous. This was another reason I felt it neccssary to widen the scope of this book and to delve more deeply into the lives and histories of its participants.

As for Adam himself, I have woven his story into that of the Tetrarchs. Although many people know of him as an influential architect, few, apart from Adam specialists, have more than a vague idea of his three-year stay in Rome, or his friends and working methods there – let alone the importance of his visit to Split and the subsequent publication of his *Ruins of the Palace of the Emperor Diocletian at Spalatro* seven years after his return to England. I have set his time in Rome within the wider context of the period and of the other artists studying there, while limiting my discussion of his buildings to those directly affected by his visit to Dalmatia, such as Kedleston, Syon, Osterley, Bowood, Saltram and the Adelphi.

An interesting postscript is that Edward Gibbon's inspiration to write his *Decline and Fall of the Roman Empire* came to him in the very year that Adam published his *Ruins of Spalatro*:

> It was at Rome on the 15th October 1764, while barefoot friars were singing vespers in the Temple of Jupiter, that the idea of writing the decline and fall of the city first started to my mind.

Gibbon's chapter on Diocletian was to include a detailed description of the palace in Split. He refers directly to Adam's publication and quoted from his preface. Adam thereby becomes one of Gibbon's sources.

My book, *Four Emperors and an Architect: Robert Adam Rediscovers the Tetrarchy*, is intended as an accessible introduction to the history and architecture of this intriguing period. It should also appeal to anyone visiting the countries concerned as there are few books in English at any of the sites. Surprisingly few people know about the Tetrarchy and most would have no idea of any close link to Robert Adam.

Alicia Salter, 2013

TETRARCHIC REIGNS
AND TIMELINE

c.1200 BC		*Illyrians settle in Balkans.*
229 BC		*Romans resist piracy in Balkans.*
AD 9		*Augustus stamps authority over whole Balkan peninsula.*
AD 103–5		*Trajan builds bridge over Danube.*
c.243/4	Diocletian born.	
Nov. 284	Diocletian elected Emperor.	
Spring 285		*Diocletian defeats Carinus at Battle of the Margus.*
285	Maximian appointed co-Emperor.	
287		*Carausius proclaims himself 'Roman Emperor' in Britain.*
293	FIRST TETRARCHY CREATED Diocletian and Maximian become Augusti and Galerius and Constantius Chlorus become Caesars.	*Carausius assassinated and replaced by Allectus.*
296	Diocletian commissions palace in Spalatro.	*Allectus defeated by Constantius Chlorus.*
297		*Galerius suffers reverse at hands of Persians.*
297–8		*Egypt rebels under Achilleus and Domitius Domitianus. Rebellion crushed by Diocletian.*
298/9		*Galerius defeats Persians. Builds palace in Thessalonica.*
301		*Edict of Maximum Prices.*
Feb. 303	*Vicennalia* in Rome.	*Edict of Persecution.*
1 May 305	Diocletian and Maximian abdicate simultaneously. THE SECOND TETRARCHY Galerius and Constantius Chlorus succeed as Augusti and Maximinus Daia and Severus become Caesars.	*Diocletian retires to palace in Spalatro.*
July 306	Galerius promotes Severus to Augustus.	*Constantius Chlorus dies in York and his son Constantine is proclaimed Emperor by his army.*
Oct. 306	Maximian's son, Maxentius, proclaims himself 'Princeps' in Rome.	*Maximian comes out of retirement.*
Late 306		*Severus defeated by Maximian and commits suicide in Rome.*
307	Constantine appointed Caesar by Galerius.	*Constantine marries Maximian's daughter Fausta.*
308	Imperial Conference at Carnuntum which is also attended by Diocletian and Maximian. Licinius declared an Augustus.	*Maximian attempts to unseat Maxentius in Rome; on failing flees to the court of Galerius.*
310		*Maximian commits suicide.*
311		*End of Great Persecution. Galerius dies.*
312	Constantine declared senior Augustus by Roman Senate.	*Constantine defeats Maxentius, Battle of the Milvian Bridge. Diocletian dies aged 66.*
313		*Edict of Milan. Marriage of Constantine's half-sister Constantia to Licinius. Death of Maximinus Daia.*
317		*Christianity declared the state religion.*
324–5	Constantine sole Emperor. END OF TETRARCHY.	*Constantine defeats Licinius at Battle of Chrysopolis. Death of Licinius.*
337	Death of Constantine I [thereafter known as the Great].	

PEOPLE MENTIONED IN THE TEXT

ALLECTUS: Usurper. Carausius's successor in Britain 393–6.

AMBROSE: Saint. Bishop of Milan 374–97. One of Four Fathers of the Church.

AMMIANUS: Author of *Res Gestae* (*History of the Roman Empire*), 325–90.

AURELIAN: Emperor 270–5. Withdrew from Dacia.

AUSONIUS: Poet in Milan c.380 who also describes Trier.

ATHENASIUS: Patriarch of Alexandria. 293–373.

BRUNIAS, AGOSTINO: artist taken to Spalatro and then England by Adam.

CARAUSIUS: Usurper in Britain 386–93.

CARINUS: Emperor 282–5; son of Emperor Carus.

CONSTANTIA: Half-sister of Constantine and wife of Licinius.

CONSTANTINE V PORPHYROGENITUS: Emperor of Byzantium 905–59.

DACIANS: People across the Danube in today's Romania.

DECEBALUS: King of the Dacians 87–106.

DEWEZ, LAURENT-BENOIT: Artist taken to Spalatro and England by Adam.

DOMITIANUS: Usurper in Egypt in 297.

EUSEBIUS: Historian and author of *Ecclestiastical History* and *Life of Constantine*.

FARLATUS, DANIEL: Seventeenth-century Jesuit, author of a history of Illyria.

FAUSTA: Daughter of Maximian, sister of Maxentius and wife of Constantine.

GRAHAME, GENERAL: Commander of the Venetian Army in Spalatro.

GRAY, COLONEL GEORGE: Secretary of the Dilettanti Society.

GRAY, THE HON. JAMES: British Envoy in Venice.

HELENA: Wife of Constantius Chlorus and mother of Constantine.

HOPE, THE HON. CHARLES: Adam's travelling companion on the way to Rome.

JULIUS CAESAR: 100–44 BC.

LACTANTIUS: Rhetor to Diocletian in Nicomedia.

LICINIUS: Emperor 308–24.

MARCUS AURELIUS: Emperor 121–80.

MAXIMINUS DAIA: Caesar to Galerius and subsequently Augustus.

MURRAY, SIR JOHN: British Resident in Venice.

NARSES: King of Persia 293–302, whose wife and family were captured by Galerius.

NUMERIAN: Second son of Carus who died in his litter.

PRISCA: Wife of Diocletian.

SEVERUS: Emperor 306.

SMITH, JOSEPH: British Consul in Venice.

TRAJAN: Emperor 98–117.

VALERIA: Daughter of Diocletian and wife of Galerius.

VALERIA MAXIMILLA: Galerius's daughter by his first wife and wife of Maxentius.

ZENOBIA: Queen of Palmyra 240–74.

CHAPTER I

ROME WAS THEIR GOAL

'Rome is the most glorious place in the world.'
(Adam on his arrival in February 1755)

Rome was it.
Everyone wanted to be there.
That is, everyone in the artistic world.

IN EIGHTEENTH-CENTURY EUROPE any aspiring artist, whatever his medium, had set his heart on visiting Rome. No longer content to acquire his knowledge second-hand, he wanted to see and experience the excitement of its ancient history for himself. This history lay in the stones, the inscriptions, the broken sculptures and the ruined buildings of the legendary city. Such enthusiasm became contagious and it soon spread across the entire continent. The origins of such an idea had been laid in the previous century in two quite separate European centres, the first in Rome itself and the second in France.

Firstly in Rome itself: what was the position there and how much respect did native Romans pay to their ancient heritage? As far as the average Roman was concerned, these antiquities had always been there and were taken completely for granted. In the early days of the Roman Republic, the Forum was described as a wet, marshy area regularly flooded by streams flowing down from the surrounding hills and of no practical use to anyone. However, over many centuries it had proved an ideal gathering point for the townspeople; commercial life of all sorts took place there, news and gossip were exchanged, and it became linked in the popular mind with the great military triumphs of victorious generals and with political tragedies such as the assassination of Julius Caesar. Just as the Forum was central to the everyday life of each Roman citizen, so it inevitably became the focal point of the huge, rambling Empire, acquiring in the process magnificent buildings both sacral, legal and political.

Such was its aura that every self-respecting ruler – which was to include Diocletian and his fellow Tetrarchs – sought to build there, using architecture as a tool with which to perpetuate their own memory. This aura did not, however, prevent scandalous events being played out in public, such as when the ex-Emperor Maximian (Diocletian's trusted ex-colleague) tore the purple robe from the shoulders of his unsuspecting son Maxentius, in full view of the attendant army, and proclaimed himself Emperor in his stead. But such events were rare, and the Forum soon became the theatre not only of

FACING PAGE: **Robert Adam turning the pages of either the** *Ruins of Spalatro* **(1764)** **or the** *Works in Architecture of Robert and James Adam* **(1774). Attributed to George Willison.**

15

ancient Roman history but also of early Christianity, when several of its famous temples were converted into Christian churches.

By the sixteenth century, however, almost all this reflected glory had vanished; handsome monuments, both Roman and Christian, were in ruins. The level of the ground had risen unchecked through the intervening centuries as decaying rubbish accumulated; cattle grazed among the abandoned buildings and noisy hordes thronged the twice-weekly markets held there. Ashamed of this derelict city, the Papacy undertook the renewal of Rome. The Renaissance popes began a process which was to gain a new momentum two centuries later. It was a mammoth task and took several generations to achieve. Successive popes restored churches, wiped away the slums, repaired aqueducts and opened up vistas along the streets (defining them with handsome fountains). Above all they completed the rebuilding of the great church of St Peter's, begun over a hundred years earlier by Pope Julius II in 1512. As part of this transformation, Pope Alexander VII decided to plant a double avenue of elms running from the Arch of Titus, near

the Colosseum, to the Arch of Septimius Severus, just below the Capitol, in 1656, following the path of the ancient Via Sacra.[2] It was a wide ceremonial route allowing much-needed access to his newly refurbished churches within the Forum.

The second event that was to prove so important to the reputation of Rome was the coming of age of the new young king of France, Louis XIV.[3] In 1652, at the age of nine, Louis had been smuggled out of Paris during the uprising known as the Fronde to the safety of his father's hunting lodge in Versailles, then deep in the country. He never forgot the experience, and once he had reached his majority decided to build a new palace out there at a safe distance from the troubled politics of Paris, where he could enjoy the best contemporary ideas in art and design.

To fulfil the young king's expectations, his first minister, Jean-Baptiste Colbert,[4] made clever use of the recently founded Académie de Peinture et de Sculpture. The Académie owed its existence to Cardinal Mazarin, who had wished to unite all the different crafts of Paris under one roof, encouraging their practitioners to work as a single professional body under one director. Colbert's plan was to extend this further by gathering a team of native artists under his own personal control, all of whom

2 This avenue remained in place until the 1880s.
3 1643–1715.
4 1619–83.

LEFT: The Arch of Septimius Severus (AD 203) in the Roman Forum.

FACING PAGE: The Colosseum (AD 72–80) in Rome, erected by Vespasian on part of the extensive grounds belonging to Nero's *Domus Aurea*.

would undergo a similar classical training, thereby eliminating the need to employ foreign artists.

The idea was good; the problem was its implementation. How was he to train the best craftsmen? Where should they look for instruction? Where would their tutors look for inspiration? It had to be Rome. Ever since the dawn of the Renaissance, the city – for all its shortcomings – had been the source of artistic knowledge and research. In spite of its endemic decay and neglect, it was here that the finest artists of each generation had found their inspiration. But such opportunities had been largely limited to native Italians; now, thanks to Colbert, young, talented Frenchmen had the opportunity to compete on equal terms with their Italian counterparts.

One of the first young scholars to benefit from Colbert's patronage was Antoine Desgodetz, sent to Rome in 1676 with instructions to make detailed, measured drawings of the classical buildings in the Forum. After nearly two years' study, Desgodetz

finally published his results in 1682 in Paris as *Les Edifices Antiques de Rome Dessinés et Measurés Exactement*. This work was to set the standard for classical research throughout Europe for nearly a century and to become the key architectural text within his native France.[5] Desgodetz had begun a movement which was to prove unstoppable and was to gain huge momentum in the following century when architectural publications on European antiquities proliferated.

ROBERT ADAM

Artists were not the only ones wanting to spend time in Rome: their future patrons were also no longer willing to be the passive recipients of knowledge gained through pattern books at home. They too wanted to come to Rome to see and learn for themselves. They were, of course, the Grand Tourists, many of them British. These young aristocrats had an enthusiastic appetite for acquiring art, but they also had the wherewithal to support promising artists during their apprenticeship in the city. Apart from sowing their wild oats and widening their horizons, they wanted to bring their purchases home to impress their friends and, in some cases, to introduce new fashions of interior design.

5 Seventy years later, during his own time in Rome, Robert Adam thought seriously of upgrading this publication, which was by then out of print and unavailable. He spent many hours making drawings and checking Desgodetz's measurements, but eventually decided that it was too time-consuming and did not ultimately serve his overall purpose. Desgodetz's two volumes were not translated into English until 1771 and 1795 respectively, many years after Adam's stay in Rome.

One of the most single-minded of the young artists bound for Rome was an unknown architect from Scotland, Robert Adam. Adam was unusually well prepared for such a visit as he had had the benefit of an excellent education in Edinburgh and, from the age of 18, a secure job as an apprentice to his father, William, one of Scotland's leading architects. William Adam was a sophisticated businessman with extensive financial interests in many other fields: investments in coal mines, salt pans, barley and timber mills – to name but a few – had enabled him to buy a small estate, Blair Adam, which still remains in the family to this day. He was obviously very fond of Robert, whom he described as having 'the sweetest disposition with the finest genius'.

Robert's upbringing, as the second son of ten children, had been unusually liberal, his parents holding regular open house to the intellectuals who gathered in the Edinburgh of their day. Edinburgh was home to many of the leading minds of the Scottish Enlightenment which had burgeoned after the Act of Union in 1707. Robert himself was hard-working and ambitious, though possibly rather dreamy at this stage, his determination tempered by an amiable charm (often remarked on by friends) and by a sense of humour evident in his letters home.

By the time he was 27, he had saved the considerable sum of £5,000 – enough to go to Rome, where he was to spend two and a half of his most formative years, 1755–7. This nest egg he owed to the regular summer work undertaken by the Adam practice for the Scottish Board of Ordnance, checking on the forts along the coast.[6] In contrast, another section of the practice entailed work on the interiors of the state rooms of Hopetoun House, where the Earl – who had commissioned an extension to the house from William Adam – treated Robert and his brother John as family. As John Clerk of Eldin was to write on Robert's death, 'The numerous family of Mr Adam and the uninterrupted cordiality in which they lived… formed a most attractive society and failed not to draw around them a set of men whose learning and genius have done honour to that country which gave them birth.'

The immediate family circle remained an important part of Robert's life even at the height of his fame, and on more than one occasion was to rescue what could have been a ruinous financial situation. When he received a long-awaited letter from the Hon Charles Hope, younger brother of the Earl of Hopetoun, suggesting that Robert accompany him on his trip to Rome, he would only accept the offer after discussing the whole matter with 'A Council and Quorum of wise and considerate friends' – ie his mother and sisters at home in Edinburgh.

Once he had the family's approval, Robert accepted with alacrity, for he saw the trip as an essential prelude to his future career. It was an arrangement that suited everybody. Hope, being a member of the nobility, could give him an entrée into Roman society, but at the same time Adam could retain his much-needed independence. Adam would pay his own way, but Hope would buy a carriage and be responsible for most of their travelling expenses. The journey out went well. Hope was only too delighted to include Adam in his invitations and the latter, for his part, had never had such an entertaining social life. Both he and his younger brother James, who accompanied them on the first leg of their journey, enjoyed themselves enormously, fitting themselves out in the latest fashions for the balls, masquerades, suppers and concerts that came their way.

Their route took them through Belgium to Paris and then south along the Rhône Valley to Marseilles and Nice. Always an enthusiast for Roman architecture, Robert was thrilled to see for himself such great feats of Roman engineering as the Pont du Gard and the amphitheatre and temples of Nîmes. It was Florence, however, that was to prove the turning point of his journey, not because of its artistic treasures, which he explored assiduously in the company of his old friend the sculptor Joseph Wilton,[7] but because of his chance meeting with the Frenchman Charles-Louis Clérisseau.[8]

CLÉRISSEAU
Clérisseau, on his way back to France, was staying with Ignazio Hugford, a friend of Wilton's who was a painter and dealer in antiquities. Hugford turned out to be an immensely valuable contact as he knew everyone in Florence and introduced Robert to all the leading artists there, some of whom, such as Giovanni Battista Cipriani,[9] were to reappear in his

6 A coastline considered vulnerable following the 1745 Stuart uprising.
7 1722–1803.
8 1721–1820.
9 1727–85.

ABOVE: The Pont du Gard, Nîmes, by William Marlow (1740–1813). The aqueduct spanned the gorge of the Gardon River, part of a 30 mile water system built by the Romans in the first century AD.

life years later. But no one was to be as important to him as Clérisseau, for the two men struck up an immediate friendship which turned out to be mutually beneficial and was to last for more than 20 years. In many respects it was an unlikely alliance, but to Robert's credit he realised almost instantly how much he could learn from this experienced architect. Although Clérisseau was never an easy colleague, he too was always determined to make the relationship work. After only one week Adam wrote home: 'I have found a gentleman who I am to carry to Rome with me, who will put me on a method of improving myself more in architecture and drawing than I ever had any ideas of.'

Clérisseau was a gifted artist and a born teacher. He had trained at the École des Beaux Arts in Paris under France's leading architectural teacher, J.F. Blondel, and at the age of 24 had won the esteemed Prix de Rome, which had entitled him to study at the French Academy in Rome. Situated in the Corso at the Palazzo Mancini[10] under the directorship of Charles Natoire, the French Academy was a branch

foundation – created by Colbert – of the Académie Royale in Paris. The establishment of the Prix de Rome in 1674 allowed the most promising French artists, sculptors and architects, whatever their financial situation, to live and study in Rome for a period of three to five years – an advantage of which their British counterparts could only dream. Such was its popularity that Clérisseau had had to wait for three years until a vacancy occurred, his arrival in Rome being postponed until 1749. Although a trained architect, Clérisseau's forte was drawing. On arrival in Rome, he had studied under Pannini, a well-known Venetian *vedute* painter, who was also the Professor of Perspective at the Academy.[11]

Clérisseau knew Rome intimately and had spent many hours sketching its antiquities. New ideas resulting from the discoveries at Herculaneum and Pompeii had influenced his technique, combining a pictorial with an archaeological approach: a technique he was able to pass on to his new pupil. His favourite medium was gouache, a form of opaque

10 Today the French Academy is in the Villa Medici just above the Spanish Steps.
11 Giovanni Paolo Pannini (1692–1765). *Vedute* is Italian for 'view' and *vedute* painters are particularly associated with Venice.

watercolour in which the water is mixed with gum with added washes of colour. His drawings display great precision and detail, and yet at the same time express a romanticism which was to prove very attractive to prospective clients. Not only could he impart these skills to Adam, whose learnt medium had been dry architectural drawings, but he could introduce him to the most important members of the artistic communities in the city, both native and foreign. His usefulness to Adam at this early stage of his apprenticeship was incalculable. From Clérisseau's perspective the arrival of Adam, a complete stranger offering him work as a tutor and a return to the life he desired above all else, must have appeared miraculous. For, following a quarrel with the Academy's director Charles Natoire, he had lost his lodging and with it his means of remaining in Rome.

It was on 24 February 1755 that the weary travellers finally arrived in Rome; they had taken four months to reach their destination. The journey had obviously tested the friendly arrangements between Hope and Adam. After only a few weeks in Rome serious differences emerged, with the result that Robert decided to set up his own establishment and hire his own lodgings. By this time he had explored enough of the city to know where he would like to live, and successfully negotiated to hire the Casa Guarnieri on the Via Sistina: an apartment with good reception rooms for entertaining, two reasonable bedrooms (a large one for himself and a smaller one for Clérisseau), and a bolthole for the disagreeable manservant, Donald, whom he had brought with him from home. In addition there was ample space for study, and above all it came with its own domestic staff.

The location, at the top of the Spanish Steps, was outstanding, with a magnificent view of St Peter's in the distance. Adam had scored a considerable triumph in obtaining this apartment for it was, and still is, in the centre of the most fashionable part of the city. As a newcomer he had made a very important statement. Robert Adam was a gentleman; he would conduct his life as such and would soon have all the necessary trappings to fulfil such a position. In a short time he knew all the most interesting people in Rome. He began to learn Italian and was overwhelmed with invitations, all of which he describes in detail in his letters home, and all of which he obviously enjoyed. A young lady whom he

ABOVE: SS Trinità dei Monti and the Spanish Steps, Rome, built in 1723–5 to link the Piazza di Spagna and the Pincian Hill.

met, Miss Diana Molyneux, wrote: 'Lord bless me is it possible that the gay, cheerful and frolicsome Mr Adam that we see at our house is the same studious, laborious and enterprising Mr Adam that we see at his own?'

LIFE IN ROME

It was at this point that Adam began to appreciate the enormity of the task he had set himself and it became clear that he was going to have to make some far-reaching choices. His long-term objective had always been to set up an architectural practice in London, but he was not the only young man with such an ambition. There were other promising young architects in Rome, all intent on making their name back in England. William Chambers,[12] a few years his senior, was already much admired for his designing skills and the Mylne brothers, Robert and William, were fellow Scots and already well known to the Adam family. None of them could compete with Adam's affluent lifestyle in Rome, but Chambers had also recently employed Clérisseau as a tutor (before a quarrel brought their friendship to an end) and Robert Mylne was sure that 'a little studye will make more than one family of architects in Scotland'.

Never very robust and prone to bouts of illness, Adam had to husband his energy, while at the same time working hard to extend his knowledge and skills. Clérisseau had set a demanding schedule of sketching expeditions to explore the major classical remains of the city. These were followed by daily drawing lessons under the tutelage of Laurent Pécheux, especially hired for his prowess in draughtsmanship.[13] Adam wrote that 'Wilton, Clérisseau and in short all my friends, tell me that in order to do anything a purpose in Rome, I must apply to drawing… I must resolutely resolve to lay aside the fik-faks of company'; and again: 'The truth is I am a very promising young man but there is much to be done.'

Adam had always known exactly what he wanted; he was ambitious and had already shown how single-minded he could be when saving up for his Grand Tour. He had a clear idea of his own worth, but could also view himself quite dispassionately. His upbringing had taught him the value of good contacts, and while working on Hopetoun House and Dumfries House he had lived as one of the family or house party, so learning to feel quite at home in such settings. His solution, at this point, was to limit his social outings to those people he thought might be useful to him on his return to London. He also embarked on a collection of paintings, sculptures and interesting 'stones' intended for sale in the future. As lighter relief, he initiated a *conversazione* (the equivalent of a French *salon*) of his own one evening a week, to which he would invite friends and fellow artists such as the Allan Ramsays, Robert Wood and Giovanni Battista Piranesi.[14]

Piranesi was to be a major influence on Adam. They quickly found they had a good deal in common and spent the summer months of that same year drawing together, making expeditions to Hadrian's villa in Tivoli and to the tombs along the Via Appia. Adam and Clérisseau also travelled to Naples to see the excavations in Herculaneum, recently opened to visitors.[15] Such a visit was not for the faint-hearted, as it involved crawling through the ruined houses underground by the light of a flickering torch. It was also necessary to keep abreast of the exhibits above ground in the Museum at Portici, which changed from day to day as new items were added daily to its displays. It was obviously important for Adam to learn about archaeological sites outside Rome, but this was expensive and, to his regret, he never managed to visit Sicily and its magnificent temples of Segesta and Agrigento. However, a trip to the 'Hadriatic Shoar' (as it was popularly known) was suggested for the following summer. Who was it that suggested this visit – an expedition which was to be such an important influence on Adam's subsequent work in England? Could it have been Piranesi? The latter was a native of Venice; and Spalatro, on the Dalmatian coast, was under Venetian rule.

Or was the journey born of Adam's excitement at the discovery of the Baths of Caracalla, or more particularly those of Diocletian, which even today remain an awesome spectacle in the middle of modern Rome? Adam had always been fascinated by the great feats of Roman architecture and had studied them before he ever left Scotland. Encountering the baths in person confirmed his conviction that an in-depth knowledge of these buildings could be of great assistance to his future architectural career. Such was his enthusiasm and admiration for the Baths of Diocletian that he planned a publication devoted entirely to them, entailing very detailed and accurate drawings, together with research into the history and origin of such an enormous structure – all of which he undertook with relish. In doing so he must have learnt a great deal about this controversial Emperor, and this may well have underlain his wish to visit Diocletian's palace in Dalmatia. The book on the baths never materialised but the visit to the palace in Spalatro was to prove invaluable.

12 1723–96. In Rome 1750–55.
13 1729–1821.
14 Allan Ramsay (1713–84), already an established portrait painter, was on his second visit to Rome and became one of Adam's closest friends; Robert Wood (1717–71); Piranesi (1720–78).
15 Workmen digging foundations for a summer palace for the ruler of Naples, King Charles III of Bourbon, had rediscovered Herculaneum in 1738. Access was very restricted. Adam makes no mention of visiting Pompeii, which – although discovered in 1748 – was not seriously excavated until 1764, after his departure from Italy.

BELOW: Head of the
Emperor Diocletian,
wearing a crown of laurel
with a jewel. (Museum of
Archaeology, Istanbul)

CHAPTER II

DIOCLETIAN

Diocletian's origins in Salona; his change of name;
appointment of Maximian and two Caesars. The situation
in the Roman Empire at his election.

'THE TETRARCHY, the Rule of the Four Emperors, Diocletian, Maximian, Constantius Chlorus and Galerius, is one of the most important periods in the history of the classical world, during which the Emperors, born in the territory of present-day Croatia and Serbia, revived within decades the power of the weakened Roman Empire, enhanced the importance of their native region and made it the centre of the civilised world.'[16]

It is no exaggeration to say that Diocletian transformed the Roman world of late antiquity. Not only did he manage to stabilise the rapidly declining power of the Empire, he also managed to halt what appeared to be the demise of the entire framework of government. Upon his acclamation in AD 284, he inherited an enormous empire, already over 300 years old, which had grown out of a proud tradition of republicanism dating back to the foundation of Rome in 753 BC. Encircling the Mediterranean Sea, the Roman Empire then extended as far as Britain and Gaul in the north-west, Spain and North Africa in the south, and the neighbouring empire of Persia in the east. Included, too, were Germany and the Balkans in the north-east, both with volatile borders along the Rhine and the Danube that had been breached continually for the past 50 years.

At first glance, Diocletian appears an unlikely candidate to have had the vision and expertise necessary to stem such a tide of dissolution. His background was unremarkable and might have been mirrored in the lives of many of his fellow officers. But he and his colleagues were the beneficiaries of military reforms passed under Marcus Aurelius Gallienus.[17] These had opened up the leadership of the army to outsiders from different parts of the Empire, none of which any longer required confirmation from Rome. Not only did they increase the speed of promotion by simplifying the formalities which had existed for so long, they also allowed decisions to be taken locally whenever they were needed. Such a move gave army commanders an extraordinary independence and was indirectly to open a path (through acclamation) to the imperium for their most successful generals. Advancement for both political and military aspir-

16 Dragoslav Srejovic, *Catalogue of Roman Imperial Towns and Palaces in Serbia* (1993).
17 AD 121–80.

RIGHT: Map of the Roman Empire under Diocletian illustrating the theoretical division into East and West and including the four imperial capitals of Trier, Milan, Thessalonica and Nicomedia.

ants had until then followed a rigid pattern of rank through various stages known as the *cursus honorum* (sequence of offices), and most provincial governors and legionary legates only reached the rank of consul, the most senior position within this hierarchy. By the time of Diocletian's election all this had been swept away and it was not necessary to get senatorial approval of his appointment as Emperor.

DIOCLETIAN

Born in 244, Diocletian – or Diocles, as he was originally known – grew up in the household of a Senator Aulinus; his father was a scribe and a freedman, which must suggest that Diocles benefited from some form of rudimentary education. Of the rest of his childhood we know very little, although Lactantius[18] recounts that the name Diocles was possibly derived from the town of Dioclea, his mother's place of birth in today's Montenegro. He lived in the neighbourhood of Salona, in Dalmatia, which was the most important centre of Roman administration along the Adriatic coast. Entering the army, he gained rapid promotion: some sources describe him as an intelligent soldier, anxious to understand the problems of his day and skilled at hiding his personal ambition under the appearance of public service. Edward Gibbon in his *Decline and Fall of the Roman Empire* describes his abilities as 'useful' rather than 'splendid'. Perhaps it was this practical turn of mind and the ability to decide which issues were the most important that enabled him to construct a framework which would outlive him and re-establish peace within the fluctuating borders of the Empire.

His greatest gift was to inspire his soldiers with confidence, and it was this sense of trust and innate fairness that was to prove the foundation of his rule, particularly once he had set up the Tetrarchy, the 'rule of four'. As a young officer he had been appointed Dux (leader) of Lower Moesia, where he commanded a sizeable Roman force on the Lower Danube. Moesia, roughly equivalent to today's Bul-

garia, was the most southerly of the four provinces of Illyricum, the others being Pannonia (Hungary), Noricum (Austria) and Dalmatia.

At 40, Diocles commanded the *Proctectores Domestici*, the personal bodyguard of the Emperor Carus, responsible for the Emperor's safety at all times. As such he was in a privileged position, with easy access to his master, who – following two victories, one on the Danube and the other on the Euphrates – died

18 Lactantius was a contemporary of Diocletian and appointed by him to teach rhetoric at his court in Nicomedia. His publication *On the Death of the Persecutors* (AD 315) is one of main sources for the life of Diocletian.

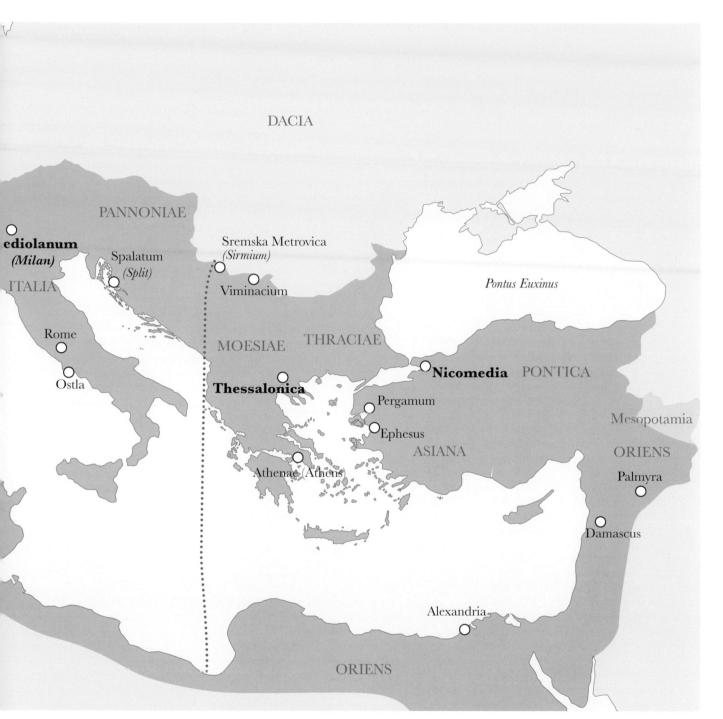

unexpectedly in August 283 while still fighting in Mesopotamia. The accounts of Carus's passing are dramatic: lying ill with fever, the Emperor died when his tent was struck by lightning and burst into flames. Gibbon relates how this storm was so violent that it turned the day into night making it so dark that no one could any longer distinguish his neighbour. The superstitious soldiers were terrified.

Carus's son Numerian – who, like his elder brother Carinus, had been given the junior title of Caesar by their dynastically minded father – had accompanied the Emperor into battle. But Numerian was a gentle, delicate man, who preferred poetry to warfare, and by the time of his father's death his health had been badly damaged by the long months of the Persian campaign. His eyes were so badly affected that he could no longer stand the bright sun, with the result that he had to travel in the shade of a litter, invisible to all around him. He left all business matters, both military and civil, to his father-in-law, the Praetorian Prefect, Arrius Aper.

Following the death of Carus and accompanied by such a delicate patient, the Roman army left the distant banks of the River Tigris, making the long journey back in a series of slow marches. By the time they arrived at the shores of the Bosphorus rumours were rife. Where was Numerian? What was the state of his health? But it was not until the imperial tent was forcibly broken into that his body was discovered. Denying any responsibility for what had happened, Aper was finally forced to announce the death of the young Emperor.

Such disturbing events called for unusual solutions. Diocles, as one of the most senior officers present, decided to halt the whole of the eastern army outside the city of Nicomedia, in the province of Bithynia and Pontus (present-day Izmit in Turkey), so that a grand council could be called to decide on Numerian's successor. The acclamation of Emperors on the field of battle was, by this time, a recognised form of succession and had been practised frequently during previous decades of unrest, but Diocles was the first to insist on such a period of consultation. The day's drama concluded with Diocletian's elevation to the purple with the cloak being laid upon his shoulders amid all the panoply of a military acclamation. Denying Arrius Aper's charge that he was responsible for Numerian's death, Diocles accused Aper himself of assassination and – in an unexpectedly swift move – stabbed him to death in full view of his troops.[19] The date: 20 November 284; the place: Nicomedia.

On hearing of his brother's death and the acclamation of Diocletian, Carinus – whom Carus had left in charge of Italy and the western provinces – wasted no time in marching east to claim his inheritance. The two armies met some months later in the Balkans to fight the Battle of the Margus (where the River Morava meets the River Danube

just south of today's Belgrade).[20] The outcome remained uncertain until Carinus's assassination by one of his own soldiers, whereupon his demoralised army surrendered.

Following this triumph, Nicomedia became Diocletian's most favoured city and he subsequently made it his eastern capital. Situated on the southern shore of the Sea of Marmara at the most easterly point of a small gulf, it would prove an excellent choice. With a good natural harbour for the arrival and supply of fresh troops, it was also a strategically sound mustering point for any military campaign into Anatolia or Syria.[21] He soon initiated an ambitious programme of imperial patronage, creating a magnificent city of which, sadly, there is no trace today.

From the outset of his reign Diocletian demonstrated a surprising confidence in the loyalty of those around him. Contrary to the practice of his predecessors, there were no executions or confiscations of property following his acclamation. Equally, many of the Emperor Carus's officers – most of whom Diocletian must have known over a long period as comrades in arms and loyal friends – were allowed to retain their former positions in the army.

Upon his acclamation, the 40-year-old Diocles adopted a new name – Gaius Aurelius Valerius Diocletianus. His most pressing and immediate need was to safeguard his own life, as over the last half century no fewer than eight of his predecessors had been assassinated.[22] He appointed a body of trusted advisors to surround him and limited his public appearances to only the most important occasions. An elaborate protocol for petitioners was introduced at his court that was to become mandatory for all the Tetrarchs. Visitors brought back reports of a richly dressed Emperor in purple and jewels who insisted on prostration in his presence. Diocletian had probably witnessed the Persian satraps insisting on such behaviour during the long Roman campaign against the Persians.

DIVISION OF POWER AND EMPIRE
A far more significant move, however, was his appointment of a co-Emperor to rule the western half of the Empire. In one sweeping gesture, Diocletian theoretically divided the Empire into two; a division which was only formalised sometime after 303 but which was to remain very flexible during his own imperium. Although a surprising change,

19 There was a prediction that Diocletian would become Emperor on the day he killed a boar ('aper' in Latin).
20 Near modern Smederevo.
21 An intriguing thought is that Diocletian's choice of capital might well have influenced Constantine when he decided to move from Rome in AD 330. Byzantium lay on the northern shore of the Sea of Marmara almost opposite Nicomedia.
22 Gallienus, Salonius, Claudius Gothicus, Quintullus, Aurelian, Florianus, Probus and Numerian.

collegiate rule had been experimented with in the past, and the idea of handing over certain powers to a successor had initiated with Augustus when he appointed Tiberius his heir, awarding him tribunician powers. The more normal practice had been to divide certain powers between members of the same imperial ruling family, as Carus had done with his sons the generation before. Diocletian's move was a new approach and was to prove very effective. In skilfully dividing the Empire into two, Diocletian had, in one swift move, halved the problems of its defence.

As his junior colleague, he selected Aurelius Maximianus, to be known in future as Maximian. Maximian had been chosen with care. He was a fellow general who had served with Diocletian under the three previous Emperors and had been present at his acclamation in Nicomedia. He came from a similar background, being a native Illyrian and career soldier, and was known for his fierce loyalty and devotion.

ABOVE: Two herms: each depicts two of the four Emperors. One of each pair wears the *pilleus pannonicus* from Pannonia. (Museum of Archaeology, Split)

Henceforth each Emperor would be responsible for his own section of the Empire, although edicts were issued, official announcements were made and coins were minted in their joint names. In a further attempt to legalise this new system, each of the two Emperors adopted a *signum* or title, which was added to their respective names. Diocletian chose the name of Jovius, recalling Jupiter, the ruler of the gods, and Maximian chose Herculius, after Hercules, the most famous of all mythical heroes. The portraits of both Emperors appeared on the newly minted coins with depictions of Jove with his orb, sceptre and eagle on the obverse side of Diocletian's, and that of Hercules and the Nemean lion or the many-headed hydra on those of Maximian. A subtle message underlay these titles: Jupiter was the father of Hercules, intimating that Diocletian was in fact the senior of the two partners. The coinage would prove a useful instrument in consolidating this newly established diarchy, the 'rule of two', for it was the custom with each new reign to issue coins in all the chief cities of the Empire. The new coins could define these concepts in pictorial terms to a population still largely illiterate, and they became key instruments of propaganda. By assuming the titles of Jove and Hercules, both Emperors could claim the legitimacy of divine parentage.

Such was the success of the dual imperium that eight years later, in 293, each Emperor appointed a deputy. Under this arrangement the two senior Emperors were known as 'Augustus' and their juniors as 'Caesar'. The new Caesars came from the same background as their Augusti. Maximian chose his Praetorian Prefect, Marcus Flavius Constantius – usually known as 'Chlorus', meaning 'pale'– who had been governor of Dalmatia under the Emperor Carus and an important supporter of Diocletian in 284–5. At the same time Diocletian picked Gaius Galerius, another experienced colleague and military commander, to be his junior. Family links reinforced this new situation with further ties of loyalty and support when the two junior Caesars both divorced their wives to marry the daughters of their respective Augusti: Constantius married Maximian's eldest daughter Theodora and Galerius married Diocletian's daughter Valeria. At the same time both adopted the family name of Valerius and were absorbed into the divine families of Jove and Hercules.

It was agreed, too, that at some indeterminate time in the future the two senior Emperors would abdicate simultaneously, to be succeeded by their junior colleagues, who would in their turn become Augusti. The new Augusti would then appoint two further Caesars – and so the succession would proceed smoothly, doing away with the uncertainty that had followed the death of so many previous Emperors. Thus the Rule of Four was established, each man making his headquarters in a different corner of the Empire: Diocletian in Nicomedia, Maximian in Milan, Constantius Chlorus in Trier and Galerius in Thessalonica. Although the Tetrarchs would, from now on, always be referred to as the Four Emperors, any representation of them in the future

would subtly underline the difference between the two Augusti and their junior Caesars.

On his accession Diocletian – as has been noted – found himself faced with an Empire on the verge of disintegration, attacked on all sides by invading tribes, its borders breached, and barbarian leaders claiming imperial power. The challenges were huge and only a man of immense ability could have overcome them. Having taken the first and most important step with the establishment of the Tetrarchy, Diocletian now embarked on a wholesale set of reforms – of local administration, of the army and of the economy – which were to occupy him for the next 20 years. One of his first moves was to separate civil and military power by appointing civilian governors to the new regions independent of their military commanders. He divided the provinces into 12 large territorial districts called 'dioceses': six in the West, three in Illyricum and three in the Orient.[23]

Frontiers in the Roman Empire varied from one geographical area to another. Some had scarcely any definition at all; others only a road; others, as in the Balkans and in Germany, a river; and others again a physical running barrier, such as Hadrian's Wall in Britain. Trajan's extension of the Roman Empire beyond the natural barrier of the River Danube had proved unsustainable, and by the end of the third century every Emperor's chief concern was to contain what already lay within the imperial borders. Many of these borders were constantly under threat, causing the army to be dangerously overstretched. On parts of the Rhine and Danube the legions were stationed at strategic points along the bank, sometimes so close to the water that fortresses were washed away and had to be rebuilt further inland. One of Diocletian's most pressing needs was to strengthen these frontiers.

At the same time he enlarged the army, created new legions of mobile troops which could travel quickly to any theatre of war, and repositioned units that already existed. By rebuilding and updating many of the camps and fortresses along the threatened frontiers, he improved the ordinary soldiers' living quarters and, as a result, their survival rates. He set in motion a massive building programme. Undefended cities were given walls, and fortress architecture was adapted to meet the new requirements. Each camp was to have only one small entrance; towers were added along the defensive

---

23 West: Britanniae, Galliae, Viennensis, Hispaniae, Africa and Italia.
Illyricum: Pannoniae, Moesia, and Thracia.
East: Asiana, Pontica and Oriens.

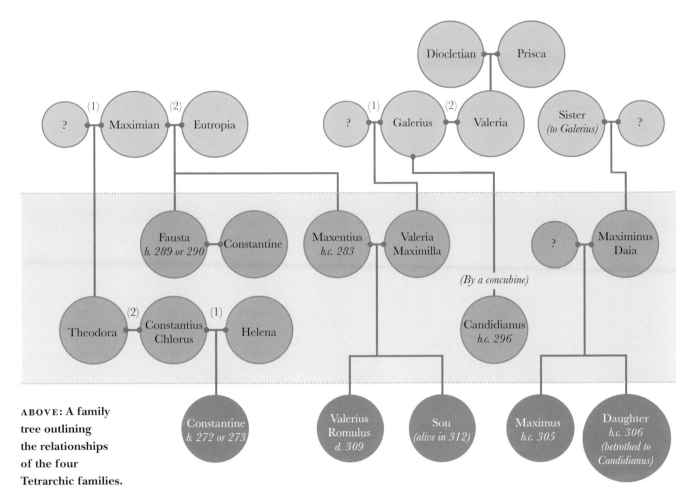

ABOVE: A family
tree outlining
the relationships
of the four
Tetrarchic families.

walls, while fan-shaped turrets were built on the corners to give an all-round view of the surrounding countryside. Both Diocletian and Constantius Chlorus followed this format when building their own camps in Spalatro and York.

All this was effected at a time when the economy was already suffering from high inflation and a debased coinage. One of the important measures Diocletian took was to ensure that every soldier received regular wages. The poor quality of the coinage was of particular concern, as coins were regularly clipped for their silver content, while many coins disappeared from circulation altogether. To counter this, Diocletian introduced special taxes payable only in silver or gold in order to gain enough precious metal for the treasury. In an effort to evade such demands, many of his subjects buried hoards of coins and silver, some of which have since been excavated: examples are

the Beaurains Hoard (Arras) c.315 discovered in 1922 in France, and the Sevso Silver in the 1980s in Hungary. The Arras Hoard, in the British Museum, has proved an extremely valuable historical tool, enabling scholars to further their research into the Tetrarchic period, while the Sevso Silver remains a mystery, with criminal overtones to this day.

Although Diocletian overcame many of the administrative and financial difficulties which had dogged his predecessors, perhaps his most enduring change was to act independently of the Establishment in Rome. The fact that he and Maximian visited the Eternal City only once, 20 years after their accession, shows how unimportant they felt it to be. By setting up his strategic centres of rule elsewhere within the Empire, Diocletian was setting a precedent which was eventually to lead to the demise of Rome as the imperial capital of the Roman Empire under Constantine. For the first time in 600 years Rome was no longer the centre of Empire, and it became apparent that 'The real Rome is where the Emperor is'.[24]

24 Used by Herodian, AD 170–240, in his *History of the Roman Empire from the Death of Marcus Aurelius* and then reiterated by the Panegyrist at the meeting of Diocletian and Maximian in Milan in 291.

BELOW: A view of modern Split showing the waterfront (the ancient *cryptoporticus*) of Diocletian's palace and the campanile of the Cathedral. The Dinaric Alps are in the background.

CHAPTER III

DIOCLETIAN'S PALACE AT SPALATRO

Adam's reasons for choosing Spalatro as the site of his original research. The difficulties he encountered on arrival. The building of the palace by Diocletian.

THE CITY OF ROME may have lost some of its political cachet under the Tetrarchs, but historically this was merely a blip. By the eighteenth century it had long since regained its original prestige and was looked upon as the centre of the artistic world.

As the time of his departure from the city drew near, after two and a half years during which he had worked extremely hard, Adam extended his remit to include domestic buildings in addition to the temples, which had taken up the greater part of his time there. The largest proportion of work in any future practice would logically be domestic; any temples that might be commissioned would only be additions to parks or landscapes under the general heading of 'follies'. This was perhaps one of the overriding reasons why he finally chose Spalatro as his one area of original research. He wrote: 'I could not help considering my knowledge of architecture imperfect unless I should be able to add the observation of a private edifice of the Ancients to my study of their public works.'

In addition to what he had heard from Piranesi, he tells us in his preface to *Ruins of Spalatro* that he had read descriptions of Diocletian's palace by both the Emperor Constantine V Porphyrogenitus and the Jesuit Daniel Farlatus.[25] He therefore knew, from his reading of these travellers' accounts, that the palace had 'never before been observed with any accuracy or drawn with any taste'.

Adam left Rome reluctantly. First he had to pack up his antiquities, which by now filled one whole room of the Casa Guarnieri, and dispatch them to an agent in Leghorn on the first leg of their journey to London. Secondly, he had to buy a trunk to house his large portfolio of drawings, which he never let out of his sight throughout the long journey home. These drawings were to prove most useful in the establishment of his practice once he had settled in London, as they illustrated his ideas to potential clients, informing and exciting them in equal measure. They demonstrated not only how conversant he was with ancient architecture, but also how he could bring his knowledge of the past

---

25 Emperor Constantine V Porphyrogenitus (born in the purple) of Byzantium wrote in the tenth century and Farlatus in the seventeenth century. Farlatus claimed that Diocletian's body had been discovered 200 years before in one of the corner towers, an idea of little credence and never confirmed.

to bear upon the present. It was the influence of
these drawings which was to transform his architecture and make him one of this country's most
successful and well-known artists.

VENICE

His journey home in 1757 was carefully planned.
In addition to Spalatro and Pola (both in Dalmatia) it was to include Venice and Vicenza. But the
visit to Spalatro did not materialise as intended.
Unexpected difficulties arose, as permission to
visit Dalmatia could only be obtained in Venice. It
was a difficult time politically since – after a short
interlude following the end of the War of the Austrian Succession in 1748 – Europe was once again
embroiled in conflict. The Seven Years War had
broken out in late 1756, with Britain and Prussia
lined up against France, Austria, Sweden and Rus-
sia. Dalmatia was ruled by Austria; Venice was her
important ally with immediate responsibility for the
security of Spalatro, and neither nation relished
the idea of an unknown Englishman visiting this
strategically important site. Adam probably did not
understand the political consequences of what to
him must have seemed a distant war, but his impa-
tience to travel before official permission arrived
was to backfire and meant that his visit to Spalatro
had to be limited to five short weeks.

Although by now Adam must have been familiar
with bureaucratic delays, his overriding anxiety was
probably financial, for he liked to travel in style and
he still had a long, expensive journey ahead of him
after he left Italy. He had in recent months been trying to persuade James, his younger brother, to join
him in Rome and wrote that, had this taken place,
they could have gone to Sicily and Greece together.
It would also have injected further capital into the
travelling purse. James, however, was not keen. He
was to have his own Grand Tour a few years later;
he had no wish to travel in Robert's shadow and
his savings were still insufficient to travel independently. He also wished to be in London on Robert's
return so as to take an active role in setting up the
new practice.

The party set out from Rome in June. Adam
shared one coach with Clérisseau and the two
young draughtsmen who had been part of his
entourage at the Casa Guarnieri, while the Allan
Ramsays followed in another. He received a warm
welcome from the British contingent in Venice and
his collection of drawings drew much admiration.
The British Resident, John Murray, and his wife,
Lady Wentworth, together with the British Consul,
Joseph Smith,[26] were very useful to him in his quest
for a permit to visit the military fortress of Spalatro.
Anxious to obtain this permit as quickly as possible,
he visited Consul Smith in his villa on the mainland
to seek his advice. To his delight he was treated to a

---

26 1674–1770.

viewing of Smith's renowned picture collection (the sale of which – to the young King George III – his brother James was to negotiate a few years later). Also in Venice, Adam ran into an acquaintance he had met on his outward journey from Britain three years earlier. A fellow Scot, General William Grahame of Bucklivie was at that moment commander of the Venetian land forces in Dalmatia. Grahame then introduced Adam to Count Antonio Marcovi, the Governor at Arms in Spalatro who was an engineer and a native of Dalmatia. As good fortune would have it, both men were about to go to inspect the garrison at Spalatro. They were to prove immensely valuable to Adam.

Permission to visit Spalatro was promised, but rather than wait until the papers arrived, Adam decided to sail for Dalmatia immediately. It was hot and he was impatient to get started. He hired a felucca, stipulating that it should have a double awning to shade the decks, and made sure that he took his own bed and bedding and a plentiful supply of wine and provisions. Adam had never been one to stint on his comforts. Once they had crossed the Adriatic, a sea well-known for its sudden squalls, he ordered the skipper to follow the coast so that should it get too hot or stormy they could all sleep on shore. The party set sail on 11 July, arriving on the 22nd.

SPALATRO

His first stop was Pola in Istria (today's Pula), some way north of Spalatro. It has handsome Roman remains to this day, including an enormous amphitheatre dating from the time of Augustus, which a few years earlier would have enthralled Adam. He did a few drawings but – discovering that two old friends from Rome, James Stuart and Nicholas Revett, had already been there the previous year – he moved on quickly. Sailing into the harbour of Spalatro, he was thrilled. The situation of this ancient city nestling inside the old Roman palace, the Romanesque campanile rising above the walls and a few medieval houses built haphazardly against them, made for a very picturesque scene. Such a setting would have had an immediate appeal. Clérisseau and the two draughtsmen would have shared his excitement, and they must all have looked upon this whole expedition as a huge adventure. The journals of earlier travellers, Adam felt, had not done it justice.

To their surprise the Adam party found themselves very unwelcome. Unable to find accommodation – Spalatro being a military outpost, there were no hotels or lodging houses available – they were forced to appeal to General Grahame and Count Marcovi. Thanks to their influence, they eventually rented an empty house, which to their dismay also required furnishing. Worse was to come. On inspecting the remains of the palace more closely, they found that much of it had been rebuilt. Old materials had been reused indiscriminately, and in order to interpret what remained they had to dig down some way into the foundations. Adam felt that he might have made some useful discoveries 'had not the repeated alarms and complaints of the inhabitants prevailed upon the Governor to send me the most positive orders to desist'.

The garrison's suspicions were increased further by Adam's and Clérisseau's sketching expeditions into the countryside – an area only recently brought under Venetian control. Once again, as in Roman times, the rugged hinterland of the Dinaric Alps had proved a problem to the invaders. The local population, already averse to Venetian domination, had enough cover there to mount sporadic raids against this unpopular occupation. As no official permission for the Adam party had yet arrived, the officers of the garrison began to suspect them of being British spies sent to test the strength of

this military outpost and reconnoitre the surrounding countryside. Adding to the uncertainty, but unknown to Adam, there were rumours of a squadron of British warships in the Adriatic.

When permission from Venice finally did arrive it was not favourable to Adam, warning the garrison to keep a close eye on the visitors. They were forbidden to go outside the town, and had to restrict their researches to the inside of the palace, well away from the sixteenth-century fortifications regularly patrolled by Venetian soldiers. Luckily, as Adam explained in a letter to his sister, they had by then completed most of the exterior work. At his suggestion a Venetian officer was allocated daily to oversee them. Instead of staying until the end of August, as they had intended, the Adam party left after five weeks of hard, dusty work in extremely hot conditions.

PALACE ORIGINS

What had they found? Did the palace live up to their expectations? Considering the problems they encountered – and that they were all amateurs in the fields of both archaeology and history – their achievement was remarkable. Today Croatian historians acknowledge that Adam's *Ruins of Spalatro* is the first scholarly study of the palace. The folio is fully illustrated with well-executed plans and drawings. Following the example of Palladio and Piranesi, he used the remains that he found there as fingerposts for his reconstructions.

As for the history behind this remarkable monument, Adam's knowledge, for all his talent at second-guessing its origins, must have been comparatively limited. His research had hitherto centred on the Emperor's famous baths in Rome. These had been built according to the accepted traditions of the time, but had not had any private input from the Emperor himself: Diocletian had not seen them until he attended their official opening in AD 303.

The palace here, however, was Diocletian's personal achievement, over which he had taken a great deal of care. He had commissioned it in 296, specifically for his retirement; the area he chose had been familiar to him since boyhood, and it is still a particularly beautiful spot, right on the sea. On early maps such as the *Tabula Peuntigeriana*, its name is written as *Spalatum*, and derives from 'aspalathos', the Greek word for Spanish broom, which flowers profusely here in the early spring. This favourable location was only a few miles east of Salona. Salona

ABOVE: Reconstruction of Diocletian's palace by E. Hébrard, 1912.

A. North Gate
   (Porta Aurea)
B. Temple of Jupiter
   (Diocletian's
   Mausoleum)
C. Vestibule & Sala Regia
D. Temple of Aesculapius
E. *Cryptoporticus*
F. Great Hall
   (Basilica below)
G. *Peristyle*

LEFT: Map of
Croatia today.

35

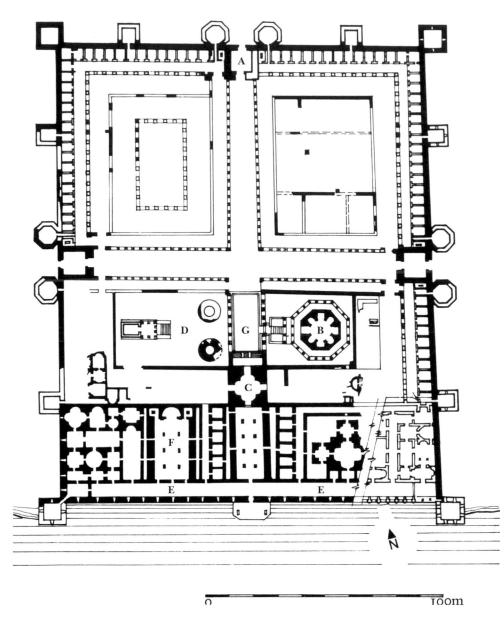

A. **North Gate**
   (Porta Aurea)
B. **Temple of Jupiter**
   (Diocletian's Mausoleum)
C. **Vestibule**
D. **Temple of Aesculapius**
E. *Cryptoporticus*
F. **Great Hall**
   (Basilica below)
G. *Peristyle*

0   100m

FACING PAGE: **The North Gate (Porta Aurea) and reconstructed view. The richly decorated façade provided a theatrical backdrop for sculpture, which might have included a statue of each of the four Tetrarchs.**

was the most important city in the area and the centre of Roman administration along this middle section of the Dalmatian coast. It was obviously an ideal situation.

Diocletian had always been an enthusiastic patron of architecture, and by the time he came to plan his palace he was a seasoned builder, well able to benefit from his past experiences. His military campaigns across the Empire had introduced him to cultures very different from his own, and Egypt and Syria were to become particular sources of inspiration to him. Later archaeological research tells us that there was already some form of construction on his chosen site, as traces of two wells

from an earlier building remain in the basement, although nothing further has been discovered. The name of the palace's architect is unknown, but there are mason's marks in the basement halls, together with the names of two Greek craftsmen: one, 'Filotas', carved on the base of one of the columns encircling the mausoleum, and the other, 'Zotikas', on a capital over the north gate. Diocletian would have known of Galerius's team of sculptors and masons working on his own palace in Thessalonica and might well have engaged a number of Greek craftsmen with similar skills to work in Spalatro.

The palace covered an area of nine acres, which sloped gently down to the sea. Good local building stone from the island of Brac and the Seget quarries near Trogir was plentiful. For the more decorative elements such as columns and capitals, Diocletian looked to the East and imported marble from Greece and granite from Egypt. Tufa came from the nearby riverbed and bricks were made locally.

Diocletian had planned his new palace as a fortress, with safety as its highest priority. The many permanent military bases he had already built across the empire had proved that a camp could supply comfortable living space as well as the necessities of defence. The rectangular castrum plan could easily be divided into four sections by the two cross streets, the *decumanus* and the *cardo*, allowing ample room for the religious and residential areas Diocletian required in the southern half.[27] Three of the four perimeter walls and their gates survive almost intact. Built of rubble and faced with large blocks of cut stone, each corner of the four walls is reinforced by a square tower, while octagonal towers frame each gate. Further towers, a total of 16 in all, add reinforcement along the length of each wall. Each of the three gates had a double entrance, one behind the other, with a small courtyard in

between, known as a *propugnaculum*, a feature with which Diocletian would have been familiar from the city of Salona. The north gate, on the landward side, was the main entrance to the palace and led directly to the imperial apartments through the peristyle (an open-air courtyard around which stood the most important buildings). Subsequently nicknamed the Porta Aurea, the 'Golden Gate', it was designed to proclaim the importance of the Tetrarchy and is decorated accordingly. Two round-headed niches at either side of this entrance originally held sculptures and were framed by columns set up on elaborate consoles. A further seven deep segmental arches appear above them, all of which were also framed by columns and consoles.

Such a theatrical backdrop must have been designed to convey a particularly important message; but what was this message? Whose images stood on those lavishly carved consoles? The Arch of Constantine, built a few years later in Rome, may possibly point the way to an understanding of this grand façade. Inserted into this Arch, together with other bits of earlier sculpture, Constantine included a small sculpted panel which depicts the famous monument commissioned by Diocletian and his fellow Tetrarchs to celebrate their *vicennalia*, the twen-

---

27 The *decumanus* ran east–west and the *cardo* north–south; the forum was often at the intersection of the two, although not in Spalatro.

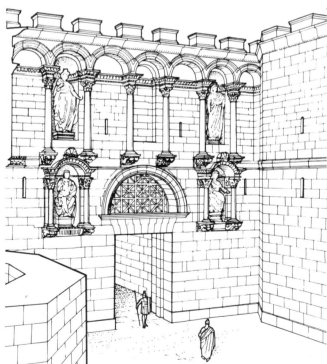

tieth year of their reigns. Forming the background to the action is Diocletian's new Rostrum, where there are five columns, four of which each support a statue of a Tetrarch, while the fifth in the centre holds a statue of Jupiter. Was there something similar here in Spalatro? On the attic storey of the Porta Aurea are five barely discernible column bases, which possibly held similar sculptures of Jupiter and the Four Tetrarchs. They were a familiar theme at the time and were repeated all over the Empire.

PALACE DESIGN

The palace was well guarded: sentry walks ran around the interior circumference of the palace walls. An extraordinary relic of these internal walkways lies in the two tiny medieval chapels inserted into the thickness of these passages and guard-rooms over the north and west gates.[28] One of these minute pre-Romanesque Christian chapels, only about a metre and a half wide, dates from the eleventh century and is in constant use today by the nuns of the small Benedictine monastery situated there. It is a fascinating twist of history that the walkways built to provide a safe passage for the Roman soldiers around the palace of Diocletian continued to fulfil the same function for generations of Christians who, many years later, also found their lives equally threatened. Being adaptable to the needs of successive generations has ensured the survival of Diocletian's palace through the ages.

The south wall overlooked the sea and was both the Emperor's window on the world and the entrance to his private apartments. A raised walkway with an open arcade provided an uninterrupted view along the seafront.[29] Articulated by half columns with three tripartite loggias set at intervals along the wall, it would have formed an impressive sight from afar. This area was for the exclusive use of the Emperor and his family: his privacy in retirement was all-important and no one anticipated any danger from the sea. A small, insignificant entrance at ground level led to the quay, while the sentries were relegated to the topmost level of the wall, leaving the middle level free of interruption. The half columns of the *cryptoporticus*, as this section is called, consisted of stone drums with the entablature breaking out over each one independently.[30] Such a decorative arrangement, which contrasts so strongly with the other three walls, suggests that this wall was covered in stucco and painted, so hiding the jointures of the column drums. The corridor along the *cryptoporticus* gave access to the Emperor's lavish apartments, which were situated immediately behind it.

Of these private apartments, only the impressive Vestibule survives today: a circular room with four semi-circular niches set into the wall. The Vestibule housed a shrine dedicated to Vesta, goddess of the hearth, hence its name. Today it is bare of its original marble panelling and mosaics, but sad as the unadorned wall may be, it is nonetheless a fascinating illustration of contemporary building methods. Narrow courses of Roman brick interspersed with those of rough stone are all held together by mortar. Relieving arches of brick were inserted into the wall for reinforcement; this was an old device used as long ago as AD 128 in the Pantheon in Rome, and still obviously thought of as a structural necessity in Diocletian's time. Any arch, once the keystone is in place, is self-supporting; inserting an arch into a solid wall will therefore give it additional strength to resist the thrust of the vault. Unfortunately the Vestibule vault no longer exists and all we are left with is a large open hole in its place, the sheer size of which underlines the necessity for strong walls. However, the beautifully carved

28 St Martin's Chapel and the Chapel of Our Lady of the Belfry respectively.
29 Half hidden, today, by houses built above the wall.
30 A *cryptoporticus* is normally a covered passage below ground lit by splayed openings above. This one is unusual, being a gallery of columns affording a continuous view of the sea from above.

FACING PAGE, TOP: Panel from the Arch of Constantine. Constantine (headless) declaims from Diocletian's Rostrum. (Note the columns and statues in the background.)
BOTTOM: St Martin's Chapel, built within the thickness of the old Roman wall of Diocletian's palace.

ABOVE: Two views of the south front of Diocletian's palace today showing remains of the *cryptoporticus*, once open with a walkway behind. (The attic storey and windows were added at a later date.)

TOP: Two views of
the Vestibule and
Mausoleum roofs taken
from the campanile.

ABOVE: A section of the
elaborately carved door
frame of the entrance to
the Mausoleum.

door frame is still there, virtually complete, standing as witness to the skill and craftsmanship lavished on this much-loved building.

Guests would have approached the imperial presence from the landward side through the Porta Aurea, continuing directly into the *peristyle*. The Emperor received them standing on the *prothyrum* – a balcony and portico combined, expressly designed to be the impressive backdrop to such an audience. The *prothyrum* stood on four granite columns above which was a triangular pediment, where surviving grooves indicate the existence of a large sculpture, possibly a *quadriga*.[31] The grandeur of the *prothyrum* suggests that the same design was possibly repeated again on the eastern side of the *peristyle* to create an equally grand entrance to the Temple of Jupiter.

The *peristyle* and the temples are at the very centre of the palace complex and, as the religious centre, were given the most elaborate architectural treatment. The rectangular *peristyle* is enclosed on three sides by an elevated arcade of granite

31 A *quadriga*, symbolising victory, is a chariot drawn by four horses, as on the Wellington Arch at Hyde Park Corner in London.

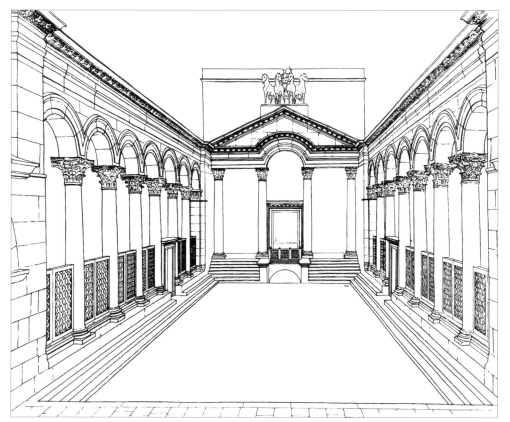

ABOVE: The *peristyle* and *prothyrum* today. The two side doors are entrances to two chapels inserted in the seventeenth century, as are the niches above.

LEFT: Reconstructed view showing the *quadriga* and the lattice work panels between the columns. Below the door to the Vestibule is the arched entrance to the basement levels.

monolithic columns, varying in colour from rose to grey. Diocletian probably shipped these and the 11 sphinxes found here directly from Egypt after his successful campaign in 297–8. Proof of the columns' reuse is the slight variation in heights, cleverly compensated for by the different-sized bases, which are carefully graded to form a level springing for the arches above.

The *peristyle* and its arches reflect some of the architectural influences absorbed by Diocletian on his travels in the East; the lintels of the three land gates, with their open arches above horizontal transoms, and the *prothyrum* indicate others. Diocletian certainly knew the delightful Temple of Hadrian in Ephesus. In a prominent position on the main street of Ephesus, it has a portico of two Corinthian columns with a pediment, below which run an architrave and decorated frieze. This then curves into a graceful arch at the centre to form a charming entrance into the tiny *cella*, the inner

32 This style is sometimes called 'Syrian' because it appeared in Syria as early as the ninth century BC. Similar arcading is also found in the third-century Propylon in Miletus and in the gateway at Perge, both in Turkey, as well as in structures built for the Tetrarchs in Palmyra and Luxor. (S. McNally, *Architectural Ornament of Diocletian's Palace in Split*, 1996.)

each Tetrarch) are by Iunius Tiberianus, Proconsul of Asia, of which Ephesus was the administrative centre. That to Diocletian reads:

Bona Fortuna
Optimo clementissimoque
principi domino nostro
Diocletiano invicto Aug (usto)
Iunius Tiberianus v (ir) c (larissimus)
procos. Asiae d (evotus) n (umini) m (aiestatati) que eius

translated as:
Good Fortune
To the most excellent and most merciful Prince, our Lord Diocletian, the unconquered Augustus
Iunius Tiberianus, of senatorial rank, proconsul of Asia
In devotion to his divine nature and majesty.

chamber.[32] The temple was built in AD 118, but the probability is that Diocletian restored it and placed a statue of himself and his three colleagues on the four separate columns in front of it. The bases of these columns, together with their original inscriptions (although now almost illegible), remain there to this day. The statues themselves, which stood on wreaths, have disappeared: they were probably made of bronze and melted down for the value of the metal at a later date. The dedications (one for

Another source for Diocletian's *peristyle* and *prothyrum* may have been two buildings in Palmyra, the Propylaea of the Sanctuary of Bel and the arch which terminated the upper colonnaded street. In both instances a tall arch is framed by a pediment supported on four columns and an elaborate carved entablature.

ABOVE: A capital from Diocletian's palace.
LEFT: Engraving of the Temple of Diocletian in Palmyra, from *Dictionary of Words and Things* by Larive and Fleury (1895).

FACING PAGE, TOP: The Temple of Hadrian in Ephesus, built to commemorate the Emperor's visit in AD 128 but restored in honour of Diocletian, as the column bases indicate.
BOTTOM: The four column bases inscribed with the name of each Tetrarch, unfortunately barely legible today.

ABOVE: The interior of Diocletian's Mausoleum. BELOW: Detail of the peristyle colonnade today, with Adam's pilaster on the left.
FACING PAGE: Engraving of the Mausoleum by L.F. Cassas, 1782. Note the two rows of free-standing columns each with an individual entablature, frieze and interlocking fans of brickwork in the dome.

MAUSOLEUM AND TEMPLES

Of the four original temples within the Palace at Spalatro, the Mausoleum, as the Temple of Jupiter is known today, is the largest and best preserved and is a combination of both Eastern and Western ideas. Octagonal on the exterior but circular within, it has eight recesses carved out of the thickness of the walls, as in Western traditions. The dome construction, on the other hand, with its interlocking fans of brickwork converging upwards towards the crown, derives from the East. Although now furnished as a medieval cathedral, the entire structure of the Mausoleum from floor to vault is still the original Roman building designed by Diocletian as his burial place. Unfortunately there is no trace of the original ceremonial entrance as this was swept away with the building of the Romanesque campanile in the thirteenth century – but, as in the Vestibule, the exquisitely carved Roman doorframe survives.

Inside the Mausoleum, which was planned as a family burial place, are two rows of free-standing porphyry columns superimposed one above the other and an elaborately carved entablature. Above is a frieze encircling the entire building with carved garlands, erotes, hunting scenes and two portrait roundels of the Emperor and his wife Prisca. When Diocletian died in 312 he was buried in a porphyry sarcophagus, set in the centre of the temple.

LEFT: Carved doorframe of the Temple of Aesculapius. BELOW: The coffered vault of the interior, with carved masques.

FACING PAGE: The basement hall (basilica). Note the six free-standing piers, the apse beyond, and groined vault.

Of this tomb there is no trace today. Ammianus Marcellinus,[33] in his history of the Roman Empire (published in 391) reported that Diocletian's rich purple shroud was stolen from his mausoleum and the thief put to death.

Opposite the Mausoleum in Spalatro were three small temples, only one of which still exists. Two of them – one circular and the other octagonal – were destroyed as the medieval town expanded and only their foundations remain. The third one, the Temple of Aesculapius, is a delightful example of a perfect small Roman temple. It stood on a podium, approached – as Adam noted – by 15 steps,[34] with a *pronaos* of six columns, four in front and two behind. Nothing of this front porch remains except, again, the beautifully carved doorframe with its highly decorated consoles, which enclose tiny busts in the foliage to either side. The interior, however, is a perfectly preserved *cella* with a magnificent cof-

fered barrel vault. The carved frieze around the wall is an outstandingly beautiful example of late Roman craftsmanship, with small animals frolicking among scrolling vegetation. Both the Temple of Aesculapius and the Mausoleum offer us an exciting glimpse into Diocletian's world and give us some idea of the care and wealth that he lavished on his final home.

BASEMENT HALLS

A staircase below the *prothyrum* leads down to the basement halls, which survive intact. It is unknown whether Adam had a chance to visit these, as his drawings of the *prothyrum* show a continuous set of steps across its entire width. Once again history has played a surprisingly beneficial role, for the halls became a dumping ground for unwanted waste materials. Only cleared since World War II, they remain complete and reflect the chambers above, which formed the Emperor's private apartments.

On the western side are a series of large interconnecting rooms of different shapes, all entered from a corridor along the southern front. The largest of them, known today as the basilica, runs north–south; it has six massive free-standing piers together with an apse and was possibly below the original *sala regia*, the main audience chamber. The room leading off this basilica contains two flights of small spiral stairs, one of which led to the upper floor of the palace and the other to the street above. Roman wooden beams, which must have supported a ceiling structure, sat in the put-holes which are still visible.

The ruins of two sets of baths remain behind the state apartments, but the most impressive suite of rooms – only recently excavated – are those in the eastern basement, which formed the substructure of the *triclinium* or dining-room. This was the venue for *symposia* or drinking parties.[35] Its shape was cruciform, with an alcove in each wall to hold the diners' couches. Reclining here, male guests could enjoy one of the most popular after-dinner pastimes, the *kottabos*. The happily inebriated diners would attempt to topple a small plate, precariously

33 325–91.
34 The reason for an uneven number being that you started and ended your ascent on the same foot.
35 The Greek word *sympotein* meant 'to drink together' at a gathering during which men could debate, plot or simply enjoy themselves, and is the origin of our word 'symposium'.

balanced on a single stand in the centre of the room, with a drop of wine flipped from a long handled spoon or a *kylix*, a flat drinking vessel. The winner's prize was the beautiful serving girl who had attended them all evening. Illustrations of this game appear frequently on plates and vases of the period.

SUBSEQUENT HISTORY

The history of the palace immediately after Diocletian's death in AD 312 is sketchy, but it seems that it was largely abandoned. The few pieces of porphyry now in the Archaeological Museum in Split may be the only surviving remnants of the Emperor's tomb. Under the early Byzantine Emperors the palace was seldom used and almost forgotten.[36] A recently discovered plan labels part of the northern section of the palace *gynaeceia* – 'the place of the women': the thinking now is that this area may have been used for the dyeing of cloth, as it was largely women who handled this process.

The fact that the palace survives at all must be attributed to extraordinary historical chance. When Salona was attacked in the early seventh century by Avars and Slavs from the north, its Latin inhabitants initially fled to islands off the coast as their Greek predecessors had done before them. But once the Avars had disappeared they returned to the mainland, seeking safety inside the impregnable walls of the old palace, still intact even after 300 years of neglect.

This new settlement was a mixture of Illyrian and Latin descendants of old Salona and newly arrived Slavs, and was to form the nucleus of the medieval city of Split, built among the ruins of Diocletian's palace. With the advent of Christianity, Split continued to grow, some sources describing it as half the size of Constantinople. It became an archbishopric. The metamorphosis of palace into city took place in AD 650 when St Domnio's relics were translated to their new home, the old mausoleum of Diocletian. The erstwhile Temple of Jupiter became the Christian Cathedral of Split and the Temple of Aesculapius, the Baptistery. The lively town within the palace walls is today full of people going about their daily lives impervious to the ancient buildings around them, giving it a vibrancy and interest that is so often lacking on ancient sites.

Two views at basement level: ABOVE: The steps to the royal apartments above; BELOW: Roman barrel vault.

36 The Byzantine Emperor Constantine v Porphyrogenitus (905–59) wrote a manual on statesmanship for the benefit of his son, *De Administrando Imperio*, which is an invaluable source for historians, in which he refers to Spalatro.

THE IMPORTANCE OF PORPHYRY

IN CHOOSING PORPHYRY as the material for his tomb, Diocletian was following a well-established precedent. Nero had been the first Emperor to do so in AD 64, since when it had become the accepted fabric for both imperial burials and other important memorials. The only source was Mons Porphyritis in the eastern desert of Egypt, and its rarity lent it a legendary aura. Both Diocletian and Galerius used it frequently and it became their favourite material for sculpted portraits.

Constantine continued this same tradition by choosing porphyry both for himself and his mother, Helena. Helena's magnificent porphyry tomb survives today in the Vatican Museum.

ABOVE: The Sarcophagus of Empress Helena, depicting Roman soldiers attacking barbarians.

Diocletian would have had a similar sarcophagus but probably not so elaborately carved as that of Helena.

Massive in scale, it is carved in deep relief and highly polished, obviously an object on which no expense was spared. Constantine was very fond of his mother and, once he became Emperor, showered honours upon her. She was proclaimed Empress (as the former wife of the Tetrarch Constantius Chlorus) and the city of her birth in Bithynia was renamed Helenopolis. The sarcophagus must originally have been intended for her husband, as it depicts victorious Roman soldiers lauding it over prostrate chained barbarians. The early Christians, following her discovery of the True Cross in Jerusalem, looked upon Helena as a saint, a fact which also accounts for the survival of the unusual memorial at Igel outside her husband's capital of Trier. Today she rests alongside her granddaughter Constantia (Constantine's daughter) who lies in an equally grand porphyry sarcophagus of 50 or so years later.

Jura Mts

Bavarian Forest

Bohemian Forest

Volhynian-Podolian Plateau

Rhaetian Alps

Bavarian Alps

ALPS

Karawanken

Dolomites

Julian Alps

Moldavian Tableland

Hungarian Plain

Apuseni Mts

Transylvanian Basin

Transylvanian Alps

Coastal lowland

CARPATHIANS

Dobruja Tableland

Walachia Plain

Serbian Mts

DINARIC RANGES

APENNINES

Balkan Mts

Black Sea

Rumelian Basin

Adriatic Sea

Rila Mts

Sar Mts

Rhodope Mts

Tyrrhenian Sea

Pindus Mts

Thessaly Basin

Aegean Sea

Ionian Sea

Sea of Crete

Mediterranean Sea

0   200
Km

50

CHAPTER IV

THE BALKANS (ILLYRIA)

*The history and topography of the Balkans; the importance of
Salona; the Via Egnatia and the Via Militaris; Trajan and
the Dacians. Early visitors to Diocletian's palace.*

HOW WAS IT THAT THE BALKANS, known in
Roman times as Illyria, had assumed such an important role in the Empire? How did it come about that
this area produced a succession of men who, against
all the laws of probability, succeeded in ruling one
of the greatest empires the world has ever known? It
is an intriguing story and, as so often, geographical
factors played a vital part.

GEOGRAPHICAL FEATURES

The Balkan Peninsula has an unusually wide variety
of climatic regions, each of which developed independently of the others. The Dinaric Alps – a continuous mountain range which runs the length of
the peninsula – made communication very difficult
between the coast and hinterland. These mountains
run in a south-easterly direction and are a continuation of the Swiss Alpine chain and the Julian Alps
outside Trieste. They continue along the Adriatic
coast for another 400 miles, through Albania and
Macedonia to the Pindus Mountains of Greece. They
form an almost impenetrable barrier to the interior;
passes are few, and lead into a bleak and desolate
hinterland where vegetation is limited to a few poljes.

Poljes form when the roof of a limestone cave
collapses, leaving a small, flat valley with very steep
sides, the floor of which is well below the level of
the limestone pavement above. Over time these valleys, which can sometimes run for tens of miles, fill
with sediment and become very fertile. The mountains themselves are limestone, which is resistant to
erosion, but the corrosive action of acid rainwater
as it percolates through the cracks eventually causes
steep, jagged escarpments, which create high-sided
gorges and canyons. Fissures and channels – often
of considerable depth – open up, hollowing out
whole systems of underground channels. The limestone is perforated with caverns and watercourses,
which appear and then disappear, only to emerge
on the other side of the mountain range, often as
torrents. Writers have compared this landscape to a
petrified sponge, honeycombed with subterranean
rivers, waterfalls and lakes. The local term used to
describe it is 'karst', meaning 'stony' or 'bare'; it is a
particular feature of the Balkans, and can be bleak,
dramatic and very frightening.

For many centuries travel between the Dalmatian coast, and its desolate hinterland on the one

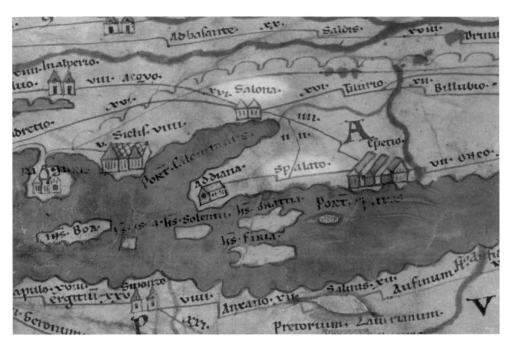

LEFT: Detail of the Peutinger Table, dating from about AD 500, showing Salona and Spalatro.
FACING PAGE, TOP: Salona, with the Dinaric Alps in the background.
MIDDLE: Keystone to the *Porta Caesarea*, Salona. Tyche Salonita wears a mural crown, and in her right hand she holds a banner inscribed MIVSF (*Martia Julia Valeria Salona Felix*, the official name of the city).
BOTTOM: Section of the *Res Gestae* (Augustus's funerary inscription) describing the subjection of Illyria.

hand and the great valleys of its inland rivers such as the Sava and Danube on the other, was almost impossible. Rivers such as the Sava and the Drava in the north flow for many hundreds of miles and collect water from countless tributaries along the way, while those which run from the Dinaric Alps into the Adriatic are short: only four rivers flow further than 18 miles before reaching the sea.[37] Immediately north of the Dinaric Alps the situation is much the same, with the rivers Ina and Drina running a comparatively short course before draining into the River Sava. To survive in such a harsh landscape, people tended to settle in small groups near rivers or along the sea, where communications were comparatively straightforward. Those few who ventured inland developed a very different independent lifestyle, which had little in common with their seafaring countrymen.

The difficult Balkan terrain was one of the factors which hindered the Romans in their attempts to establish control over Illyria. The offshore Dalmatian islands had been first settled by the Sicilian Greeks. These islands are also offshoots of the Dinaric Alps, but broken down and submerged over the centuries. Their strategic value has never been in doubt. The Greek ruler of Syracuse, Dionysius,

was the first to seek control over both the Tyrrhenian and Adriatic Seas, by creating a safe 'moat' of water to each side of the Italian peninsula in order to safeguard his trade routes. He could control the Tyrrhenian Sea from Sicily but he needed a similar base in the Adriatic. His solution was to fortify one of the islands off the northern Illyrian coast, namely Issa.[38] The Greek rule was short, and after Dionysius's death in 367 BC the native Illyrians regained control of the region, striking a mutually supportive agreement with the Romans who, in those early days, had no territorial ambitions upon the area. But later, after the Dalmati, another Illyrian tribe on the mainland, began to mount piratical attacks on their fellow tribesmen and islanders, the Romans were gradually drawn into local conflicts over the following centuries, eventually making Salona – the future childhood home of Diocletian – the centre of their administration.

SALONA

Salona, midway along the Dalmatian coast, was a natural successor to the island of Issa. It was already a merchant and trading settlement, situated conveniently close to the sea. With the benefit of a natural harbour and a belt of islands to protect its shoreline, it had the added advantage of comparatively easy access to the hinterland, through one of the few passes of the Dinaric Alps. In such an unrivalled position, it grew to be the most important Roman

---

37 The Zrmanja, the Kirka, the Cetna and – most exceptionally – the Neretva, which is 225 miles long.
38 Vis, as it is called today, was to be a vital link for the Allies in Word War II to Tito and his partisans.

city in this area of the Balkans, and under Roman administration the native economy grew rapidly. Farming, stockbreeding and fishing were the traditional occupations in addition to which a flourishing new trade had developed, the weaving and dyeing of cloth. Dalmatian cloth remained an important industry long after Diocletian's death. Two new trades introduced by the Romans were brick-making and stonemasonry, produced in private, municipal and military workshops. There are still bricks visible in the vault of Diocletian's Mausoleum in Split stamped 'Dalmatia', and, as has been mentioned, there was plenty of good quality building stone on the nearby islands of Brac and Trogir.

In 48–47 BC, Salona had chosen to side with Julius Caesar in his struggle with Pompey, with the result that it became a Roman colony and was given the name of *Martia Julia Salona* – a distinction bringing with it many sought-after privileges. In earlier times, Roman colonisation had taken place very slowly, and principally within the Italian peninsula: the practice of establishing colonies for retired legionary veterans on the captured land of some former enemy had been very rare. Julius Caesar, however, promoted this policy vigorously, finding it a useful means of retaining control of newly conquered areas.

The title *Martia Julia Salona* put Salona quite literally on the Roman map, encouraging the arrival of both army veterans, who were given grants of land in the surrounding area, and ordinary Roman citizens. Other towns along the coast also became colonies,[39] so ensuring that Rome had a secure base in Dalmatia for the immediate future. Augustus continued his predecessor's policy, and was able to claim in the *Res Gestae*[40] that he had founded colonies in most of the existing provinces.

VIA EGNATIA AND VIA MILITARIS

It was Augustus who brought Rome's protracted struggle to subdue the area to a triumphant conclusion in AD 9. Much of his success was thanks to an early road system set up by previous generations of Roman governors across the Balkan Peninsula, which he in turn extended to cover the whole area. On his arrival in the Balkans, there had been only

39 Pola (Pula), Zadar, Narona (Vid), Epidaurus (Cavtat) and Aquum (Čitluk), to name the most important.
40 *Res Gestae Divi Augusti* ('The Deeds of the Divine Augustus') is the funerary inscription engraved on a pair of bronze columns placed in front of his mausoleum in Rome. Subsequently it was inscribed on temples throughout the Empire, and a copy exists today outside the Ara Pacis in Rome.

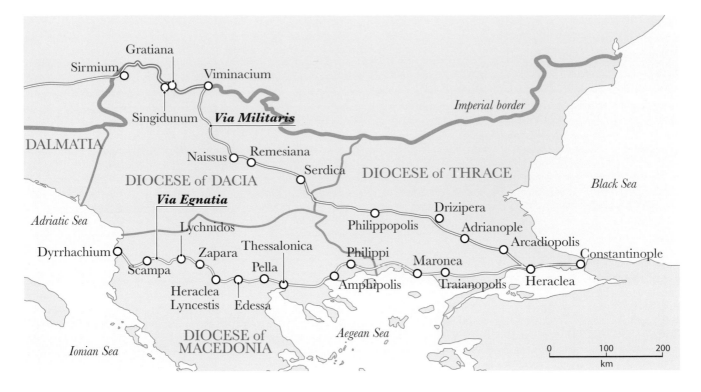

one road that ran in a west–easterly direction, the Via Egnatia, built almost 120 years earlier.[41] This was the main route between Rome and the Eastern Empire, leading from the Via Appia in Rome, south to Brindisium (Brindisi), across the Adriatic to Dyrrhachium (Dürres) on today's Albanian coast and finally to Thessalonica and the Hellespont.[42]

Another route, running parallel to the Via Egnatia but following a more northerly path beyond the Dinaric Alps, was needed to serve the inland valleys of the Sava and Drava rivers – two large and important waterways which run parallel to each other and form part of today's Croatian border. Augustus opened up this great military highway, the Via Militaris, connecting northern Italian settlements such as Aquileia and Trieste in the west and following the course of the River Sava past Siscia (Sisak, Croatia) to

its confluence with the Danube at Belgrade, then the fortress of Singidunum. From here the road turned south, running through present-day Serbia to Naissus (Niš) and Serdica (Sofia) before finally reaching Byzantium (Constantinople) and the Bosphorus. For 400 years this route was the axis that ensured the cohesion of the Empire: the main link between its eastern and western sectors. In addition to the Via Militaris, Augustus constructed eight short roads running north from the Dalmatian coast to the Sava Valley beyond the Dinaric Alps, and south along the coast to Ragusa (Dubrovnik), Dyrrhachium and beyond.

Augustus's campaign of AD 9 allowed the Romans to stamp their authority over the entire western half of the Balkan Peninsula, establishing their frontier along the River Danube. As the *Res Gestae* puts it, 'Through Tiberius Nero, then my stepson and legate, I brought under Roman authority the Pannonian peoples which no Roman army had approached before I became *princeps* and advanced the boundaries of Illyricum to the banks of the Danube.'[43]

Along this stretch, known as the Middle Danube, the river acts as the dividing line between the Balkans and the Great Plain of Hungary, and its immense width was to prove an effective bulwark against the barbarians for several years to come. Augustus, after his long struggle to establish peace, had willingly settled for such a frontier, as did

41 A key source for the Via Egnatia is the *Tabula Peutingeriana* or Peutinger Table (held in the Austrian National Library, Vienna), called after the scholar Conrad Peutinger (1465–1537), who acquired it in 1508. It consists of a long strip of parchment, a copy of the original, which dated from *c.* AD 500. It displays the Roman Empire with highways and cities in schematic form. Seas are coloured green, the land is parchment-coloured, the roads are thin red lines and the buildings are yellow. Another source for the Via Egnatia is the Antonine Itinerary (Bibliothèque Nationale, Paris). This is a codex and consists of a list of places and distances for the use of the Roman army and for delivery of the post. Called after Antoninus Pius (reigned *c.*138–161), it may date from AD 150, if not earlier, but it was certainly revived in the reigns of Caracalla and Diocletian. For a distance of 535 miles it was marked out with milestones, which denote repairs undertaken by different Emperors and form a valuable record of its history.
42 The ancient name of the narrow strip of sea, now known as the Dardanelles, dividing the Balkans and Europe from Asia Minor.
43 *Res Gestae*, Chapter 30.

most of his successors. But Trajan,[44] who came to power in AD 98, felt that the threat from the well-organised Dacian army under their aggressive King Decebalus was sufficient to justify a new series of campaigns. Dacia was rich in minerals such as gold and salt, and would provide much-needed extra living space for Roman citizens.

TRAJAN AND DACIA

In AD 101, on his first campaign, Trajan created a double bridge of boats to ferry his army across the Danube. The campaign was only partially successful. Realising he needed a reliable supply route to maintain his army on any future long campaign, Trajan commissioned his architect and engineer, Apollodorus of Damascus,[45] to build a permanent bridge across the Danube.

The Emperor had already eased the movement of traffic up and down the river by digging a channel to by-pass the dangerous cataracts known to the Romans as the *Porta Ferrea* (Iron Gates), which until then had blocked all navigation upstream. A few

FACING PAGE: Map showing the route of the Via Militaris (orange) and Via Egnatia (green).

ABOVE LEFT: The Danube at the point of the 'Iron Gates'.
ABOVE: A pier of Trajan's Bridge.

miles south of them, the Danube, though still wide, had a constant height of eight metres, and it was at this spot that Apollodorus chose to build his bridge. Over 1,100 metres long, the bridge was built on 20 brick piers, each about 45 metres high. The piers rested on piles sunk deep into the riverbed. To drive the piles into the water, each individual section of river had to be pumped dry to allow drilling into the subsoil beneath the water. Wooden arches, which supported the road above, rested on these brick piers. Today the remains of two piers are still visible on either side of the river, while seven more have been detected using underwater sonar technology. Trajan's remarkable achievements are commemorated by a plaque, the *Tabula Traiana*, set up on the cliffside on the river bank. It reads:

The Emperor Caesar, son of the divine Nerva, Nerva Trajan Augustus Germanicus, great pontiff, tribune for the fourth time, father of the country and consul for the fourth time, has conquered the mountain and the river and opened this road.[46]

---

44 AD 53–117. Reigned 98–117.
45 Born in Damascus, Apollodorus also designed Trajan's Column in Rome and Trajan's Arches in Beneventum and Ancona.
46 One hundred and fifty years later the Emperor Aurelian, believing quite literally that it was a bridge too far, abandoned Dacia and destroyed Trajan's Bridge. Contemporary engineers, however, have endorsed Trajan's choice of site by building a modern bridge only a few yards from this point today.

The completion of the bridge is one of the incidents from the Dacian campaign recorded as a pictorial scroll on Trajan's Column, commissioned as the centrepiece of his Forum in Rome. Much admired and copied by subsequent Emperors, it was to be an inspirational monument for the Tetrarchs. Attempts to decipher and reproduce the individual scenes presented a continual challenge to antiquarians and artists of later centuries; one of the many who made such illustrations and subsequently engraved his own prints was Piranesi, a close friend of Robert Adam.

None of Diocles's friends growing up with him near Salona 130 years after Trajan's reign can have guessed that one day their playmate would return there as Emperor, ushering in a new era for the city. In addition to building the splendid palace which bears his name, he ordered the refurbishment of the city walls and the main gate of Salona, the Porta Caesarea. Built at the time of Augustus, this made an impressive entrance to the city: it was two storeys high, the upper storey being richly decorated with fluted half columns and composite capitals either side of arched window openings. The aqueduct carrying water from the Dinaric Alps had been incorporated into the city walls and reached its distribution point here in a *nymphaeum*[47] situated just inside the gate. There was also a second inner courtyard – the *propugnaculum* – a device that Diocletian was to incorporate into his own palace a few

years later. Evidence of the town's continued prosperity is the survival of a keystone inserted in the mid-fourth century to commemorate the moment it had become a colony: the inscription reads, '*Martia Julia Valeria Salona Felix*'. The figure of Tyche Salonita – the personification of the city as Tyche, the goddess of Fortune – wears a mural crown and holds a standard in her right hand inscribed with the initials MIVSF, while her left hand rests on a granary barrel full of ears of corn (see p. 53).[48]

The local inhabitants, however, were not the only ones who profited. The Balkans' wealth of minerals, in particular gold and silver, was exploited intensively by the Romans. Pliny the Elder describes how as much as 50 pounds of gold could be extracted from some mines in a single day. Nero's Domus Aurea – 'the Golden House' – attests to the quantities and importance of the gold that was transported to Rome. Archaeological remains in the area also point to an important industry in lead and silver mined by immigrants – Pannonians, Celts, Italians and Greeks – but administered by freedmen under the control of a Roman supervisor. Sometimes even members of the imperial family held these profitable posts. Serving soldiers were often responsible for the security of the mines, preventing smuggling and maintaining communications. This trade was so valuable that the road which ran north from Salona to Sirmium on the Danube (where Diocletian had his first palace) was known as the Via Argentaria in honour of the large quantity of silver it carried.

---

47 Monument dedicated to the nymphs.
48 Now in the Archaeological Museum of Split.

RIGHT: Relief panel on the Church of St Maria del Giglio, Venice, depicting a plan of Spalatro which shows Venetian fortress walls encircling the original walls of Diocletian's palace.

FACING PAGE: Gold aureus of Trajan and his column.

HISTORY, 1000—1800

Although Salona fell into decline under the Byzantine Empire, the strategic importance of the Balkan Peninsula was undeniable and no ruling power within the Adriatic could ignore it. Before long, the rise of Venice as an important maritime power brought this Dalmatian coastline full of small islands and inlets into focus as a safe haven for potential enemies. To counter any such threat, by the year AD 1000 Venice had assumed suzerainty over the area.

A fascinating reflection of the strategic importance of Dalmatia appears on the façade of the Church of St Maria del Giglio in Venice. When the wealthy Barbaro family commissioned the new façade in 1680, they included relief maps of six important cities into their sculptural programme – their importance underlined by the reliefs being situated at eye level. Two of these maps depict ports along the Balkan coast, Zara (now Zadar) and Spalatro.[49] The artist emphasises the huge sixteenth-century fortifications surrounding the city of Spalatro, added by the Venetians to surround the medieval city within the ruins of Diocletian's palace. By the eighteenth century, very few people apart from the Venetians visited Spalatro and there is little documentation of its Roman ruins. Piranesi, however, would have known of the handful of travellers who had visited the site and had left their impressions. Men such as Cyrus of Ancona, Andrea Palladio and Fischer von Erlach had written about it, information which Piranesi no doubt imparted to Robert Adam.[50]

The earliest antiquarian to leave a written description of Spalatro was Cyrus of Ancona[51] in his *Commentaries*. These were in the form of a diary in which he noted down his archaeological discoveries; they eventually filled six volumes. Working as a young man in the port of Ancona, initially as a book-keeper and later as an inspector of the port, Cyrus's job took him to all parts of the eastern Mediterranean. His training had taught him to transcribe in great detail. Curiosity about the fine arch built by Trajan, the gateway to the port area of Ancona,[52] gave birth to what was to become a consuming passion. Hearing of his research, the Pope of the day, Eugenius IV,[53] invited Cyrus to Rome, where he became something of a celebrity. Cyrus had passed through Dalmatia in 1436, remarking on Diocletian's palace as he did so, but it was the survival of the ancient monuments in Ionia and Greece that concerned him the most. The Ottoman Turks and their ruthless passage up the Balkan Peninsula were a constant threat. It was during one of these journeys that Cyrus also came across Galerius's palace, in Thessalonica, another remarkable Tetrarchic ruin.

49 The others being Rome, Padua, Crete and Corfu.
50 Andrea Palladio 1508–80; Johann Bernhard Fischer von Erlach 1656–1723.
51 Cyrus of Ancona 1391–1453/5. His *Commentaries* were destroyed by fire in 1514. Sparse information as to his life and work comes from his biographers.
52 Ancona was the port from which Trajan had embarked for his Dacian wars. Apollodorus, once again, was the architect of the arch.
53 1385–1447; Pope 1431–47.

Palladio's journey to Spalatro would undoubtedly have aroused Adam's curiosity, for his father, William, had worked within the Palladian vocabulary all his life, teaching his sons a healthy respect for the master. Palladio had travelled to Spalatro as part of his tutelage under his patron Giangiorgio Trissino. Trissino had taken this promising young stonemason under his wing and renamed him Palladio after Pallas Athene, the Goddess of Wisdom. Three years later he took him to Rome, the first of several visits during which Palladio made detailed drawings, often reconstructing the buildings as he thought they must have been in their prime. It was during this period that he visited Spalatro, where he is recorded as making a drawing of Diocletian's palace with appended notes.[54]

The third author to have commented on Diocletian's palace, whose work Adam would undoubtedly have also studied, was Johann Fischer von Erlach, a contemporary of Antoine Desgodetz. Fischer von Erlach had arrived in Rome from his native Austria in 1671 and spent sixteen years there studying the theory and history of architecture; his interest lay in architectural evolution and the way that buildings over the years had been adapted to suit different cultures. The dramatic siege of Vienna by the Ottoman Turks in 1683 must have alerted him to the Balkan lands which lay along the borders of the Austrian Empire. He had obviously heard of Spalatro, for when preparing his history of architecture many years later he asked for contemporary drawings to be sent to him from the city.[55] He finally published his own research as the *Entwurff Einer Historischer Architectur* in 1712; a translation first appeared in English in 1725 as *A Plan of Civil and Historical Architecture*.

But what else did Piranesi tell Adam about the current situation in Dalmatia? Very little, it would appear; the same is true of the friends he made in Venice before his departure. Had Adam been warned of the delicacy of the situation, he might have been less headstrong, less arrogant and faced less opposition when he got there.

The Balkan territories were then an unsettled and difficult area. By the time of Adam's visit they had been under Turkish occupation for 300 years, and the Austrian forces had only recently succeeded in re-establishing their authority over the northernmost section of the peninsula. The difficult task of driving the Ottomans out of the Balkans after their defeat in the Battle of Vienna in 1683 was to occupy Austria and her allies for another three hundred years until a final resolution was reached following World War I. At this point Austria had managed a partial solution by establishing a 'military frontier' along the line of the Sava River, which, at the same time, was also the Venetian frontier with Dalmatia. But further allied progress was painfully slow. The area around the 'military frontier' became a haven for unwelcome immigrants of all kinds, among them the Uskoks, who were to prove a serious irritant for the Venetians. The Uskoks were Catholic refugees who had fled north to escape the Ottoman advances on Bosnia and Croatia. They settled, with the tacit approval of the Austrians, in the mountains behind and along the coast to the north of Spalatro. There they hid in the many coves of the Dalmatian coast, from which they mounted piratical attacks on Venetian ships. This made for a very uneasy relationship between the Austrians and the Venetians and led to many disagreements.

The Venetians for their part felt very isolated. In addition to the Uskoks in the north and the Austrians in the hinterland, unco-operative allies at the best of times, there was the immensely successful Republic of Ragusa to the south. Ragusa[56] – through skilful diplomacy with the Sublime Porte over a long period – had established itself as one of the safest staging posts for merchants travelling overland through Ottoman-occupied lands to Greece and Constantinople. Lacking such friendly relations with the Ottoman Empire, the Venetians had had to devise their own alternative route to the East, through Spalatro. By the eighteenth century this had become a successful reality. It was then that Spalatro's docks and warehouses were developed, the walls reinforced, and a lazaretto established to care for the sick. In addition a shuttle service of small, specially built galleys shortened the crossing between Spalatro and Ancona on the Italian coast. This investment had paid off handsomely, and the direct trade between Constantinople and Venice soon equalled that of Ragusa. But such a difficult history and such a hard-won victory still resonated with the Venetians, which was why they kept a permanent garrison in Spalatro. Adam should have been warned.

54 Palladio published his treatise *The Four Books of Architecture* in 1660. It was translated into English in 1715.
55 Made by Spon and Wheeler for their publication *Voyages d'Italie, de Dalmatie, de Grèce, et de Levant* (1678).
56 Today's Dubrovnik.

TRAJAN'S COLUMN IN ROME

TODAY TRAJAN'S COLUMN stands in isolation, but originally – painted in bright colours – it stood between two libraries, both with viewing galleries from which it would have been possible to see the upper sections. The column illustrated Trajan's *Commentarii*, his own narrative of the two Dacian wars written as a scroll – a document which has long since been lost, but was inscribed as a spiral, which may explain the design on the column itself. On one panel both Trajan and his engineer Apollodorus attend a sacrifice to celebrate the completion of the bridge across the Danube; others show not only battle scenes but also sieges of individual towns, with the Emperor

addressing his troops. Made of Carrara marble, the column sat on a marble plinth which was to contain the Emperor's ashes after his death in AD 117.

Jacopo Ripanda was the first to draw the entire scroll, while suspended in a basket; he then proceeded to engrave 130 plates to illustrate a *History of Warfare* in 1579 by Alonso Chacon. Later still, in the seventeenth century, Giovanni Giacomo de Rossi repeated this feat – thanks to Louis XIV, who subsidised the erection of a scaffold, and to whom his book is dedicated. Casts were taken from his drawings, some of which were later acquired by Piranesi. In 1864 a cast was taken for the newly established Victoria & Albert Museum, in London; it still forms the centre of the Cast Courts – cut in half because of its great height.

ABOVE: Detail from Trajan's Column, Rome: the Emperor, on horseback, enters a well-fortified city at the head of his army.

BELOW: View of the confluence of the Rivers Danube and Sava from the cliff, in the foreground, on which the Romans built Singidunum. Belgrade can be seen in the distance.

CHAPTER V

DIOCLETIAN AND GALERIUS IN THE EAST

Diocletian establishes himself in Illyria and the Far East, overthrowing the usurper in Egypt. Galerius's victory over the Persians. Monuments in Alexandra and Luxor.

IN HIS PREFACE to the *Ruins of Spalatro*, Adam introduces Diocletian with a flourish. He describes Diocletian as a man 'who in his munificence and example revived the Study of Architecture and excited the Masters of that Art to emulate in their Works, the Elegance and Purity of a better age.' Was this hyperbole to encourage sales in the London of 1764, or did he genuinely believe that Diocletian had initiated great architecture?

Had Adam lived today, the most recent excavations in Thessalonica and Trier might have justified his claims as they prove how original so much of the Tetrarchic architecture was. Diocletian was certainly aware of the importance of architecture and its symbolic power to impress, his many palaces being constructed with this in mind. His travels both before and after he became Emperor were central to this education, and many of the ideas he introduced into his own palace architecture were adapted from elements he had seen in Persia and Egypt. He was open to new ideas and materials, and

started to build suitable palaces soon after his acclamation. His influence on his fellow Tetrarchs was considerable and all four Emperors left large palatial enclaves, sections of which still remain today. Only that of Maximian in Milan has disappeared completely while those of Galerius in Serbia and Thessalonica rival Spalatro in size and complexity. Constantius Chlorus's palace in Trier continued to expand under his son Constantine, and it remained popular with his successors for many generations.

Serbia, at the heart of the Balkan Peninsula, was the central hub from which all four Emperors had set out on their successful military careers. At the time of the Roman Empire this area of Illyria was known as Upper Moesia; to its west was Dalmatia and to the east Thrace.[57] Two of the Emperors, Maximian and Constantius Chlorus, were born there, and and possibly Galerius too, but he certainly returned there to make it his final home, building a magnificent retirement palace just as his mentor, Diocletian, had done in Spalatro. In the early days of his rule Diocletian also spent long periods in Upper Moesia reinforcing the frontiers along the Danube.

---

57 Roman Thrace was bordered by the Balkan Mountains in the north, the Aegean Sea in the south and the Black Sea and Sea of Marmara in the south-east. Today it forms part of what is now Bulgaria and Turkey.

Having secured this section of the Danube in the Battle of the Margus in AD 285 against Carinus, Diocletian chose to set up his own headquarters some hundred miles further west on the River Sava, at Sirmium in Lower Pannonia.[58] Here the Sava formed a natural barrier between the Great Plain of Pannonia (today's Hungary) and Upper Moesia, but it was vulnerable to serious incursions by the tribes of the Marcommanii and the Sarmatians. Sirmium became the favoured city of both Diocletian and Galerius – and of future Emperors until well into the fourth century. Situated on the important Via Militaris, it grew into one of the largest cities in the northern Balkans. Such is the interest of archaeologists in the excavation of ancient Sirmium today that joint Yugoslav, American and French teams – wishing to have complete control of the site in the 1970s – offered to relocate the modern city elsewhere.

The scattered sites of third- and fourth-century houses, granaries and public baths, as well as an elaborate hypocaust (underfloor heating) system – quite possibly belonging to a large and important

palace – are visible today. Recently the remains of a huge circus lying within the line of the Roman wall were discovered. This circus may possibly date to Licinius or Constantine, members of the Second Tetrarchy and Diocletian's successors, both of whom also built extensively here. Should it turn out that this circus/hippodrome is connected to the palace buildings nearby, the complex could be as significant as those palaces built at Thessalonica or Constantinople. As in Spalatro, stone, marble

58 Sremska Mitrovica, Serbia.

FACING PAGE: Two views of the ruins of Sirmium Palace, showing an extensive hypocaust. LEFT: Provinces of the Roman Empire in the Balkans, showing the settlements of Sirmium (Sremska Mitrovica), Singidunum (Belgrade), Felix Romuliana (Galerius's Palace), Naissus (Niš), Serdica (Sofia) and Dioclea (Diocletian's birthplace).

and even porphyry were imported from a considerable distance to supplement the use of brick (the natural building material of Pannonia). Diocletian attached great importance to the furnishing of this palace and among such works which survive is a *quadriga*, the chariot of which is drawn by deer rather than the normal four horses.[59]

An interesting point, which Adam would not have appreciated in the eighteenth century, is that prior to the Tetrarchy no *palatium* or *basileion*,[60] designated for an emperor and his court alone, had existed outside Rome. Previously, an emperor visiting a city would have stayed in the residence of the provincial governor, as Constantius Chlorus did on his visits to Eboracum (York). The Tetrarchs required a more impressive symbol to reflect the importance of their positions and the abiding power of their imperium. Each Emperor chose a strategic point on the imperial road network on which to establish his residence – sometimes a virgin site, but at other times a site already used by a

provincial governor or as a military base, as in Trier.

In appointing Galerius as his Caesar, Diocletian chose a man who clearly admired him, and over whom he continued to have a considerable influence until his own abdication. Sources differ as to the date of Galerius's birth, but the consensus is that it was sometime between 250 and 260. He was born either near Serdica (now Sofia in Bulgaria) or possibly near Gamzigrad in Serbia and was originally known as Maximinus, taking the name G. Maximinus Valerius Galerius on his elevation to emphasise his kinship to the imperial family. In his youth he tended cattle, acquiring the nickname of 'Herdsman' – *armentarius* in Latin – which he continued to use for the rest of his life, for he associated the title with Romulus, the most celebrated of Roman shepherds and founder of the city of Rome.

As a young man Galerius joined the army, becoming one of the top-ranking officers at Diocletian's court. He is described as a big man of great strength, rough in manner and most daring on the field of battle – and also a heavy drinker. Nothing is known of his father except that he was described as a peasant. His mother, Romula, was termed a 'barbarian' – which, although undoubtedly a term

59 Curiously, deer were used to illustrate victories that had occurred in the north of the Empire, while elephants pointed to victories in the south. The *vicennalia* coin illustrates the former.
60 The Latin and Greek words respectively for a ruler's abode. *Basileus* is Greek for king or sovereign.

of abuse, points to her as a foreigner among the Greek-speaking Balkan people. In Romula's case it probably meant that she came from across the Danube, from Old Dacia (today's Romania). Quite possibly she was one of those Roman citizens whose family had lived contentedly under Trajan's occupation and, wishing to remain under Roman rule, had migrated south of the Danube after Aurelian abandoned Dacia in *c.* AD 275. Whatever the truth of her origins, Galerius was devoted to her and named his palace Felix Romuliana after her.

GALERIUS ATTACKS THE PERSIANS

In 297 Galerius was dispatched to the Far East to subdue the Persians, who, with their large and highly organised army, had been causing trouble for several generations. The Sassanid rulers had become particularly aggressive opponents determined to restore the glory of ancient Persia. Galerius's first encounter with the enemy proved indecisive and Diocletian, it is said, shamed him by making him walk for a few miles in front of the Emperor's carriage in full view of his own troops:

Diocletian received him with such indignation that he had to run for a few miles before his

carriage, garbed in his purple. He gained with difficulty his request that his army should be restored to its full complement from the frontier troops of Dacia and that he should attempt another military engagement.[61]

Whether this humiliating story is true or not, Galerius's second attempt was better thought-out and proved to be one of the most successful victories of the Tetrarchy. Gathering an army of seasoned troops who had already fought alongside him in Pannonia, he moved to attack the Persians, choosing as his battle site not the wide open plains where the Persians and their heavily mailed shock troops excelled, but the mountains of Armenia, where they had little space to manoeuvre and construct their battle orders. The enemy King of Kings, Narses, was wounded and barely escaped with his life; but his accompanying household, harem and treasures were all abandoned on the field of battle and carried back to Thessalonica as booty. The spoils were enormous and their transport caused considerable problems, as demonstrated by a long procession of pack animals on the commemorative arch Galerius was to build in Thessalonica. Narses's wife and family were treated with courtesy as

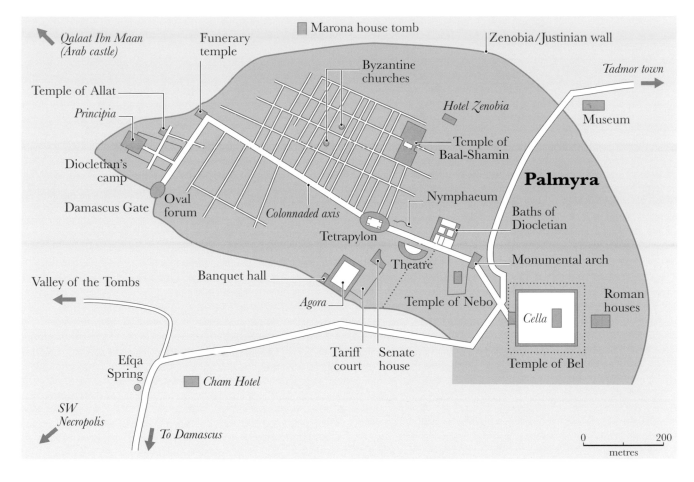

Qalaat Ibn Maan
(Arab castle)

Funerary temple

Marona house tomb

Byzantine churches

Zenobia/Justinian wall

Tadmor town

Temple of Allat

Principia

Hotel Zenobia

Museum

Diocletian's camp

Temple of Baal-Shamin

Palmyra

Damascus Gate

Oval forum

Colonnaded axis

Nymphaeum

Baths of Diocletian

Tetrapylon

Monumental arch

Valley of the Tombs

Theatre

Temple of Nebo

Roman houses

Banquet hall

Agora

Cella

Efqa Spring

Cham Hotel

Tariff court

Senate house

Temple of Bel

SW Necropolis

To Damascus

0   200
metres

honourable prisoners at Daphne near Antioch and were eventually returned to him unharmed.

Galerius continued his pursuit of the Persians, marching still further east, crossing the River Tigris and capturing the Persian capital of Ctesiphon, just south of today's Baghdad. Hearing of his Caesar's triumphs, Diocletian – who was then in Egypt – hurried to join Galerius at Nisibis (Nusaybin in Turkey). Here Diocletian joined in the celebrations, acknowledging Galerius's great victory and awarding him all the traditional honours which went with such a triumph. At the same time he introduced some restraint during the negotiations, using his diplomatic skills to construct a fair and lasting peace while putting an end to any possible ambitions Galerius might have had to go it alone. This treaty maintained peace in the area for many years, establishing the most stable frontier of the period.

To achieve this, Diocletian constructed a new road – the Via Diocletiana. This led from Egypt to the Euphrates, and roughly 100 miles of it can be

61 Festus, *Breviarum* 25 (published 369–70).

FACING PAGE: The Eastern Roman Empire.
ABOVE: Plan of Roman Palmyra showing the colonnaded street, the Baths of Diocletian and Diocletian's camp at the western end of the town.

traced even today. Along it he placed new watchtowers and forts, often near readily defended ravines, thereby controlling the all-important water points. There were no barriers along the road, but it was patrolled by cavalry and two new legions were stationed in the vicinity – one at Palmyra, an important frontier town and road junction, and the other some distance behind.

PALMYRA
Diocletian gave his new legion in Palmyra, the 'Illyrian Legion', accommodation in the north of the city, still known as the 'Camp of Diocletian'. He considered Palmyra to be one of the most important posts along his Via Diocletiana and vital to the security of his eastern frontier. One of the more unusual characteristics of these eastern cities, which survive even today, is their colonnaded streets,

LEFT: The colonnaded streets of ancient Palmyra, a particular feature of these eastern cities. The brackets on each column would have held statues.

FACING PAGE, TOP: Pompey's column, in Alexandria, erected in 291 to hold a statue of Diocletian.
BOTTOM: Diocletian's Gate, Philae, Egypt, a triple arched gate approached from the sea by an impressive flight of steps.

which give the urban panorama a stately grandeur unknown in the West.[62] Most of the columns have brackets halfway up their shafts intended to hold statues of important citizens living or dead, and handsome entablatures which run the entire length of the street. In Palmyra, breaking the line of this colonnade is a fine portico of four columns and a pediment which marks the entrance to the Baths of Diocletian. In addition, Diocletian's governor of Syria, Sosianus Heirocles, added a huge garrison camp to the western section of the city, just inside the Damascus Gate. Elements of the magnificent architecture of Palmyra were to be repeated in Diocletian's own new palace in Spalatro.

Stabilising the frontier that ran from north to south was not, in itself, enough. Diocletian had also to secure roads for the long-distance caravans coming in from Mesopotamia, which were vital for the movement of goods from east to west. New practical additions to the frontier lines included armament factories at all the chief outposts, which were entirely under state control and ensured that supplies could be shipped speedily to any area of unrest. Textile factories were also established, an idea soon to spread to all parts of the Empire. These state factories supplied uniforms and cloth-

ing on the spot and once again simplified the supply chain in such a remote area. The *gynaecia* (similar to those in Diocletian's palace at Spalatro) manufactured woollen goods, whereas the *linyphia* manufactured linen goods with raw materials imported from Egypt.

After nearly ten years of constant warfare the frontiers of the Eastern Empire were finally secure. To achieve this Diocletian had raised a significant number of new legions, all stationed along the newly secured borders. Diocletian was as familiar as his quartermasters with the needs of each soldier – how much food, fuel, clothing and equipment was needed for each legion. But enormous funds were now needed to pay and equip this huge army; how could he raise the necessary new taxes?

In spite of his efforts to stabilise the economy and prevent the debasement of the coinage, problems that had consistently dogged previous Emperors, the money raised through taxation had failed to keep abreast of the state's needs, and inflation continued to rise. Taxation of agricultural land had, until then, been applied at a standard rate and no longer matched the expected output; certain fertile areas such as the Nile delta were undertaxed while those in mountainous areas, such as Dalmatia, could not possibly meet their fiscal requirements. Always the practical man, Diocletian introduced an

62 Others are Apamea, Jerash and Petra.

innovative and simple solution. In future, instead of a fixed tariff chargeable throughout the Empire, an estimated yearly budget of state needs would be broken down, divided and allocated to the different provinces. This would then be divided further so that eventually each city, even each field, would be matched to its expected contribution.

No Roman ruler had, hitherto, attempted such a detailed analysis of the state's fiscal needs. In the past newly conquered territories had been allowed to continue their indigenous systems of monetary collection, and, although their administration was then taken over by Roman officials, the latter also liked to work the system to their own advantage rather than that of the state, so very little progress had been made. In another attempt to stabilise prices and control inflation, Diocletian introduced his famous Edict of Prices, published in 301. A copy of this remarkable document, in the Museum of Cyrene in Libya, sets out in great detail the prices allowed for different commodities, as well as fixing wages for labourers; it even accuses profiteers of robbing a soldier of his pay to settle his debts the very moment he received his wages. Any infringement was punishable by death.

DIOCLETIAN IN EGYPT

While Galerius had been busy in Persia, Diocletian had had his own problems in Egypt, where insurgents in Alexandria – possibly provoked by the new tax laws – had proclaimed a usurper, Lucius Domitius Domitianus, as Emperor in June 297. Egypt was the largest and most important province of

the Empire; it was essential not only to the wealth but also to the health of Rome, as it was by far the largest producer of foodstuffs – in particular grain, but also wine, oil and sugar cane. Alexandria was a great metropolis, second only to Rome in size and learning, and it held out against Diocletian with surprising determination. It took the Emperor nine months to recapture the city, after which he exercised a terrible revenge, killing all the revolutionaries and refusing any pleas for mercy.

At the same time, hearing that the city was suffering from famine in the aftermath of the siege, Diocletian ordered that a portion of the corn sent annually to Rome should be diverted to the people, and allowed them exemption from taxation. As a tribute to Diocletian's generosity and to commemorate his victory over the Alexandrians, Posthumus – the Prefect of Egypt – erected an enormous monolithic column, known today as 'Pompey's Column': a total misnomer. The Greek inscription makes clear that it was in honour of Diocletian and originally had an equestrian statue of the Emperor at the top.

The rest of Egypt capitulated quickly, and Diocletian soon imposed the same military and civil reforms which had been so effective in other parts of the Empire. He divided the country into three provinces, settling Egypt's southern border with

Nubia at Elephantine Island,[63] just above the First Cataract. Diocletian was above all a realist and in this way he established a useful buffer zone between Egypt and the Africa beyond. At Elephantine Island the River Nile changed character alarmingly. The current increased, and the level of the water fell five metres in a series of eddies and dangerous falls over a distance of three miles. The Romans could utilise these cataracts to form a natural boundary which required little additional defence. Like so many others before him, Diocletian wanted to leave his mark on the country. On the island of Philae[64] there are the remains of the gate he built, possibly to mark the end of his journey, a magnificent tripartite arch of which only the side arches survive.

To ensure future Roman control in Egypt Diocletian extended his defensive measures throughout the country. Either he built camps around the great temple complexes or he stamped his authority on existing temples, adapting their architecture to suit his purpose. An intriguing example of the latter was discovered in 1916–17 at the major Temple of Ammon in Luxor. Egyptologists, over recent years, have tended to show little respect for any such Roman additions, ruthlessly destroying any traces that remained. But here, on one of the most important sites in the whole of Egypt, there is still evidence of Diocletian's efforts to superimpose a Roman dedication upon this ancient temple.

Diocletian's first move here was to construct a new Roman camp to encircle the ancient buildings. The ruins of these walls are still visible today and are in the process of being excavated. He also built a new northern entrance, on a different axis from that of the original temple. In this way the Roman army could have direct access to the river, a useful point of entry should any emergency arise. Remains of the four column bases which used to support

---

63 Today's Aswan.
64 The original island of Philae was submerged with the creation of the Aswan Dam in 1960–70, and the temples moved to nearby Agilka Island. But Agilka Island is now known by the name of the original island, Philae.

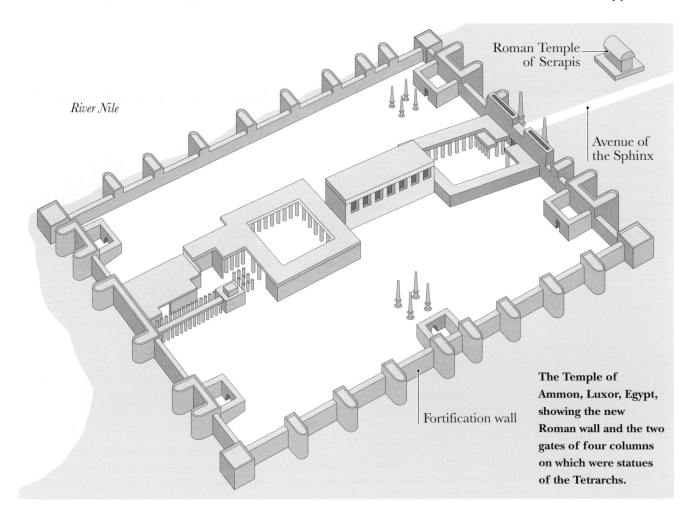

The Temple of Ammon, Luxor, Egypt, showing the new Roman wall and the two gates of four columns on which were statues of the Tetrarchs.

River Nile

Roman Temple of Serapis

Avenue of the Sphinx

Fortification wall

four large statues of the Tetrarchs mark the crossing of the two major roads in the camp, the *decumanus* and the *cardo*.

At the same time, Diocletian remodelled one of the great central halls of the Temple of Ammon as a *sala regia* – a ceremonial audience chamber dedicated to the Tetrarchy, dated 296–7.[65] The room held the standards of the legion stationed in Luxor. Such an ambitious reconstruction meant adapting the ancient Hypostyle Hall as this was the first area to be crossed en route to the new chamber. Hypostyle halls lacked any directional emphasis – something considered essential by the Roman architects. Their solution was to insert walls between certain columns, so creating a large, wide corridor leading straight to the new chamber. Within the new *sala regia* itself, the eight huge columns which had originally supported the roof were dismantled and their drums used to build a new raised floor. A flight of steps – unknown in an Egyptian temple, where everything was on a single level – rose from this Hypostyle Hall, marking out the new entrance and chamber. In the chamber itself an imposing apse housed a square canopy supported on four columns, which would have covered either a throne or an altar. The frescoed walls depicted a procession of figures holding precious objects in veiled hands

Two views of the Temple of Ammon, Luxor. **ABOVE:** The extra storey added to the Hypostyle Hall. **BELOW:** Bases of the four columns which originally held statues of the Tetrarchs and formed one of the two new entrances added to the temple under Diocletian.

---

65 Originally this hall was one of a sequence of three halls, which terminated in the Holy of Holies, the most important of the three, housing the sanctuary of the Shrine of the Temple Deity.
66 These frescoes were originally thought to represent Christian saints in a converted Coptic church, but John Gardner Wilkinson's watercolours point to the above interpretation (Ioli Kalavrezou-Maxeiner, *Imperial Chamber at Luxor*, Dumbarton Oaks, Vol 29, 1975). Further work on their preservation has been done recently by the American Research Center in Egypt. The symbol of veiled hands continued into Christian art, often used when depicting the Virgin.

and approaching a figure in a chariot, on the wheel of which was the word 'Diocletian'. Some attendants are richly dressed while others look after the spirited horses. Although already in poor condition when the archaeologist Sir John Gardner Wilkinson recorded them in the mid-nineteenth century, they still convey an energy which reflects their importance. Research in the 1950s suggested that this might have represented a *proskynesis* – an act of homage initiated by Diocletian in the early days of his reign, as already mentioned – or, alternatively and more likely, an *adventus* to celebrate his victory over the usurper Domitianus.[66]

The celebration of an *adventus* had grown out of an ancient Egyptian religious tradition whereby the sacred images of the gods paid honorary visits to one another on special feast days of the year. The Egyptian high priest would carry the god's image ceremoniously down the River Nile accompanied by an armada of small boats. In later years this honour was extended to the Pharaoh, when the same sacred images were carried out of the temples to greet him on his visit. The tradition continued into the Greek and Roman period and was adopted by the Roman army. The clue, in the case of these frescoes, is the veiled hands, which are obviously carrying something exceptionally precious as a gift to someone special.

Another tetrastyle, similar to the one already mentioned, exists on the opposite side of the camp, but this time it is dated a few years later – 308–9. This is of particular interest as it bears an inscription to the successors of the First Tetrarchy. For, following the abdication of Diocletian and Maximian in 305 and the death of Severus in 306, Galerius appointed Licinius as the second Augustus and Constantine and Maximinus Daia as their Caesars.

Following his suppression of the Egyptian uprising, Diocletian returned to Nicomedia and Galerius made his way back to his capital in Thessalonica, where he received a hero's welcome. Galerius's victory over the Persians had transformed his standing within the Empire and the huge captured booty had made him a rich man. His new palace in Thes-

ABOVE: Sir John Gardner Wilkinson's sketch of the converted chamber, depicting the frescoes of the Imperial Cult.

RIGHT: Detail of the niche in the same room today.

salonica stands as a monument to his achievements even today – in particular the great Arch, which depicts his triumph in fascinating detail. Was this the moment when Galerius realised how powerful a propaganda tool sculpture might be? None of the other Tetrarchs made any attempt to describe their lives in such detail. This simple 'Herdsman', delighted with his team of Hellenistic craftsmen, adopted the medium with great enthusiasm and was to continue to make good use of it for the rest of his life.

BELOW: The Arch of Galerius,
Thessalonica. The Arch
spanned the Via Egnatia and
formed the grand entrance to
Galerius's palace.

72

CHAPTER VI

GALERIUS IN THESSALONICA AND SERBIA

Galerius's Palace, Arch and Mausoleum in Thessalonica. Depictions of Tetrarchs and works of art in his Palace of Felix Romuliana, Serbia.

DIOCLETIAN'S PALACE in Split may astonish visitors by the beauty and integrity of what remains, but the ruins of Galerius's palaces run it a close second and are almost unknown outside the Balkans. His palace in Felix Romuliana is enormous and has large sections of decorative work still intact; his Arch in Thessalonica is unique and tells an absorbing story. Each Tetrarch had chosen the site of his capital with care; Diocletian had set an exciting example in Nicomedia where he began to build a palace immediately after his election in AD 284. Galerius followed suit when he picked the ancient city of Thessalonica in what was then Southern Moesia (today's Macedonia in Greece). Thessalonica was not a virgin site as for many years it had been an important crossing point on the Via Egnatia. Galerius chose his site wisely as it had an excellent harbour and was also the start of a major maritime route running south to the Greek islands and along the coast of Ionia as far as Alexandria.

The construction of this new capital was an enormous undertaking and lasted many years. As in Spalatro, it was based on a *castrum* plan with the two major roads, the *cardo* and the *decumanus*, running at right angles to each other within an outer wall. In this case the *decumanus* ran alongside the already existing Via Egnatia, and the crossing with the *cardo* was marked with an enormous triple arch. This arch and its sculpture vividly illustrate the grandeur and magnificence of Tetrarchic architecture, but they are surprisingly little known.

Galerius built his palace in c. AD 300 around a processional route of galleries and colonnades, which led directly to the harbour.[67] Was he looking back to the grandeur he would have seen in the colonnaded streets of Palmyra and Apamea? Colonnaded streets were a common feature in Eastern towns but never became popular in the West. They added a visual splendour which is evident even today among the Roman ruins of Syria. The processional route in Thessalonica was exceptionally grand and formed the pivot around which all the main palace buildings lay, dividing the Mausoleum in the north from the residential quarter in the south. Little in the residential quarter survives apart from the octagon, but there was a wing overlook-

---

67 Today the Greeks in Thessalonica call this route the 'Kamara'.

73

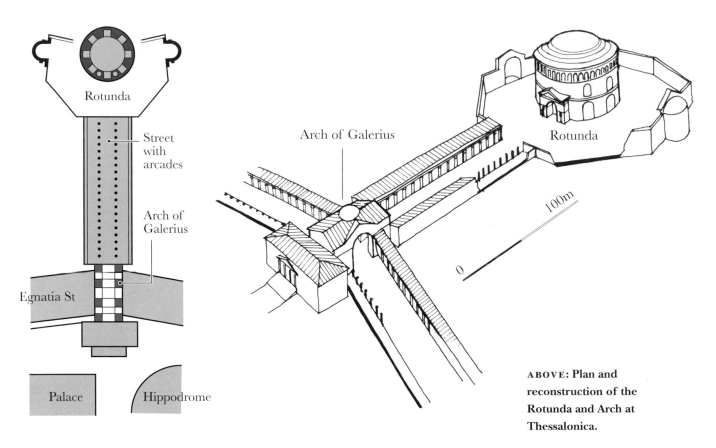

Rotunda

Street with arcades

Arch of Galerius

Egnatia St

Palace

Hippodrome

Arch of Galerius

Rotunda

100m

0

ABOVE: Plan and reconstruction of the Rotunda and Arch at Thessalonica.

ing the sea and a large hippodrome stood on the opposite side.[68]

Excavations in Thessalonica began in 1960, but little is visible today as the greater part still lies under the modern city. Remains of a temple, a large courtyard and a large apsed hall have come to light, of which the octagon is the most interesting, with walls which stand up to 0.6 metres high. Eight-sided as the name suggests, it has large semi-circular alcoves inside, all of which were elaborately decorated. A few years ago archaeologists discovered an arch of marble decorated with plant and scroll patterns, together with relief busts in circular frames: it fitted one of these alcoves perfectly. As a beautiful design in its own right, it gives us a tantalising glimpse of the original grandeur of these palace interiors.

Another intriguing find was a black and white floor mosaic with a cross and a palm, both Christian symbols. Why did Galerius – a man, as we shall see, long entrenched in his distrust of the Christians – commission such a mosaic? Did he, after his sudden

change of heart at the end of his life, order the builders to insert the palm and the cross to ensure that his successors, Maximinus Daia and Licinius would continue his new policy after his death? It remains a mystery.

Galerius was determined to outdo Diocletian. This may have been a riposte to the insult that Diocletian had paid him following his initial defeat by the Persians, for Galerius's victory is triumphantly displayed on the great triple arch which survives. The Arch itself was designed as an 'octupylon', ie it had eight piers (of which four survive). In simple terms this means that a second arch of exactly the same design ran parallel to it, separated by about nine metres. The three openings of each section lay opposite one another, the two central ones for wheeled traffic and the four outer ones for pedestrians. The Via Egnatia ran through the central arches and the whole composition was linked together by an elongated dome. It stood on a platform above the surrounding area so that steps from the pedestrian arches led down to ground level. It was not originally a free-standing structure, as it is today, but was attached to a wall on both sides, thereby forming a most impressive entrance into the palace.

---

68 All Tetrarchic palaces appear to have had a hippodrome, similar remains being found in Antioch, Sirmium, Trier, Milan and Rome.

Scenes from the Arch of Galerius, Thessalonica:
LEFT: Galerius in battle unseats the Persian ruler Narses, who falls from his horse. The enemy wear Phrygian caps, and one of them kneels beneath Galerius's horse. The Emperor's victory is indicated by the eagle above his head.

LEFT: From the left Diocletian, and Galerius, seated beside him, stretch their hands to welcome the kneeling figures of Mesopotamia and Armenia, newly released from the Persian yoke. Below are symbols of the Tigris and Euphrates.

LEFT: Galerius in military uniform sacrifices at an altar, with Diocletian, in civic dress, to his left.

The Arch in Thessalonica is unique not only for its architecture but also for its sculpture, much of which has survived in situ. All eight piers were originally covered in three rows of sculptured reliefs, which must have been carved off-site before being hoisted into place. The few inscriptions which survive seem to suggest that the sculptors were Greek. They tell a fascinating story, describing history in the making. The Arch was started in 298–9 and dedicated at Galerius's *decennalia* in 303. Portraits of the four Emperors, two on each outer side of the Arch (all now lost), faced east and west respectively, reflecting the division of the Empire. Diocletian and Galerius faced east towards Thrace, whereas Maximian and Constantius Chlorus faced west to Italy, Gaul and Britain. As elsewhere in the Empire, the sculptural programme here symbolised the unified rule of the Tetrarchs.

Although Galerius had not seen Trajan's Column, he would have known of it. The panels in Thessalonica can be read, like Trajan's, as a history of the Emperor's military success, told as a series of detailed pictorial events. Each zone or strip describes an individual incident: for example, Galerius on horseback addressing his cavalry in mountainous Armenia with elephants in the background. At another point he fights the Persians, differentiated by their Phrygian hats, and is seen in the very act of striking Narses, who falls off his horse. The eagle above Galerius's head indicates his victory.[69] In the panel below, two small Victories each hold a wreath ready to crown the two senior Emperors, Diocletian and Maximian: the two Augusti are seated and the two Caesars stand behind.

Finally, Galerius receives the surrender of the city of Ctesiphon and captures the Persian harem. The iconography is interesting both for the story it tells and for the outstanding quality of the art. Reading from the left, Galerius and Diocletian stretch out their hands in welcome to two kneeling female figures who represent Mesopotamia and Armenia, both provinces newly released from the Persian yoke. Maximian sits on the right with Constantius Chlorus to his right again. The two

heads under an arch on the very bottom of the panel represent the rivers of the Tigris and the Euphrates.

Despite being in such poor condition, the sculptures in Thessalonica open a door into the thinking of this bygone age. One of the best-preserved panels shows Galerius in battle dress, accompanied by the figure of Peace, sacrificing at an altar. The altar has two reliefs, one of Jove and one of Hercules, the *signa* of Diocletian and Galerius. Nearby stands Diocletian himself; in contrast to Galerius, he is in civic dress, graciously conceding that he is not the actual victor. He is, rather, the architect of order, accompanied by Jove whose universe is symbolised by the zodiac. The technique used on the panels – deep carving with little use of the drill – would suggest that the sculptors had learnt their trade carving sarcophagi. The depiction of the narrative has similarities to sarcophagi, when many figures have to be inserted into a limited field.

The climax of the processional way to the north is the Rotunda, the shape of which echoes the great circular *calidarium* of the imperial baths in Rome. It has survived remarkably well. Started in 306, the year after Galerius became an Augustus, it was intended as his mausoleum – though in fact it was still unfinished at the time of his death five years later, and he was buried next to his mother Romula in his homeland of Serbia. Only when Constantine the Great converted the building into the Greek Orthodox Church of St George was it finally completed.[70]

---

69 South pier, west face.
70 Both the Rotunda and the Arch are examples of a typically Ionian method of building. Without the volcanic sand used to make Roman concrete, builders in the Aegean had perfected an alternative method of creating domes and arches using bricks. Instead of the bricks being laid radially or parallel with the axis of the arch, or being simply used as a facing, they are laid end to end along the curvature of the arch.

LEFT: The sculpture of the Four Tetrarchs in Venice. Note one of each pair is bearded, and they wear identical swords and the *pillei Pannonici* which would have had a jewel at their centre. Note also the white marble foot which is a replacement of that lost in transit from Constantinople to Venice after the Fourth Crusade in 1204.

FACING PAGE: The Rotunda, Thessalonica.

Originally surrounded by a ceremonial enclosure, the Rotunda was enormous – far larger than Diocletian's Mausoleum. The walls were six metres thick and eight square recesses were hollowed out of the walls on the interior. Above were similar smaller recesses housing a ring of large windows. Lining the interior were marble panels similar to those in other Tetrarchic buildings, such as the Basilica at Trier, with mosaics above. At the top was a shallow dome, on the outside of which was an outer open-air gallery which helped to buttress the thrust of the dome.

The two outstanding monuments built by Galerius in Thessalonica and Felix Romuliana illustrate the ambitions of the Tetrarchy better than any other surviving buildings of the period. Each individual Emperor may have only ruled a quarter of the Empire, but this was no barrier to their architectural ambitions. Is it possible to picture these fascinating Emperors, and to engage with their unity and their loyalty to each other? The idea that four men could co-exist and rule without rancour was a novel one. Works of art were the only instruments available to convey the confidence and harmony they enjoyed, a concept many of their subjects must have found hard to understand after the unrest of the previous few years.

Several pieces of porphyry heads and figural compositions still exist, particularly in Serbia, where Galerius set up a sculptural workshop at Naissus (now Niš) which was to become famous for its skilled artisans. Most of these craftsmen, many of whom Galerius had brought back with him from Thessalonica, had been trained in the Hellenistic tradition, which gave them an edge over their Balkan counterparts, and much of the work we now associate with the Tetrarchy probably originated there. Before building in Thessalonica, Galerius had planned a new palace at Felix Romuliana (possibly the place of his birth), near today's Gamzigrad. These new workshops for sculptors, mosaicists and fresco painters were established with the express purpose of furnishing his new home.

The only complete sculpture of this period to survive today is the porphyry group of the Four Tetrarchs which stands just outside St Mark's Basilica in Venice. Originally this group stood on a bracket, such as those seen on the colonnades in the main street of Palmyra, and would therefore have been viewed from below. Painted statues would have stood at intervals on these brackets and must have presented a remarkable sight to any visitor arriving in this city of the desert. Both Galerius and Diocletian, after their experiences of fighting in the East, would have been familiar with such a concept, so it is possible that this sculpture originated in the East, possibly Syria.

Each Tetrarch wears a long *paludamentum*[71]

LEFT: Two views of a rather damaged head of Galerius wearing a jewelled crown with little busts of the Tetrarchs in between the jewels. The head is now in the museum at Zajacar, near Naissus.

FACING PAGE, TOP: The entrance gate to Felix Romuliana. Note the typical courses of stone interspersed with Roman brick.

BOTTOM: A decorative niche on the lower storey of one of the entrance towers at Felix Romuliana.

draped over his left shoulder. The brooches fastening the cloaks were studded with coloured stones or jewels. Here the four Emperors stand shoulder-to-shoulder, identical in height and pose, the epitome of fraternal affection. They have almond-shaped eyes and dramatically arched eyebrows with furrowed brows, all to become distinctive characteristics of Tetrarchic art. Divided into two pairs, they wear identical Roman military uniforms, their right arms thrown across each other's shoulders and their left hands clasping the eagle-headed hilts of their swords. The whole composition symbolises valour and *Concordia*. The only difference between the four is that one of each pair has a beard, emphasising his position as an Augustus rather than as a clean-shaven Caesar. They wear the *pilleus Pannonicus* – a cylindrical hat from Pannonia – which identified them as Illyrians and would also, like the brooch, have had a jewel at its centre. The unknown artist, restricted by the fact that each man should be an exact replica of his comrade, used the play of folds on the skirts of the cuirasses and the upper sleeves to great effect – his only way of displaying his own personal talent and individuality.

This sculpture was taken by the Venetians from the palace of Constantine the Great in Constantinople during the Fourth Crusade in 1204 and brought back to Venice as booty. Along the way one of the Emperors' feet went missing; the Venetians replaced it with a marble one, but recently a porphyry foot of exactly the same dimensions was

discovered in Istanbul – proof of a theft committed many centuries ago.

A more likely origin than Syria for the Venetian Tetrarchs is Galerius's workshops at Naissus. Another similar fragment still exists there. This second piece has an identical head, with the same cropped hair and cylindrical hat. The face is beardless; the eyes are big and wide open, with moulded pupils. Behind the head there is a broken section which served to connect it with those of the other three Tetrarchs. Like its prototype, it is carved of porphyry. Yet a third porphyry head, this time of

71 A cloak or cape worn by senior military commanders.

Galerius only, is in the museum in nearby Zajacar, a few miles up the road from Naissus. This was also part of a figural group of which only a few tiny fragments remain, but is perhaps the most unusual of all. The Emperor is now triumphant: he holds a globe in his left hand and is being crowned with a wreath by a figure of Victory, of which only a hand remains. The face is badly damaged and the missing nose destroys its proportions, but the eyes (like the ears) remain unscarred, and share the almond shape and arched eyebrows of the Venetian Tetrarchs. The rest of the face is less of a mask than those in Venice; it has a double chin and soft cheeks, thereby giving a truer reflection of the Emperor's real appearance. In this case the hair is smoothed so as to emphasise its contrast with the elaborate crown. The crown, the most important part of the composition, is most delicately carved: it consists of three ellipsoid jewel settings with four tiny busts placed in between each jewel. Each bust is individualised, with a separate head and shoulders, the whole composition worked in minute detail. The skill and patience required to work such small surfaces is another example of the extraordinarily

high standard that existed in this quiet corner of the Empire. It is both a remarkable achievement on the part of the artist and an entirely new method of illustrating the unity of the Tetrarchy. Here we have the portrayal of a confident Galerius who wears the Tetrarchy *in* his crown.

FELIX ROMULIANA

Galerius's retirement palace of Felix Romuliana near the small village of Gamzigrad in Serbia mirrors his remarkable change of fortune and the new circumstances in which he now found himself. In contrast to the Palace in Thessalonica, much of it still remains, as well as interesting pieces of the sculpture and mosaics with which it was furnished. Galerius's original idea had been to imitate Diocletian's palace in Spalatro: the ground plan was similar and it was designed first and foremost as a fortified camp/palace. Following his elevation as an Augustus in 305, however, it was rebuilt on a far larger scale, illustrated by the existence of two parallel sets of walls. The first set of walls encompasses an area of 3.8 hectares, with east and west gates flanked by octagonal towers, very similar in both size and design to those of Spalatro. Outside

FACING PAGE, TOP: The Fountain Courtyard of the residential wing of the Palace at Felix Romuliana. BOTTOM: Decorative niche on the upper storey of an entrance tower.

RIGHT: Decorative pilaster strip on the east gate at Felix Romuliana, depicting the Second Tetrarchy. Above are Galerius and Constantius Chlorus, and below are their Caesars Severus and Maximinus Daia.

these and surrounding the entire area is a second set of walls, built only a few years later, which ranks among the most monumental and best-preserved fortifications of this late classical period.

The two main gates of these later walls are most imposing. They have huge octagonal towers to either side, constructed of hewn stone and brick with niches to hold sculptures and reliefs, several of which have been unearthed. Handsome columns and triangular pediments framed these niches, transforming the bare brickwork of each tower. These triangular pediments framed the lower niches of each tower, while a simple arcade of a similar design marked the upper level. This is a far more sophisticated design than Diocletian's at Spalatro, and the whole impression on any visitor would have been one of immense grandeur. Instead of eliminating the original walls and towers, as might have been expected, Galerius retained them and incorporated them into the new fortification system to form a *propugnaculum* such as we saw in Salona and Spalatro. It had the added practical advantage of forming a covered path all around the inside of the palace walls at ground level, with an open-air walkway above.

One of the most interesting features of the eastern gate was a carved stone pilaster strip designed as if it were a military standard, with three small medallions depicting the Tetrarchs. It marks the change of rule that occurred in 305 when Diocletian and Maximian abdicated simultaneously and Galerius and Constantius Chlorus moved up to take their place. Two of the three medallions show the two new Emperors and their Caesars, Severus and Maximinus Daia, all draped in *paludamenta*. Diocletian and Maximian are not forgotten, however: the third row shows the two retired Augusti, wearing only simple garments – a toga and a cloak – to illustrate their new status. This was an ingenious way of illustrating both the contemporary political situation and the continuity and history of the Tetrarchy.

Many such examples must have existed, but only a few survive – one of them at Luxor in Egypt.[72]

No expense was spared in the furnishing of the palace, as recent excavations have shown. The site has never been built over and even today remains isolated. Excavated mosaics found here represent gods such as Dionysius, Hercules and Aesculapius, all of whom share an interesting association with apotheosis. They tell us yet more about Galerius. Each of these gods had a mortal mother and a divine father, a theme with which Galerius must have associated himself. After his triumph over the Persians in 298, Galerius celebrated his *quinquennalia* – his fifth anniversary as a Caesar – by declaring himself a second Romulus, underlining his identification with the founder of Rome.[73] At the same time he declared himself the new Alexander and a son of Mars. Seven years later, in 305, while Felix Romuliana was still under construction, Galerius became an Augustus and, as such, was himself in line for deification.

However, the plans for his own deification changed when his mother Romula died. He had already dedicated the palace to her, and it seems he now wanted to deify her too. Archaeologists in Serbia puzzled over the ownership of this palace for many years, searching for a dedicatory inscription or clue as to its ownership; their efforts were finally rewarded in 1984 by the discovery of an inscription to 'Felix Romuliana'. Romans used the adjective 'felix' as a prefix to describe gods, Emperors or regions as being sacred; 'Romuliana' was obviously derived from Romula.

Galerius's interest in Dionysius is another clue to his intentions. Dionysius had deified his mother, Semele, plucking her out of the underworld and taking her to Mount Olympus after his triumphant expedition to India.[74] Galerius planned to pluck Romula out of obscurity, in the wake of his own eastern journeys through Persia and Mesopotamia.

The discovery of the remains of two mausolea on a nearby hill, excavated between 1989 and 1992, provides further evidence. Tradition had it that this hill overlooking the palace was a sacred site, and as such would have been a suitable choice for the

72 See Chapter 5.
73 One of the sculpted panels on the Arch in Thessalonica shows him, as a young man, with the motif of Romulus and Remus being suckled by the she-wolf on the breastplate of his cuirass.
74 Dionysius was thought to be the first god to bridge the Euphrates and cross to India (Pausanius).

form of a circular *tholos* surrounded by a portico of 12 columns.

Deification of an Emperor was by now an established tradition: both Julius Caesar and Augustus had been sanctified on their deaths. The very first example of this – conveniently for Galerius – had been Romulus, who as founder of Rome had risen to heaven. Hercules, one of the two patron deities adopted by the Tetrarchs, had also ascended a huge funeral pyre on the instructions of the Delphic oracle and his earthly body had thereafter disappeared entirely.

Although most Emperors were cremated at death, it is highly unlikely that their actual bodies were burnt on the funeral pyres. Rather, a wax image was placed on a rectangular timber-framed pyre; as the pyre was lit, an eagle was released, soaring heavenwards amidst the flames. The Panegyric of 306, which touched on the apotheosis of Constantius Chlorus, talks of 'How the Sun himself took you to heaven, welcomed you into his chariot which was almost visible'. The precedent was there and Galerius followed it faithfully.

With the advent of Christianity the practice of such pagan rites came to an end. This memorial site was to be the last apotheosis of the Roman world.

mausolea. Near them were two further mounds – all that remained of the two funeral pyres, during the burning of which the deceased was deified. Like any holy site it had its own *temenos* or precinct, and it was approached through a tetrahedron (four-sided) arch, of which some small traces remain. Built in 305, Romula's tomb was hexagonal and sat on a square podium; it was faced with marble and decorated with mosaics. Galerius's mausoleum dates from 311, and was larger and more imposing than that of his mother, being a dodecahedron in the

ABOVE: Model of the entrance of Felix Romuliana. Note the earlier interior wall and small towers compared to the huge towers of the later walls.

RIGHT: Remains of the two mausolea of Galerius and his mother Romula together with the mounds which marked the place of their funeral pyres.

FACING PAGE, TOP: Inscription: *Felix Romuliana;* **BOTTOM:** Mosaic (now in the museum at Zajecar) of a seated Dionysius holding a cup and thyrsu, surrounded by vine branches and the panther, which had drawn his chariot, at his feet.

BELOW: The second frontispiece to the *Ruins of Spalatro* [Plate II]. The inscription reads: *General Plan of the Town and Fortifications of Spalatro showing the situation of the Ancient Palace of the Emperor Dioclesian. Also the Great Bay and Harbour, the Lazaretto, the Mountain Margliano, the Fort Grippe, the Suburbs and the Adjacent Grounds.* In the left background is the Portico of the Temple of Aesculapius and on the right is the interior of the Mausoleum.

CHAPTER VII

PUBLICATION OF THE *RUINS OF SPALATRO*

The Dilettanti Society, Stuart and Revett, Dawkins and Wood.
Adam's early practice, his brother James's stay in Rome and
negotiations to buy Consul Smith's collection.

'This jaunt to Dalmatia with my four people makes
great puff even in Italy and cannot fail doing much
more in England.'
(Robert Adam, letter home, 6 July 1757)

IN THE MID-EIGHTEENTH CENTURY few travellers
ventured into the Balkans. Political events made
travel difficult; to visit Venetian Dalmatia required
official permission – not easy to obtain, as Adam
had found to his cost. The history of this area has
continued to be difficult right up to the present day
with the result that many archaeological discoveries, already well known to native historians, are only
now becoming accessible to western scholars. Had
Adam known of the existence of Felix Romuliana,
how much further might he have ventured? Even
to Adam, Spalatro was very much a second choice;
he would have preferred to explore Sicily or even
Greece and had always hoped to persuade James to
accompany him. Nevertheless, to focus on Dio-

cletian's palace in Dalmatia was a clever decision:
it was close at hand and had never been properly
surveyed before.

He took advice widely, particularly from Sir
James Gray, the British Envoy in Venice, brother
of Colonel George Gray, the influential secretary
to the Dilettanti Society in London. What other
publications had already appeared and what was the
likelihood of success once he returned to England?
Adam was only one of many who planned to record
their travels abroad and looked upon them as
money-making enterprises. A few years before his
arrival in Rome two pairs of British travellers had set
out to study the classical antiquities of the Eastern
Mediterranean, venturing beyond the Italian shores
for the first time, encouraged and sometimes subsidised by the Dilettanti Society. Their works were to
be of enormous importance to Adam.

The Dilettanti Society, founded as a dining and
social club by a small group of British aristocrats
in 1732, had became an important player in the
rush to record Greek and Roman remains.[75] The
first trip it had helped to sponsor was that of James
Stuart and Nicholas Revett, who travelled to Greece

---

75 'The discovery of classical models represented the pinnacle of beauty,
whether architectural or other, becoming the driving force behind eighteenth-
century archaeology.' Jason Kelly, *The Society of the Dilettanti* (2009).

in 1751, four years before Adam's arrival in Rome.[76] Stuart and Revett had already been in Rome for six or seven years when, almost on a whim while on holiday in Naples, they decided to embark on an expedition to Athens to measure the Greek antiquities there.

STUART AND REVETT

This was an exciting time for classicists of all nationalities, as Italian archaeologists continued to uncover new sites – particularly those in the area of Naples. There the King, Charles III of Bourbon, kept everyone in suspense as he slowly unveiled the excavations being discovered almost daily in Herculaneum. But there had not been the same interest in exploring the lands of Ancient Greece, as the territory still held considerable dangers for any traveller, putting off all but the most intrepid explorers.

James Stuart was 30 years old on his arrival in Rome and had supported himself by conducting Grand Tourists around the city as a *cicerone*, assisting them in purchasing works of art. A fatherless boy from a poor background, he had come a long way. As a child he had studied under Lewis Goupy, the well-known London fan painter, learning mathematics and teaching himself Latin and Greek at the same time. He became a skilled draughtsman. Revett, seven years his junior and – by contrast – a gentleman of means, met Stuart in Rome while studying painting. They had ambitious plans for their journey to Greece and were full of optimism. There were to be three volumes illustrated by 191 plates, all of which they planned to engrave themselves. Their enthusiasm was infectious and their plans appeared feasible, persuading the Dilettanti Society to supplement Revett's private income. They prepared carefully. Prior to their departure they spent time studying the architecture, history and topography of Greece. They also crossed to Istria, in the Balkans, to draw the famous Roman temples and amphitheatre in Pola (Pula today).

Greece was considered dangerous on many counts: plague, bandits and the Ottoman rule were real difficulties, as both Stuart and Revett were to discover to their cost. They left in January 1751 and did not return for two and a half years – far longer than any of their contemporaries who were undertaking similar research. In spite of their influential contacts, which included the British Ambassador to Constantinople, another member of the Dilettanti Society, they encountered difficulties all along the way, even to the point of being threatened with death. Nonetheless, they eventually managed to draw nearly all the principal monuments of antiquity in Athens.

As was to happen to Adam in Spalatro, their meticulous method of measuring and drawing aroused the suspicions of the local garrison. A Turkish force had stationed itself on the southern ridge of the Acropolis, and initially forbad any drawings of the Parthenon or the Acropolis – so Stuart and Revett were restricted to recording the monuments in the lower town, such as the Tower of the Winds, the Choragic Monument of Lysicrates and the Forum. An outbreak of the plague delayed them further still, so that on their return to England they decided to publish a few plates individually rather than attempt a comprehensive folio. These plates met with great acclaim and they became celebrities overnight. The completed volume of their *Antiquities of Athens* did not appear until 1762 (by which time the two had fallen out, with Stuart buying Revett's interest in the project), but – as the first accurate survey of Greek classical remains – it caused similar excitement.[77] Stuart acquired the nickname 'Athenian' by which he is known to this day, and despite a natural indolence and the gibes of caricaturists and satirists, found that plenty of work came his way.

DAWKINS AND WOOD

Stuart and Revett, in their turn, owed a great debt to two explorers of the Levant, James Dawkins and Robert Wood.[78] This pair set a very high standard with the publication of their two volumes *The Ruins of Palmyra* in 1753 and *The Ruins of Baalbec* in 1757. Robert Wood was working in Rome as a tutor and secretary when John Bouverie and James Dawkins, both wealthy collectors, invited him to join them on their travels to Asia Minor. Bouverie died of fever on the outward journey but Wood and Dawkins continued on to Palmyra in Syria.

Their approach to their task was completely new. In addition to the illustrations, they were determined that the extraordinary history of this exotic city should play an important part in their

---

76 James 'Athenian' Stuart (1713–88); Nicholas Revett (1720–1804).
77 Reproductions of the major buildings on the Acropolis were not published until 1789, a year after Stuart's death.
78 James Dawkins (1722–57), son of a wealthy Jamaican merchant, and Robert Wood (1717–71).

book. The extra research required was more than compensated for, they felt, by the added interest it would give their readers.

On the fringes of the Roman Empire, Palmyra's legendary queen, Zenobia, had made a strike for independence in AD 267, conquering Egypt and establishing an independent Palmyran kingdom which stretched from the Nile to the Bosphorus. Only after seven years did the Romans manage to re-establish their authority, capturing the queen with difficulty and taking her to Rome as a hostage. Short-lived as this independence may have been, her fame lived on, and the area was still unsettled when visited by Diocletian 23 years later. Diocletian, anxious to strengthen the frontier of this remote section of the Empire, picked Palmyra as the pivotal point along his new road, the Via Diocletiana. He extended the fortifications of the city, building a large military camp to the west, much of which would have been still visible during Wood and Dawkins's visit.

Palmyra was beyond the reach of most contemporary travellers. It had a reputation as one of the most exciting cities in the Middle East, but also one of the most dangerous. Earlier travellers had suffered unexpected attacks by wild Bedouin tribes

ABOVE: A view of Split showing the harbour and palace with the campanile in the foreground and the modern town stretching away towards the mountains behind.

living in the surrounding hills who were suspicious of the explorers' motives: why should anyone travel such a distance to survey a ruined city? Had they come to plunder its treasures? Even local rulers could not guarantee safe conduct, although the Pasha of Damascus did provide Wood and Dawkins with a large escort of armed Arab horsemen and animals. In the event, the two arrived safely with their retinue of 200 and found their efforts well rewarded. Roman monuments in Syria are still extraordinarily well preserved, largely because of the dry, unpolluted air, so that the sharpness of their carved detail survives better on buildings there than on those in Italy itself.

Surprisingly, Wood spent only 15 days here; he and his architect Giovanni Battista Borra, whom he had recruited in Rome, must have worked at an extraordinary speed. Their recording of the inscriptions and details of the individual orders and ornamental mouldings, all of unprecedented accuracy, was to become a useful resource for British architects in the future.

Wood broke new ground in his publication of 1753 and it was to have a lasting influence on all such archaeological books in the future. As well as accurately measured drawings he included topographical views, enhancing the visual content. This novel approach widened its appeal, making it more accessible to non-specialists. His name was made, and he was elected a member of the Dilettanti Society in 1763.

None of this was lost on Adam. Such ideas, together with Piranesi's, were to be a huge influence on his own publication. As a result, he included the historical background to the palace of Spalatro in his preface and insisted on topographical views by Clérisseau. Adam always looked upon Wood as a close friend as one who had regularly attended Adam's weekly *salone* at the Casa Guarnieri. His advice and experience would have been invaluable to Adam at this stage of his development.

ADAM'S RETURN

Adam's return to England was carefully planned; the groundwork had been laid by his friends who had worked hard on his behalf. Allan Ramsay, arriving a few weeks ahead of him, had proposed him for election to the Royal Society of Arts, and Charles Hope had alerted his immediate circle of friends. Adam had sent Piranesi's newly published *Campus Martius* back to London with instructions to James to circulate it among his acquaintances. Piranesi was highly regarded among the cognoscenti in the capital and the impressive dedication to his friend Robert Adam was useful publicity. The engraved medal of the dedication page bore the inscription on the reverse: '*R. Adam. Academar. Div. Lucae. Florent. Bononien. Socius Romae MDCCLVII.*'

On the obverse it had the heads of Adam and Piranesi encircled by the inscription: '*IO.BAPT. PIRANESIUS ROBERTUS ADAM ARCHITECTI.*' Piranesi had given Adam an impressive curriculum vitae, describing him as a member of the Academy of St Luke in Rome, of the School of Design in Florence and of the Institute of Bologna.

Adam arrived home in January 1758. He was 30 years old, and so anxious to get started on his career that he delayed visiting his family in Edinburgh for several months. James was in London to greet him and their first priority was to find somewhere to

FACING PAGE: The title page of Piranesi's *Campus Martius*, 1762, which is dedicated to the 'most famous' (*celeberrimus*) Robert Adam.

live, to unpack Robert's treasures and to publicise his return. His precious collection of drawings, still stowed away in their trunk, had already proved their usefulness as even the customs official at Harwich had so enjoyed them that he had allowed Adam to import them duty-free. By the end of the month Robert and James had found furnished lodgings in St James's. Knowing the value of a good address, Robert felt it was imperative that they have a proper venue to entertain and show off his drawings, as these were to be his initial point of contact with any prospective clients.

Robert's first move was to hold an open house, inviting friends to inspect his portfolio of drawings, which was soon to be enlarged by his collection of marbles, newly arrived from Leghorn. John Clerk of Eldin later wrote 'that with his taste, his productions and his manners everyone went away enchanted'. But entertainment did not necessarily transform itself into commissions. Robert Wood, now an Under Secretary of State, had failed to find him any governmental commissions and initially the Earl of Bute – soon to be Prime Minister and a fellow Scot, who could have been so useful to Adam – was impervious to any suggestions that he might help. To make matters worse, Adam's old acquaintance in Rome, William Chambers, who had returned to London three years earlier and whom he had always feared as a potential rival, appeared well on the road to success.

Chambers's career path had been most unusual and quite unlike Adam's. Whereas Adam's had been largely practical, Chambers had – belatedly – chosen an academic route. At the age of 27, having worked for the Swedish East India Company for several years, he enrolled at J.F. Blondel's École des Beaux Arts in Paris – the most professional school of its day[79] – to study architecture, thereby becoming fluent in both architectural history and, more unusually, architectural theory.

Chambers, like Adam, had had a lean time on his return from Rome, particularly as by then he had a wife and two small daughters to support. The few designs he had submitted to would-be clients had found no favour at all. Once again, he decided that a change of direction was necessary: he would

---

79 Clérisseau was also an alumnus of the École des Beaux Arts.

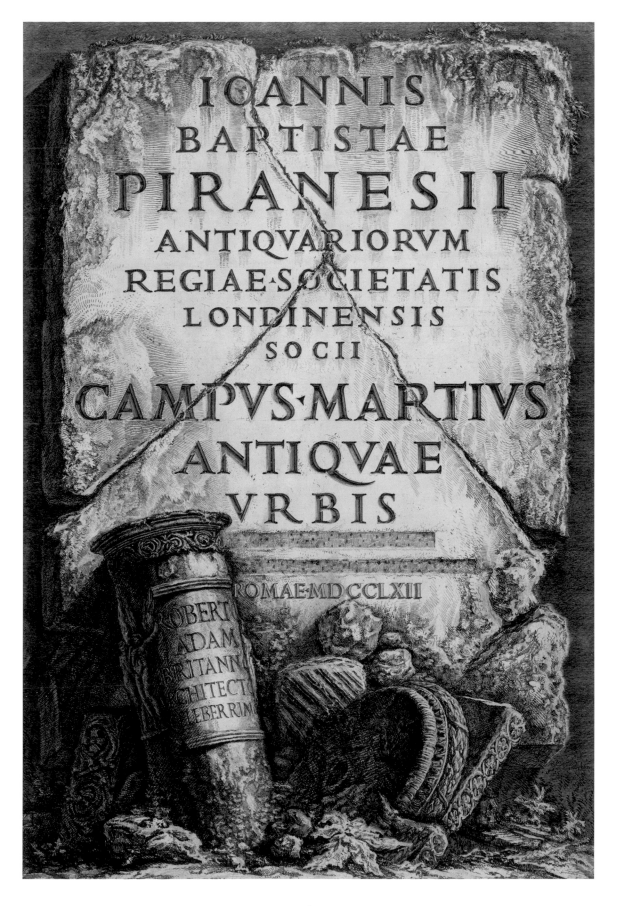

attempt to capitalise on his unusual knowledge of Chinese architecture with an illustrated publication. In 1757 he published *Designs for Chinese Buildings, Furniture, Dress, Machines and Utensils*. The book did not arouse much enthusiasm, because the vogue for Chinoiserie was waning; however, it found favour in a most unlikely quarter, the court of the Dowager Princess of Wales, Princess Augusta. Her husband, Frederick, had died unexpectedly in 1751 at the age of 44[80] and at the time of his death had been designing an 'exotic' garden at Kew. His widow, keen to continue her husband's interests, took her maternal duties as the sole surviving parent very seriously. Impressed by Chambers's wide-ranging knowledge, she appointed him architectural tutor to her son George, the young Prince of Wales. Chambers's training and his deep understanding of French architectural theory were unique among his contemporaries in London; he expected his royal charge to assimilate such theories, and put him through a strict routine of history and drawing.

Architectural training in the eighteenth century was largely practical. Many of Adam's contemporaries had trained as stonemason/sculptors, moving on to architecture once their training was complete: James Paine and Matthew Brettingham were notable examples, as was Sir Robert Taylor. This remained the norm even after the foundation of the Royal Academy in 1768, which was established with the express intention of filling this educational gap. Chambers's appointment to the Prince of Wales was to have far-reaching consequences for Adam's future which no one could then have foreseen, for once the Prince succeeded to the throne as George III, no other architect could rival Chambers for influence in royal circles.

Adam, who was having difficulty making any headway in his practice, planned to follow Chambers's example and move on with his publication: his brother James wrote that 'Bob designs to make his first work the ruins of Spalatro'. But, as he was to find to his frustration, the preparations necessary to complete the project were enormous and were to a large extent out of his hands. Much as he admired Robert Wood, Adam felt that the standard of the final engravings of Palmyra was poor. Determined that his should be of the highest quality, he had commissioned an experienced Italian engraver to work on the Spalatro drawings. His choice as head of the team was Francesco Bartolozzi, who was to prove excellent.[81] He had paid Bartolozzi an appreciable advance before he left Venice, and agreed that it should be his name that should appear on the finished plates rather than those of Clérisseau and his team of draughtsmen.[82] Progress was very slow and it was agreed that James should go out to speed things up and take control of the whole process.

JAMES ADAM IN ROME

Adam had learnt from Consul Smith that Clérisseau had been showing his drawings around Venice. General Grahame was once again called upon for help, since – as a result of the Seven Years War – travel through France was very difficult. Grahame agreed to smuggle James out of England dressed as a Jacobite officer in June 1760. Once in Rome, James followed Robert's footsteps to the letter, even to the point of hiring an apartment in the same building, the Casa Guarnieri. His suite, on the floor below, was larger than Robert's had been, and his entourage included Clérisseau, with whom he got on very well, George Richardson – who had travelled out with him – and a team of three engravers. To this he added a footman, a cook, a valet and a coachman: 'Some people here say I travel with a greater family than the Duke of Marlborough and the Abbé Grant says he never knew artists half so magnificent as I and my brother,' he wrote.

Calling himself 'Cavaliere', James enjoyed the social scene to the full – so much so that even the tolerant Clérisseau grew impatient and threatened to walk out, taking his team of engravers with him. The stipulation that James should concentrate on those things which Robert had failed to achieve, namely a journey to Sicily and Greece, fell on deaf ears. To be fair to James, the European political scene made travelling uncertain, and in the end the proposed trip to Greece was abandoned as too dangerous.

In the meantime, Robert's career in London had begun to improve. He had already bought a house in Lower Grosvenor Street, to which he summoned his two unmarried sisters, Jenny and Betty, to act as housekeepers and Willy, the youngest brother, to

---

80 He was hit on the head by a cricket ball in a freak accident.
81 Bartolozzi (1725–1815) was subsequently invited to Britain, becoming an engraver to George III. He was to become a founder member of the Royal Academy and was responsible for engraving its diploma certificate.
82 Clérisseau had his quiet revenge, which must have escaped Adam's editorial eye. On the tomb chest outside the Mausoleum (plate xxviii) he wrote: *Hic jacet corpus clerissi pictor* ('Here lies the body of the painter Clérisseau'). In the same engraving Bartolozzi put his name on a fountain in the foreground.

assist in the business.[83] He had hoped to continue working as a partner in the Edinburgh business, but his brother John's patience was wearing thin. John had agreed to subsidise Robert's two assistants, Brunias and Dewez, on their journey to England, but – having already lent him the capital to buy his house – would now only commit himself to support Robert for a further year. Robert swiftly built a gazebo in the garden behind, in which to show off his marbles and paintings as a means of attracting potential clients: 'a handsome collection of Pictures, Bronzes and plaster casts of the most beautiful mouldings of ancient Architecture, together with an infinite number of sketches of Antique ceilings discovered in the roofs of the Palace of Nero, the Baths of Caracalla, and Diocletian.'[84] In November 1761 Lord Bute, finally acknowledging Adam's potential, recommended him to the King and he was appointed Joint Royal Architect to King George III, a title he shared with William Chambers. He had also met two possible patrons, Nathaniel Curzon and Sir Hugh Smithson.

The Prince of Wales had succeeded as King George III the previous year, aged 22. Like his two brothers, he was a serious student of the arts: their mother had made sure that all her sons had had a thorough grounding in this field. To his chagrin, George had not been allowed – by virtue of his position – to visit Rome, but both the younger princes spent time there. The King had loved architecture from a young age, and was keen to increase the Royal Collections to keep pace with those of other members of the aristocracy; he was also an enthusiastic bibliophile, and soon after his accession let it be known that he was anxious to replace the 9,000 books which had been given to the nation by his grandfather in 1757.

In the few months left before his return from Italy, James became an important link in the chain of Adam influence, performing a new role as a 'purveyor of fine arts', in which he proved a skilled negotiator. Robert had commissioned him to find antique statues for the Ante-Room of Syon House, which he was redesigning for Sir Hugh Smithson.

James settled on a copy of the Uffizi Apollo and a couple of statues from Florence, all of which are still *in situ* at Syon. Through Lord Bute – an influential father figure who had known the King since childhood, and by now an enthusiastic supporter of the Adam Partnership – James won the commission to broker the sale of the Cardinal Albani's collection of rare prints and drawings to George III.

Robert had known both the Cardinal[85] and his librarian, Johann Joachim Winklemann, while in Rome and had always admired the Cardinal's extensive collection, now newly housed in the recently built Villa Albani. Negotiations proved delicate because the Papacy, concerned at the loss of so many antiquities, had recently passed a law forbidding any further exports; the British, with their voracious appetite for collecting, were particularly suspect. But Cardinal Albani, by virtue of his family connection, was able to bypass any such obstacles and – thanks in no small part to James's charm and skill – a satisfactory deal was concluded, with the King buying the collection for the large sum of 3,000 guineas.

James was to follow this triumph with further successful negotiations between the King and Consul Joseph Smith for the enormous array of artefacts acquired during Smith's time in the Venetian Territories, including paintings, drawings, prints, books and manuscripts, gems, coins and medals. Lord Bute had recommended that the King buy them in their entirety, and the sum of £20,000 was settled on for what remains one of the most prized sections of the Royal Collection.[86] James's charm led people to like and trust him, a gift which was to be of enormous help to the Adam Partnership in the difficult times which lay ahead. He and Clérisseau rejoined Robert in London in October 1763; he had been away for just over three years.

James and Clérisseau brought back the precious copper plate engravings for the *Ruins of Spalatro* with them. In London the copper plates by Bartolozzi were given titles and their plans were elucidated, with key letters being added. The commentary on the plates and introduction came next. Robert had, in the interval, sorted out the difficulties of writing an introduction. He was well aware that his talent for drawing did not necessarily enable him to write, and knew of the difficulties that had beset Stuart and Revett on this very issue – difficulties which had finally led to the end of their long and fruitful

---

83 Margaret (Peggy) and Helen (Nelly) were married and remained in Scotland.
84 According to John Clerk of Eldin, husband of Adam's niece Susan and his biographer.
85 1717–68.
86 Part of Smith's collection forms the nucleus of the British Library, and is featured today in the central lobby as the King's Library.

partnership. Soon after his arrival home Robert had written a full and frank description of his journey and difficult time in Dalmatia. He described how he had always been an admirer of the imaginative and striking buildings of Diocletian's reign, including his baths in Rome, his huge palace in Nicomedia, and other buildings erected under his inspiration in Milan and Palmyra. He argued, too, that the revival of the 'art of architecture' should be attributed to the Emperor and his colleagues.

Adam sent this first draft up to Scotland to be vetted by his cousin William Robertson.[87] Robertson edited it, leaving the first 21 pages largely intact but rewriting the last 30 pages or so.[88] In the end Adam dispensed with this too and wrote a second, more concise preface, which is the one that was finally published.

PUBLICATION: 'RUINS OF SPALATRO'

The work Adam put into this production was enormous, and the result is a well-researched and deeply thought-out folio, which remains a most interesting document even today. The text, backed up by footnotes, is impressive proof of the knowledge he had acquired during his two and half years in Rome. Here he summarises the history of Spalatro and the reflections and writings of previous observers (a few of which, such as the Emperor Constantine v Porphyrogenitus and the Jesuit Daniel Farlatus, are also quoted by Edward Gibbon in his *Decline and Fall of the Roman Empire*). It is obvious he had read extensively around his subject. Adam begins modestly, acknowledging his debt to Wood and Dawkins: 'Following the success of the *Ruins of Palmyra and Baalbeck*, I now present the fruits of my labours to the public.'

He goes on to explain that he was attracted to this particular site because it was a private residence rather than a public work. Anxious that his voyage 'might produce entertainment to the public', he gives a detailed description of the palace, its topography and location, noting its pleasant climate even in the midst of summer. Taking his cue from Palladio and Piranesi, he goes on to explain that his plates illustrate different aspects of various sections of the Palace. They move from general views to reconstructed plans, and then to detailed

FACING PAGE: Frontispiece to Adam's *Ruins of Spalatro*, showing a section of the *cryptoporticus* and the aqueduct in the background; the figures in the centre are possibly Adam and Clérisseau sketching.

drawings of doorframes, friezes etc. They give a view of the buildings as they were in his day and as he thinks they might have appeared in their prime. The sections, plans and diagrams used to illustrate these details are beautifully produced. Halfway through the preface he acknowledges Clérisseau by name, which somewhat makes up for the lack of attribution beneath the finished engravings. In an endearingly British way, Adam ends up by worrying about the Emperor Diocletian and his survival during the winter months. He had searched everywhere for signs of chimneys and fireplaces, but had come to the conclusion that the heating must have come from the hot air being pumped through pipes in the wall.

The illustrations open with a frontispiece depicting the buildings of Spalatro as a *caprice*, taking various different architectural features that existed within the palace and moving them around to form an attractive composition – a sarcophagus, a sphinx, a small section of the *cryptoporticus*, a console and fluted column from the Porta Aurea. Beneath the sphinx is a carved medallion of Diocletian, while the aqueduct features in the background. Clérisseau used this *caprice* technique to great effect to whet the reader's appetite.[89]

The title itself is inscribed on a large sarcophagus:

Imperatoris Diocletiani palatii
Ruinae
Prope Salonam

It is complemented on the following page by a general view of the bay and fortifications together with a plan. Figures were added to all the drawings and in some cases the buildings shifted around. In a plate of the interior of the Mausoleum, now one of the better-known illustrations, all the medieval additions – such as altars and the pulpit – were stripped out, and contemporary figures added. It described the two superimposed orders, the contrasting niches and the brick arches of the dome.

Subsequent plates give concise details as to the decoration and mouldings, all of which would provide patterns for future use and all of which survive in excellent condition to this day. One of the most

IMPERATORIS
DIOCLETIANI PALATII
RVINAE
PROPE SALONAM.

interesting plates is that of the *peristyle* and *prothyrum*, the ceremonial approach to the Emperor's private apartments. As the pavement level of the *peristyle* arcade is lower than its surroundings, three broad steps on each side give access to the upper podiums. The *prothyrum* itself was originally approached by three separate flight of stairs, two on either side leading up to the Vestibule and a central one which descended to the basement area and out into the south gate on the quay. In the sixteenth century this central staircase had been walled up and two chapels built into the portico. This is what we see in Clérisseau's drawing. It would appear that when Adam visited no one knew of this original arrangement.

Adam was obviously intrigued by the arcade of the *peristyle*: he found it unusual and wondered about its origin. Diocletian, as we know today, had seen similar designs in the East and used them not only his palace but also in his baths in Rome. Adam mentions that he had seen a drawing by Palladio in Lord Burlington's collection of a similar arcade along the main façade of the baths in Rome, but that because 'that part of the baths have been destroyed

w of the Peristylum of the Palace

since Palladio's day, I am obliged to quote his authority instead of appealing to the original itself'.

Adam's interpretation of Diocletian's palace remains remarkably accurate to this day even after further extensive excavations and studies by contemporary archaeologists. In spite of the debris there, Adam's team seems to have been able to survey some sections of the basement area, which they assumed to have been the bath complex. But the medieval buildings built inside and up against the palace walls which he saw then, remain there still.

With its huge vaults, high ceilings and different-shaped rooms leading off one another, the undercroft probably recalled those chambers they had seen in Diocletian's baths in Rome. They correctly assumed that the upper storey – which even then had completely disappeared – had originally echoed those lower basement halls and that the apartments for Emperor and Empress were arranged symmetrically around the central axis which led from the peristyle through the Vestibule into the Great Room, the *sala regia*. The gradation of room size from large to very small interested Adam, and this aspect of the palace planning has become

ABOVE: Capital in the peristyle which Adam adapted so frequently, calling it the *Spalatro Order*. RIGHT: The *cryptoporticus* [Plate VII].

clearer in recent years with the removal of debris from the basement halls.

During the time that James was in Italy, Adam had managed to gather an impressive list of subscribers to support his publication, headed by the King and Queen Charlotte; the King's mother, Princess Augusta, Dowager Princess of Wales; his brother the Duke of York; and the younger Princes, William and Henry. He had even persuaded the King of Prussia to subscribe: Frederick the Great, Britain's ally in the Seven Years War, was also a keen architect. A further 28 foreigners, including the Venetian Ambassador, had also agreed to subscribe, as well as members of the aristocracy, scholars, connoisseurs and artists.

The external appearance of the folio had been planned with care, different colours being allocated to different categories of recipient: scarlet morocco leather bindings for the royal family, blue for Knights of the Garter, green for Knights of the Thistle, a Scottish Order, and brown for everyone else. The finished work was announced in the *Public Advertiser* for 22 March 1764. It was received with great acclaim. Adam sold 544 copies by subscription alone. Edward Gibbon was one of the very few dissenting voices: 'There is reason to suspect that the elegance of his design and engravings has somewhat flattered the objects which it was their purpose to represent.'

Clérisseau would have disputed this. He wrote several years later, when back in Paris, and publishing his own drawings independently of Adam: 'J'ai concentré 30 années a étudier les précieux restes de l'Architecture antique; à mesurer scrupuleusement ce qu'a publié Desgodets... de Varonne, de Pola en Istrie et tous les fragments qui subsiste tant à Spalatro en Dalmatie qu'à Naples.'

By the time Adam's book was published in 1764, it had taken him seven years and proved a costly and frustrating project. He must, at times, have wondered whether it was all worthwhile. But from an historical standpoint it remains one of the great architectural works of the eighteenth century, and stands alone as a depiction of Diocletian's palace 1,450 or so years after its foundation.

What happened to Adam's precious pictures after the publication of *Ruins of Spalatro*? Sixty-four of the originals were sold to Josiah Taylor at the final Adam sale (10 July 1828, lot 71), but that par-

ticular album is now lost. Clérisseau kept a second set in Venice, of which only five survive (they were sold to Catherine the Great for the Hermitage). A few years ago a set of 20 plates was found in the Archaeological Museum of Zagreb with an Italian text but no attribution to Adam. These plates had been re-engraved in 1784, 20 years after the original English publication. The set was dedicated to John Udney, the British Consul at Leghorn in 1776, who had succeeded Joseph Smith as Consul in Venice. It was a very restricted version and contained no plans, sections or reconstructions.

BELOW: Coin of three
Emperors minted by
Carausius, depicting
from the left Carausius,
Diocletian and Maximian.
Inscribed CARAUSIUS ET
FRATRES SUI.

CHAPTER VIII

CONSTANTIUS CHLORUS AND TRIER

Background of Constantius Chlorus and his struggle against Carausius. The Saxon Shore fort of Portchester. The Rhetorical School in Autun. Expansion of Constantius's capital, Trier.

ON HIS WAY BACK TO BRITAIN, Adam travelled through Germany, but he never visited Trier – the capital of the third member of the Tetrarchy, Constantius Chlorus. Had he done so, he would have discovered another fascinating Roman palace, bigger and even more impressive than Diocletian's in Spalatro.

Of the four Emperors, Marcus Valerius Constantius Chlorus seems to have been the most loved. Both Lactantius and Eusebius praise the mildness and benevolence of his rule, whereas they are extremely critical of the other three. Is this because, as Christian historians writing only a few years later, they were sympathetic to the father of Constantine I who had introduced religious toleration with the Edict of Milan in 313?[90] The Venerable Bede, when writing his *Ecclesiastical History* in about 731,

echoes the same sentiments and describes him as 'Constantius, a man of exceptional kindness and courtesy, who had governed Gaul and Spain during the lifetime of Diocletian, died in Britain.'

Constantius Chlorus was born in Naissus in about AD 250. Unlike the other Emperors, we do know something of his parentage. His father, Eutropius, came from a patrician Dardanian[91] family and was a prominent citizen in his own right. His mother, Claudia, was also well born and is thought to have been the niece of the Emperor Claudius Gothicus.[92] Constantius himself never traded on this imperial connection, but his son was to find it a useful tool when trying to establish his own claim to the *imperium*.

Like the other Tetrarchs, Constantius Chlorus established his early reputation in the army. Posted to the southern Balkans, he became the Governor of Dalmatia under the Emperor Carus. Some ancient sources suggest that Carus had thought of adopting him as his heir instead of his own dissolute son Carinus. A more likely reason for his appointment as a Caesar in 293 was his service as Praetorian Prefect under Maximian, whose loyal and trusted

---

90 This followed the withdrawal of Diocletian's Edict of Persecution three years earlier.
91 In AD 6 the Dardanians had been conquered by Augustus and became part of the province of Upper Moesia (an area of present-day Kosovo).
92 The Emperor Claudius Gothicus (213–70; reigned 268–70) came from either Sirmium or Naissus. The sources are very unreliable. The link with the Constantinian dynasty is very doubtful and was probably initiated as a tool to legitimise Constantine and his successors.

colleague he had been for some time. Like Galerius on his appointment as Caesar, Constantius Chlorus cemented this relationship by divorcing his first wife, Helena (mother of his eldest son Constantine), and marrying Maximian's daughter Theodora, with whom he had six further children. He also adopted Hercules as his protector or *signum* and took the same family name of Valerius. As the newly appointed Caesar he was assigned to the province of Gaul, making Trier his capital.

Gaul had become a contentious province in recent years; it had a history of constant warfare and usurpation of power by leaders of local tribes. Successive Emperors, in the recent past, had largely ignored Gaul as the Empire's Danubian and Eastern provinces were considered the most under threat. With Constantius Chlorus's arrival, Maximian, who had until then been in overall charge of the Western Empire, moved his headquarters to Milan, making Spain, Italy and Africa his theatre of operations. One of the most difficult areas to patrol for both Emperors was the Rhine frontier, which stretched from Lake Constance to Katwijk (now

the Dutch port of Katwijk aan Zee), a border 560 miles in length. The Romans made no attempt to maintain a solid front line along the river, as it was acknowledged to be an impossible task.[93] Instead, they looked upon the Rhine as a means of communication and of supplying outposts further north. It was, however, the lateral rivers such as the Meuse, the Moselle and the Saar that were considered the most important, for it was on these that the Romans established their administrative centres. Trier, on the Moselle, which became Constantius Chlorus's capital, fell into this category.

The Rhine Delta, however, was in class of its own. Without any clear line of river, it was a particularly difficult area to police, and had become a useful haven for pirates attacking the coasts of both Gaul and Britain. Katwijk itself was an important strategic centre on this coast at a point where the Rhine flowed into the North Sea; it was also the port of departure for Britain.

Three tribes were particularly troublesome: the Saxons, the Franks and the Alamanns. Many such tribes had, in times past, left their homelands in the east and over generations had moved inexorably west along the line of the Upper Danube, across Bohemia to the Rhine and into Italy through the Brenner Pass.[94] Unlike those tribes threatening the Danube frontiers, these peoples formed federations among themselves and became at least partly

---

93 Archaeologists have recently discovered evidence of Germanic populations living in disused Roman villas, which had been built there in order to maintain peace along this frontier (in today's Belgium).
94 Constantius Chlorus himself was to invite large numbers of Saxons and Franks beyond the Rhine to settle in northern Gaul.
95 The Menapians were a Germanic tribe who had made their home in the Rhine Delta.

integrated into the Empire by joining the Roman army as native units. Their leaders often adopted the same clever tactics as Diocletian and Maximian, using the ranks of the military as a ladder of advancement. They were appointed local leaders and allies of Rome; but – as had become clear under Maximian's watch – this system could backfire dangerously.

CARAUSIUS

When appointed Caesar in 293, Constantius Chlorus's most pressing problem was that of the imposter Carausius, who had rebelled and set himself up as an independent ruler in Britain six/seven years earlier. Maximian had spent the eight years following his appointment as Augustus trying to subdue the unrest in this area. Finding himself forced to fight simultaneously on both land and sea, he had entrusted the safety of the Gallic and Britannic coasts to a native Menapian – Carausius.[95]

The main Roman naval base was at Ravenna in the Adriatic, but smaller Roman fleets patrolled the Channel, the Rhine and the Danube. Carausius had distinguished himself fighting under Maximian in northern Gaul in 286 and had won the Emperor's confidence. Skilled as a pilot, he was appointed commander of the *Classis Brittanica*, the Roman fleet based in the English Channel as a protection against the Frankish and Saxon pirates.

Maritime trade along these coasts was well established, and the temptation to work the system to his own advantage was too strong for Carausius, once he was in overall command. Rumours were rife and hearing of this, Maximian was incensed, and ordered Carausius's immediate execution. The Emperor had not, however, taken into account the great personal following which Carausius now commanded within Gaul. Many of the tribal mercenaries within the enlarged Roman army owed their advancement to him alone, and were entirely

RIGHT: Map showing the course and delta of the Rhine and illustrating the position of Katwijk.

FACING PAGE: Medallion of a wreathed Constantius Chlorus holding a traditional *scipio* (eagle-tipped sceptre) and raising the province of Britannia from her knees while receiving a crown from the winged Goddess of Victory. Minted in Trier in 296. The obverse inscription reads FL VAL CONSTANTIUS NOB CAES (Flavius Valerius Constantius Noble Caesar), and the reverse PIETAS AUGG. PTR (two Gs denote two Augusti).

committed to his cause. On hearing of Maximian's sentence of execution, Carausius fled to Britain, winning further support from the legions stationed there.[96] He was no fool, and rather than attacking the nearest point of the island, the south, which was well defended, he sailed east and landed on the north coast of Britain, defeating the Roman governor in a battle near Eboracum (now York). Thereafter he made Britain his headquarters. In an unusually clever move, he declared himself a co-ruler with Diocletian and Maximian.

Carausius was no brutish soldier: he ruled his new realm with skill and tact and with the approval of his new subjects. Following well-known Roman practice he established a mint, from which he issued coins with a portrait of himself and the two other Emperors side by side with the inscription PAX AUGGG.[97] Diocletian is in the centre with Maximian on his left and Carausius on his right. On the obverse is the inscription CARAUSIUS ET FRATRES SUI (Carausius and his brothers). He also minted silver coins, the first to have been issued with proper silver content for a long period, all of which ensured his popularity with the ever-important army. As a result the two ruling Emperors faced an unprecedented problem, for not only was Carausius challenging their rule and claiming parity with them, he was also successfully legitimising his claim in a way which must have appeared to most his subjects as reasonable and law-abiding.

The difficulty of dislodging Carausius may have been the reason for the installation of the two Caesars in 293. Although Maximian had successfully stabilised the eastern frontier of the Rhine in 289, his previous attempt to remove Carausius had proved a miserable failure. Neither he nor Diocletian could risk another failed campaign in the West. Constantius Chlorus's first task, therefore, was to confront Carausius. He chose as his battleground the small settlement of Bononia (today's Boulogne) on the north coast of Gaul. Carausius was on this occasion severely defeated, but was able to escape

back to Britain only to be find himself supplanted there by his finance minister, Allectus, who had seized power in his absence. Carausius was summarily assassinated and Allectus proclaimed ruler in his place in 293.

Constantius Chlorus was in no position to confront this second Usurper immediately; he had neither a navy nor a port from which to launch his attack. He worked on both problems simultaneously. First, he set up shipyards along the banks of the Moselle at his base in Trier, on the eastern side of Gaul. This was not the most convenient place, as the ships would have to be transported to the west by river and portage, but his overriding concern at this point was safety. At the same time, he picked the same small settlement of Boulogne, the scene of his recent victory, as the best place in which to build his new harbour, building a mole across the bay to prevent any ships or supplies being sent back across the Channel to Allectus in Britian. Conveniently situated on the northern shore of Gaul and within easy reach of the British coast it meant he could bypass Katwijk and the Rhine Delta with which the usurpers were so familiar.

THE SAXON SHORE

The British fleet, the *Classis Brittanica*, now under Allectus's command, cautiously withdrew to Clausentium[98] on Southampton Water, whence it could block any enemy sailing up the Solent. Britain was well prepared for such an invasion. Known then as the *Litus Saxonicum* or 'Saxon Shore',[99] this south-eastern coast of the island was protected by a line of forts stretching from 'Portus Adurni' (Portchester) in Hampshire to the Wash in Norfolk. The forts all date from the late third century and those of Pevensey in Kent and Portchester[100] may have been built by Carausius himself. Both share similar architectural features and in certain aspects echo their continental counterparts.

Portchester sits on a low-lying tongue of land which projects into the natural harbour of present-day Portsmouth. It was close to the open sea and yet linked on its landward side to the local road system. Portchester's strategic situation was to prove essential to British coastal defences well into the eighteenth century. The Romans enclosed the four hectare site with huge walls, in front of which (on the seaward side) was a double ditch. The walls were laid out symmetrically and punctuated by 20 hollow

96 Literary evidence for Carausius and his successor Allectus are two panegyrics, one of 289 delivered to Maximian in Trier by Claudius Mamertinus and the second, ascribed to Eumenius, delivered in 297.

97 The three Gs denote three Emperors; minted in 292.

98 Bitterne, today a suburb of Southampton; sea port for Venta Belgarum (Winchester).

99 It is not known why the Romans called this the Saxon Shore: possibly because the forts were a defence against Saxon pirates or because the garrison was of Saxon origin.

100 Portus Adurni, mentioned in the *Notitia Dignitatum.*

101 Julius Asclepiodotus.

RIGHT: The *Notitia Dignitatum* showing the nine forts of the Saxon Shore: Portchester, Pevensey, Lympne, Dover, Richborough, Reculver, Bradwell-on-Sea, Burgh Castle and Brancaster.
BELOW: A contemporary map of the Saxon Shore forts.

RIGHT: The *Notitia Dignitatum* showing the nine forts of the Saxon Shore: Portchester, Pevensey, Lympne, Dover, Richborough, Reculver, Bradwell-on-Sea, Burgh Castle and Brancaster.

BELOW: A contemporary map of the Saxon Shore forts.

D-shaped towers, of which 14 remain. These walls were three metres thick and they stood to a height of six metres, being built in a series of horizontal layers of flint held together by mortar and strengthened at intervals by courses of limestone and brick tiles. The foundations reached down into 1.5 metres of solid chalk. Along the interior face was a wall-walk, as in Spalatro. To build such a large camp required an enormous amount of material. (It has been estimated that, in the case of Pevensey, 1,600 boatloads of building materials were needed.)

Three years later, by late 296, Constantius Chlorus had assembled two large fleets, one based in Boulogne under his own command and the other further south along the River Seine at Rotomagus (Rouen)[101] under his Praetorian Prefect. This second fleet sailed for Britain (following mistaken orders) but, due to thick fog, was able to avoid capture by the British fleet and anchored just south

of it in Southampton Water. There the Roman commander burnt his ships and marched for London to meet Allectus. Allectus, in turn, led his army southwest with all speed to counter this surprise invasion. He never envisaged the two-pronged attack planned by Constantine Chlorus. The strategy worked perfectly: Constantius Chlorus and his army were able to land in Kent unopposed. Allectus, meanwhile, was defeated meeting his death in battle,[102] giving Constantius Chlorus the time to march to London, where he was given a triumphant welcome. Medallions were struck to celebrate this great victory showing Constantius Chlorus wearing a laurel wreath of victory and inscribed FL VAL CONSTANTIUS NOB CAES (Flavius Valerius Constantius Noble Caesar). On the obverse he is once again crowned with a wreath, this time by the figure of Victory, and holding a spear he is raising the province of Britannia from its knees. It was minted in Trier in 296.[103]

---

102 Thought to be in the region of Silchester.
103 Part of the Beaurains Hoard (Arras) *c.* 310–315, acquired by the British Museum in 1924.
104 Of the 12 Latin panegyrics which survive, five date from the Tetrarchy.
105 Then Augustodunum.
106 The Moselle flowed into the Rhine at Koblenz south of Cologne, which was the base of the *Classis Germanica* (German fleet).
107 Both the above date from the second half of the first century AD.

Constantius Chlorus's victory over the British caused a great stir and he became an immediate hero, though just as Galerius's title of *Persicus Maximus* was shared simultaneously by all four Tetrarchs, so that of *Britannicus Maximus* became universal to them all. The Panegyric of 297 was written to celebrate the event and coins were minted in Constantius's new capital, Trier, to mark the occasion. This panegyric emphasises the difference between the two Western Emperors.[104] Maximian is described as an energetic and successful soldier, but Constantius Chlorus, with such an outstanding record behind him, is depicted both as a successful general and a man responsive to the needs of the provinces over which he ruled.

TRIER

Having achieved a lasting peace, Constantius Chlorus turned his attention to rebuilding Gaul's cities. He imported skilled craftsmen to restore their architecture, giving local populations the confidence to return home. In this way he was able to regain the loyalties of the local Gallic community leaders, who looked upon him as their own particular Augustus. One reason for this popularity was his interest in the Schools of Rhetoric which had been such important centres of learning within Gaul before the upsets of the early third century. Autun[105] was a case in point: once one of the most famous of these schools, its buildings now lay in ruins and all teaching had ceased. Constantius Chlorus, aware of the need for good publicity, had already appointed a well-known rhetorician, Eumenius, as his *magister memoriae*, the equivalent of a private secretary today. As such, Eumenius was a member of the Emperor's extensive court and had accompanied him on several campaigns.

Eumenius came of a Greek family which had settled in Gaul, and his grandfather had run the School of Rhetoric in Autun. Eumenius, by now a wealthy man in his own right, requested permission to dedicate a large portion of his own money to the school's restoration. To strengthen his case, he recalled the Emperor's generosity which had enabled him to make this offer. The text of the speech he gave at the reopening of the school, in front of the governor of the province in the Autun's main square, repeats the same message once again. The text of this speech survives to this day.

Following the reconquest of Britain, the fron-

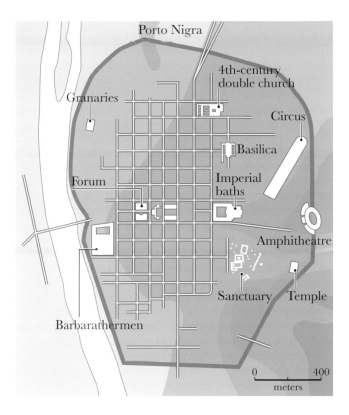

FACING PAGE: Two views of the Roman wall at Portchester, the lower showing the original Roman stonework interwoven with courses of brick.
ABOVE: Map of Roman Trier, showing the wall, Porta Nigra, Basilica, Imperial Baths and amphitheatre.

tier defences of northern Gaul and Germany were reorganised. Forts, similar to those of the Saxon Shore, were built along the coasts of northern Gaul. Trier, in eastern Gaul, already fulfilled many of the newly formulated criteria of frontier organisation, being easily accessible both from the Rhine and from the interior of Gaul and Belgica. It lay at a particularly important junction, where the road from Lyon crossed the River Moselle en route to a major crossing of the Rhine in the north.[106] Under Diocletian's reforms Trier became the capital of the new province, Belgica Prima. As such it underwent a massive reorganisation, eventually becoming one of the most important Tetrarchic capitals in the Western Empire.

The Roman bridge, the forum, the public baths and the amphitheatre all pre-date the arrival of the Western Tetrarchs. The huge size of the amphitheatre indicates its early importance, rivalling those of Nîmes and Arles.[107] But it was the Emperor Constantius Chlorus and his son Constantine who created the city, which, in its magnificence, became known as the 'Second Rome'. Constantius Chlorus retained the work of previous generations, but added extensively to what was already there. Recent dendrochronology of the surviving timbers in the cellars under the amphitheatre show extensive new work from this period. These cellars housed the complicated machinery necessary for the dramatic presentations made above ground in the arena itself. Here were the hoists for the cages which, on reaching the surface, would spring open to allow a lion or tiger to leap dramatically into the arena, to the delight and horror of the crowd.

PORTA NIGRA

One of the most iconic buildings in Trier, which also just pre-dates Constantius Chlorus, is the Porta Nigra, an enormous gate to the north of the city and the only one of the original gates to survive.[108] As a gate to the city its chief role was obviously defensive, but the large arched openings on the

108 The reason for its survival is that it became a Christian church after the death of St Simeon, who had lived there as a hermit for the last seven years of his life (1028–35).

upper level, and the extension of the towers on its inward face which form a courtyard, are unusual. Was this intended as the beginning of a grand processional route into the city as in other Tetrarchic foundations? Certain other details such as the capitals, which have been left as simple blocks, and the interior, which is devoid of any decoration at all, seem to suggest that the Porta Nigra was never finished. It is strange that Constantius Chlorus did not complete this structure, given that it was the main entrance to the city on which he had lavished such limitless money and care.

Disentangling the work of the father from that of the son is an almost impossible task but Constantius Chlorus undoubtedly laid the foundations of the greatest buildings which survive in Trier today, chief among them being the Basilica and the Imperial Baths. To use the term basilica – a building used for commercial and judicial purposes – is, in terms of Roman architecture, incorrect. A throne room or *sala regia* would describe its role better, but it has been known as the Basilica for many years. It stands within and on top of a complex of buildings which had already served as a *palatium* for previous gen-

erations of governors. It is the only such Audience Chamber to survive in any of the Tetrarchic palaces and, as such, gives us a valuable insight into their courtly ceremonial.

THE BASILICA

The Basilica, when first built, had two long narrow courtyards to either side of it. At right angles to and across its entrance was a third building. It was as long as the Basilica itself, but only half its width. Midway along this chamber's length were two wide openings opposite each other; the first led directly into the Throne Room/Audience Chamber (ie today's Basilica) while the second, marked on the exterior by a projecting portico, led outside to the Forum. (In other words, this room formed the cross of the T-bar on the ground plan.) This portico was the grand entrance to both the first room and the Throne Room. Standing at the centre of it, the petitioner would have had an uninterrupted view of the 70 metres along which he would have to walk to reach the Emperor.

The ceremonial for such an occasion was very strict: Diocletian had devised it at the very beginning of his reign, and each Tetrarch had to observe

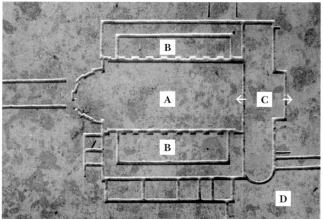

FACING PAGE: The Porta Nigra exterior.
TOP: The Basilica today. Originally it had two sets of wooden galleries beneath the two rows of windows and the small square windows lit the stairs.

ABOVE: Plan of the palace:
A. Basilica (Throne Room/ Audience Chamber)
B. Two surrounding courtyards
C. Approach Chamber
D. Forum
→ Openings: One to the Forum and one to the Audience Chamber.

it in detail.[109] The Emperor sat behind a curtain on a raised dais at the far end of the Throne Room, protected by members of his imperial guard. The name of the petitioner was called. He approached the throne together with his sponsor from the back of the hall. On arrival at the Emperor's feet, the petitioner had to perform a *proskynesis*. With arms thrown across his chest, a gesture symbolising a fettered prisoner, he prostrated himself before the Emperor and made his plea from that position. On completion of the interview, the applicant had to exit backwards. A *proskynesis* originally formed part of an elaborate religious ceremonial practised by the ancient Greeks: in adopting it for secular purposes, Diocletian was once again underlining his divine position.

The sheer size of the Basilica and its unlikely survival give us a rare insight into the grandeur of such a Throne Room. The interior was magnificent.[110] It is a huge uninterrupted space with an apse at its northern end set behind a large arch, under which stood the Emperor's throne. It is lit by two rows of round-headed windows, which wrap themselves around the whole exterior. The inner walls still have the holes into which clamps were driven to secure the great marble slabs which lined the walls. The apse was probably coffered and covered in gold leaf and the floor was covered in *opus sectile* – black and white mosaics, laid in a geometrical pattern. In scale this building is comparable only to the Basilica of Maxentius in Rome, built in 308, and could have been the prototype for it, since Maxentius would have known Trier well.[111]

The exterior presents a forbidding spectacle. Two galleries ran below each line of the windows; these were supported by strong horizontal timbers, which slotted into the walls and were braced by struts set at an angle below them. Discoloration of the brick is today's only clue to their original position. The walls were plastered to resemble stucco. It must be remembered that this façade would never have been seen in its entirety, as the exterior courtyards would have allowed only a partial view. The contrast, therefore, with the wide-open expanse of the Throne Room would have been enormous.

109 Athanasius (293–373), Patriarch of Alexandria, gives a detailed description of such an audience.
110 St Ambrose, who had grown up in Trier, used the same design when he began to build St Simpliciano in Milan. It was to become the favoured plan for large Christian churches well into the future.
111 See Chapter 11.

THE IMPERIAL BATHS

The Imperial Baths, the *Kaiserthermen*, in the south-eastern section of the city rivalled the Basilica in both size and grandeur. They covered an area similar to that of the nearby Forum. Contemporary with the Baths of Diocletian in Rome, they were one of the largest sets of baths outside the imperial city. Constantius Chlorus cleared away a whole neighbourhood of local houses to make room for the huge exercise ground, the *palaestra*. Those invited to use the Baths would have gathered in the *palaestra* to socialise, watch the young gymnasts and follow their individual interests in the adjoining library and study rooms.

A magnificent gate formed the entrance to the baths. The huge rooms in which the bathing took place – the *tepidarium*, the *calidarium* and the *frigidarium* – were arranged in a well-established pattern. One room followed another in logical succession, each one flanked by smaller rooms to either side: the *tepidarium*, the warm room, was the first, next came the hot baths, the *calidarium*, and finally the cold plunge baths, the *frigidarium*. In the overall design special emphasis was given to circular and semi-circular forms, the whole revolving around a

FACING PAGE: Interior of the Basilica. Note the arch under which the Emperor would have received applicants; the apse was coffered and covered in gold mosaics and the walls clothed with marble slabs at the lower level.

ABOVE: The Imperial Baths: exterior of the *calidarium*.

BELOW: Interior of the *calidarium*. Note the courses of brick and multiple rows of retaining arches.

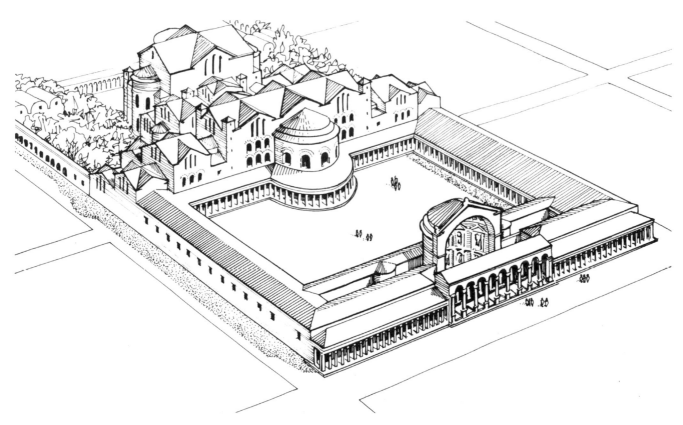

ABOVE: Reconstruction of the Imperial Baths illustrating the entrance and *palaestra* colonnade with bath buildings in the background.
BELOW: Underground passages and service chambers of the Imperial Baths.

circular core. Even the staircases in each corner of the *calidarium* followed a spiral pattern.

As in the Basilica, the interiors were lavishly decorated. To service such a large complex, elaborate tunnels and passages existed underneath, providing access to the hypocaust heating and drains. Water was supplied by an aqueduct eight miles long, which ran in an entirely closed channel. Water for the baths would have been heated in massive cylinders of soldered bronze metal, placed near the furnaces alongside the *calidarium*. Strangely, there is no evidence that these furnaces were ever fired or that the necessary water pipes were installed, which must point, once again, to the buildings being incomplete.

Constantius's palace in Trier extended over 900 square metres, today covered by the Cathedral, Bishop's Palace and public gardens. It far exceeded in area the buildings of any earlier settlement. Ausonius, the poet upon whom we rely for much of our knowledge of Maximian's Milan, paints a magnificent picture of Trier. Between them, father and son created a city of such grandeur that successive generations of Emperors were also content to make it their home. Such an achievement must surely be the best testimonial of all.

THE IGEL COLUMN

INDEPENDENT PORTRAITS of Constantius Chlorus are rare, but according to local legend the third-century Igel Column, a few miles down river from Trier, depicts him, his first wife, Helena, and their son Constantine as a boy. The parents stand to either side of their son, above which small panels describe the daily life of Secundinius, a wealthy cloth merchant who raised this handsome monument to commemorate both his own and the imperial family. Reliefs describe many details of mercantile life along the river: bales of

cloth are inspected for their quality and horses tow laden boats upstream. The column forms a valuable historical document of Gallo-Roman life and was once brightly painted. It is now under the protection of UNESCO.

ABOVE: Two views of the Igel Column with a depiction of Constantius Chlorus, Helena and their son Constantine as a boy.

The first is in situ; the second is a reconstruction in the Archaeological Museum painted to illustrate its original colouring.

BELOW: *The Triumph of Caesar* by Andrea Mantegna (1489–92). Caesar sits in his chariot holding an ivory sceptre and a palm, and is crowned with a wreath of laurel. Flames, banners and standards precede him as the cavalcade passes a triumphal arch, yet another symbol of victory.

CHAPTER IX

MAXIMIAN IN MILAN AND ROME

Maximian, his capital city of Milan and the Tetrarchic work in Rome. The 'vicennalia', the Edict of Persecution, and the simultaneous abdication of Diocletian and Maximian.

MAXIMIAN IS THE MOST ELUSIVE of the Tetrarchs. As a reigning Emperor he outlasted the other three, not because of his ability but because of his reluctance to relinquish power and his desperation to retain the 'purple' which had been thrown his way so unexpectedly. Assessing his artistic contribution in Milan is difficult, because very little survives of the transformation he wrought there, but he undoubtedly became a great builder in Rome. However, although he rarely visited Rome, several buildings which survive to this day date to his imperium. The city came within his jurisdiction and he undertook, albeit at a distance, the supervision of the Tetrarchic works commissioned there.

Diocletian may have had his reservations about Rome, but he was very aware of the need to rebuild and repair any of the ancient buildings which had been destroyed by the devastating fire of 284, just before his acclamation. These buildings had historical overtones which had resonated down the centuries and their survival was all-important. In Diocletian's enforced absence, it fell to Maximian to oversee the renovations, initiated in 298. Consequently – and

this is an intriguing thought – it is likely that these buildings and the inevitable problems thrown up during their construction were discussed many times within the Emperor's family circle. His son Maxentius certainly inherited his father's interest in architecture, and in his turn was to commission some of the finest structures of antiquity.

Maximian, like his colleagues, was an Illyrian. He was born just north of Sirmium in today's Fruška Gora. It is a hilly, poorly cultivated area and his parents struggled to make a living as shopkeepers. He had virtually no education and was a wild, capricious boy, but was well suited to the army and had a most successful career serving under Diocletian. Gibbon is chillingly dismissive of him and describes him as: 'Ignorant of letters, careless of laws; the rusticity of his appearance and manners, still betrayed in the most elevated fortune, the meanness of his extraction.'

However, Diocletian knew him well and could see beyond this rough, unappealing surface. The two men shared an official birthday and Maximian always held Diocletian, his senior by ten years, in high regard. The pair complemented each other,

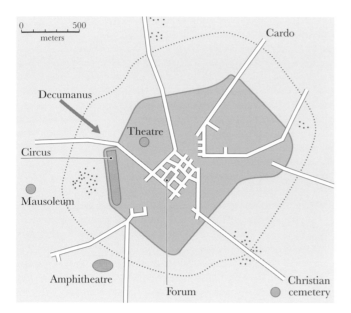

the one far-seeing with an extraordinary talent for mastering detail and the other tough, fearless and willing to carry out any task, however unpleasant. It proved to be a most successful partnership and survived for 20 years.

Some commentators believe that Maximian had been singled out by Diocletian many years before the events of 285 made their partnership a reality, for it was only a few months after the decisive Battle of Margus, in the summer of that same year, that Maximian was declared a Caesar in Milan. Diocletian's tact in dealing with Maximian was all-important: he never resented Maximian's success in battle and always awarded him his justly won military honours. Maximian, for his part, was always willing to follow Diocletian's lead, and prior to his elevation as an Augustus in 293 he looked upon himself as a son to Diocletian, a relationship which was confirmed when he took Diocletian's family name of Valerius.

The panegyrist Mamertinus describes the meeting of Diocletian and Maximian to celebrate their *decennalia* in Milan (Mediolanum) in 293 as the meeting of two deities – declaiming that, had the two Emperors ascended the Alps together, their bright glow would have illuminated all Italy. An extravagant piece of rhetoric this may have been, but Mamertinus's words proved strangely prophetic of the importance Milan was to have for Maximian.

112 The Alemanni originated near the River Main; they had attacked Gaul and were the first barbarian tribe to invade Italy.
113 Ausonius, *Clarae Urbes*, v.

Strategically situated at the centre of a busy road system which linked up with the river network running from the Po Valley into the Adriatic, the city allowed him to keep a watchful eye on the Alpine passes to the north, and was to prove a useful base when his mobile troops had to confront the Alemmanni in Raetia (Switzerland).[112] Establishing Milan and Aquileia as the central cities of his reign (both are marked on the Peutinger Table) brought great benefits to the Italian peninsula as a whole.

MAXIMIAN'S PALACE

Milan's geographical position has meant that each subsequent generation has adapted and reinvented the city to suit its own needs. Maximian's city, which was universally admired and written about, did not outlast his *imperium*. Only a few years later, it became an important centre for the newly established Christian religion with the result that Maximian's city soon disappeared. The whereabouts of the Imperial Palace, the mighty Baths of Hercules – which rivalled those of Trier in their grandeur – and the circus are all known, but tragically little remains.

One of the few items to survive is an enormous red porphyry bath, which had belonged in the Emperor's palace and now serves as the baptismal font in the Cathedral. The Baths of Hercules are reputed to have been huge. Fragments of floor mosaics and a section of a large statue of Hercules still exist, together with a statue base inscribed, *Imp(eratori) Caes(ari) M(arco) Aur(elio) Val(erio) Maximiano P(io) F(elici)*. In naming his baths after the demi-god Hercules, Maximian recalled the *signum* given him by Diocletian on his elevation as an Augustus. The 12 mythical labours of Hercules must have provided plenty of material for the interior decoration of these baths.

The amphitheatre in Milan was even larger than that of Trier and was only exceeded in size by Rome and Capua. The poet Ausonius ranked Milan as the seventh among the cities of the Empire and gives us a tantalising glimpse of its beauty.[113] He wrote in c.380 that 'The city is huge and surrounded by a double circle of walls. There is a circus where people gaze at spectacles, a theatre with tiers of seats, temples, the fortified imperial palace, the mint, and the Herculean quarter, the section called after the famous Baths of Hercules. The colonnaded courtyards are adorned with marble statues and the walls are surrounded with fortified towers.'

TOP: Column base in the Archaeological Museum, Milan, destined for an honorary statue of Maximian:
IMP(ERATORI) CAES(ARI) M(ARCO) AUR(ELIO) VAL(ERIO) MAXIMIANO P(IO) F(ELICI) INVICTO AUG(USTO)

ABOVE: Porphyry bath from the Imperial Baths of Hercules, now used as a baptismal font in Milan Cathedral.

ABOVE RIGHT: The bell tower of the church of San Maurizio was originally one of the massive towers of Maximian's circus.

RIGHT: Ruins of the Imperial Palace.

FACING PAGE: Plan of Maximian's Milan. The Imperial Palace lay between the Circus and the Forum.

There were numerous freshwater fountains and streets lined with colonnades offered shade from the unremitting sun in summer and shelter from the cold north winds in winter. The remains of such a colonnade – sixteen free-standing columns centring on an arch in the Piazza of St Lorenzo today – once marked the *temenos* of a temple. They were moved here at the end of the fourth century to form a courtyard for the new Christian church. Still visible beneath one section of the Church of St Lorenzo is the huge platform on which it was built. This was made from large stone blocks, friezes and half columns, all spoils from the nearby amphitheatre. Outside the city, beyond the double row of walls, were a succession of palaces and villas stretching far into the countryside. Though little is left of Maximian's Milan, the remains of Trier and Thessalonica help us to appreciate the lost magnificence of his imperial city, and also demonstrate the rivalry that compelled each Emperor to try to equal – if not outdo – the achievements of his colleagues.

St Ambrose, writing at much the same time as Ausonius, refers to Milan in much the same way as

the historian. He mentions Maximian's mausoleum in one of his episcopal letters.[114] Maximian's mausoleum lay outside the city walls, as Roman law forbad burials within the city. The design was very similar to those of both Diocletian and Galerius and, like theirs, it lay within a fortified precinct. For many years it survived as a rotunda, alongside the early Christian church of St Vittore al Corpo. A drawing of about 1570, by a little-known draughtsman from the Netherlands,[115] depicts it as an octagon with small windows, the top wall lit by a small gallery. The present church of St Vittore al Corpo is the second church on the site: it was built between 1560 and 1580, when the original Romanesque church was demolished and its relics transferred to the present building. Maximian's mausoleum, which had stood alongside it, was pulled down at the same time. Plans to incorporate the Emperor's mausoleum into the second church came to nothing.

The intriguing question therefore remains: was Maximian's mausoleum ever converted into a Christian chapel as were those of Diocletian and Galerius? If so, what an irony it would be – for the first church arose as a direct result of the Edict of Persecution proclaimed by Diocletian in 303. Legend has it that Victor Maurus, had been a favourite member of Maximian's Praetorian Guard; he was executed on the Emperor's specific orders after his repeated refusals to give up his Christian faith. Following his canonisation as St Victor ('Vittore' in Italian) the site of his martyrdom became a popular shrine, the first church being built to accommodate the numerous pilgrims who visited it.

As so often happened, Maximian's mausoleum was never used. He died in 310, following a second enforced retirement, by committing suicide. After his death, his successor Constantine I ordered all references to Maximian to be destroyed – an act known in the Roman world as a *damnatio memoriae* ('a damnation of memory'). The site of his death remains questionable; was it in Marseilles, where he had been defeated in battle by his son-in-law Constantine I? The medieval *Chronicle of Navaliciense* tells of his sarcophagus being present there in 1054, when it was destroyed by the then Bishop of Arles.

In contrast to the paucity of surviving material in Milan, there is a substantial body of work inaugurated by the Tetrarchs – and built largely under the supervision of Maximian himself – which still exists in Rome. The Chronographer of 354 records this

114 Ambrose (*c.*337–397) was raised in Trier. He was appointed Bishop of Milan in 374. (Letter: *Ep.*53.4.)
115 Fabrizy. The mausoleum then stood alongside the early Romanesque church.
116 As witnessed in Mantegna's *The Triumph of Caesar* at Hampton Court, a series of nine paintings depicting the ceremonial triumph of Julius Caesar, painted for Francesco Gonzaga *c.*1485–92 and later purchased by Charles I.

LEFT: Sketch by Fabrizy, *c.*1570, of St Vittore al Corpo before the destruction of Maximian's eight-sided mausoleum which had been incorporated into the Christian church.
BELOW: Coin of Maximian inscribed: IMP(ERATOR) C(AESAR) MAXIMIANUS AUG(USTUS).

FACING PAGE: Roman colonnade in the Piazza of St Lorenzo, Milan.

work: 'Many public works were constructed by these Emperors: the Senate House, The Forum of Caesar, the Basilica of Julia, the Theatre of Pompey, two porticos, three nymphaea, two temples, Iseum and Serapeum, the New Arch and Diocletian's Baths.'

Diocletian only visited Rome on one occasion – in November 303, to celebrate the *vicennalia*, the twentieth year of his reign and the tenth year of the Tetrarchy. The occasion was marked with great acclaim and rejoicing, and took the form of a very elaborate 'triumph'. A 'triumph' was the highest

honour of all, originally only granted to a general and attached to a specific victory.[116] By the early fourth century, however, it had become the exclusive right of an Emperor and had been extended to include all the successes of his particular reign, whether military or not.

The Romans placed great store by ceremonial. A triumphal procession would assemble in the Campus Martius, a huge area just below the Capitol. The senators and magistrates headed the parade, followed by trumpeters, spoils of victory such as gold and silver, arms and armour, and artistic treasure. Priests and acolytes holding sacrificial instruments and vessels followed white oxen whose horns had been gilded and decorated with garlands for the impending sacrifice to Jupiter. The victorious general/Emperor brought up the rear, together with his triumphant army, his captives and hostages.

Ten years earlier Diocletian and Maximian had chosen to celebrate the tenth anniversary of Diocletian's reign, the *decennalia*, in Milan rather than Rome. This had aroused great resentment among the senatorial families of the Eternal City, but the senators in Rome could no longer expect an Emperor to come to them as he had in the past: they now had to meet him at the place of his choice. In view of the importance of such an anniversary, however, works of art had nonetheless been commissioned in Rome.

VICENNALIA

The *vicennalia* was a much more important anniversary and an occasion the two Emperors could not ignore. To mark the event, the pair appeared together in Rome for the first and only time during their reigns. One of the conditions introduced by Diocletian when establishing the Tetrarchy had been that each Emperor should benefit equally from the achievement of the others. As a result they all shared the same titles regardless of whether they had served in that particular theatre of war. So during the *vicennalia* Diocletian and Maximian celebrated all the successes and victories of their combined reigns, including those of their Caesars.[117]

Soldiers in full armour, wearing laurel wreaths and carrying the standards of their legions, pro-

cessed from the Temple of Jupiter on the Capitol to the Forum below. The two Augusti, dressed in purple tunics decorated with rich golden embroideries, sat in two golden chariots drawn by white horses or possibly even elephants. Coins minted to celebrate the occasion portray the scene so vividly described by Lactantius. They show the two Emperors identically portrayed, seated in similar chariots, each holding a globe in his right hand and a short sceptre in his left with an inscription which reads: CONCORDIA AUGG.NN.[118] Different peoples from all over the Empire took part in the ceremony, including some of Galerius's Persian prisoners. Orators wrote panegyrics, and Diocletian commissioned an elaborate monument to commemorate the event. Money was distributed on at least three occasions and events were arranged at which the Emperors could expect a loyal acclamation.[119] The Roman crowd, however, proved surprisingly unco-operative, making their displeasure obvious. Twenty years of being ignored by the reigning Tetrarchs found a serious voice: the newly built baths and arches were no substitute for a living presence. Most of the populace had never had the opportunity of witnessing such a spectacle, or registering disapproval in such a direct manner. Diocletian's response was to leave the city as soon as he reasonably could.

Perhaps Diocletian had imagined that the restoration of the Forum which he had delegated to Maximian would compensate for his failure to make a personal appearance in the city and be seen as a concrete demonstration of his concern. He was certainly aware of the importance the ancient city held in the minds of every Roman citizen all over the Empire. Indeed, these ancient Roman buildings were a constant source of inspiration to all the Tetrarchs, and the work which took place during the Tetrarchy outstripped that of their immediate predecessors. Septimius Severus had been the most recent Emperor to make an architectural impact on the Forum, with the construction of his great arch 100 years before. An inscription in gilded bronze lettering on the attic storey proclaimed the success of the Severan family in establishing their credentials as ruling Emperors. Like the Tetrarchs, they had originated from an outpost of the Roman Empire – present-day Libya. This edifice was the inspiration not only of Diocletian's Arcus Novus and Galerius's Arch in Thessalonica, but also that of their successor, Constantine the Great.[120]

---

117 It is unlikely that either Caesar, Constantius Chlorus or Galerius was present on this occasion.
118 Munich, Munzkabinett: Aureus of Diocletian. The double GG denotes two Augusti.
119 Such an event is called a *congiara*. An example is depicted on the Arch of Constantine.
120 The Arch of Constantine was built in 315.
121 The Rostra took its name from the prows of captured enemy warships which were embedded into the wall behind. This tradition was copied elsewhere and continued for many hundreds of years. In nineteenth-century St Petersburg similar prows were embedded into a column rather than a wall.

TETRARCHIC BUILDINGS IN ROME: THE ROSTRUM

Maximian's first task had been to redesign the Rostrum,[121] the platform from which all-important matters of state were announced. The Rostrum, just below the Arch of Septimius Severus, had been a focal point in the Forum since the time of Julius Caesar. Maximian wanted to give it a more impressive appearance by adding five huge columns – four to hold statues of the Tetrarchs and the fifth and central one to hold a statue of Jupiter. The shafts were rose red granite with white marble capitals carved with Medusa heads. Jupiter's column was larger than the rest and its base bore the words 'Vicennalia Imperatorum'.

ABOVE: A freely interpreted reconstruction of the Roman Forum. In the foreground is Diocletian's new Rostrum of five columns to hold statues of the Four Tetrarchs with Jupiter at their centre. To the left is the Arch of Septimius Severus, to the left of which is the Basilica of Aemilia; in the centre are the Temple of the Divine Caesar and behind it the Temple of Vesta.

FACING PAGE: The Decennalian Monument. Two winged victories hold a shield inscribed CAESARUM DECENNALIA FELICITER (Happy Tenth Anniversary of the Caesars).

LEFT: Panel from the Arch of Constantine with Diocletian's Rostrum in the background, one column of which supports banners.
BELOW LEFT: Diocletian, crowned by a Victory, sacrifices at an altar; Mars (left) and Roma (far right) look on.
BELOW: The Decennalian Monument: a procession of four Emperors with globes and short batons.

Only one of these five column bases remains today. It is known as the Decennalian Monument (Tenth Anniversary Monument).[122] The sculpted reliefs on this column base are symbolic of everything the Tetrarchy wanted to convey and, thanks to their relatively good condition, they hold an important message for us too. On the front face of the column base are two winged victories holding up a shield, on one of which is written *Caesarum Decennalia Feliciter* ('Happy Tenth Anniversary of the Caesars'). Another face depicts the *suovertauralia*, a popular Roman ceremony in which a bull, a ram and a pig are led in procession, each animal elaborately adorned for the occasion, before being sacrificed to Mars. The underlying message of such an ancient ritual was to ask Mars to purify the land and provide a fruitful harvest. The four Emperors themselves appear on the third face. They lead a procession, holding globes in their right hands and short batons in their left – symbols of both kingship and military

122 The Decennalian Column was found in 1547.

rank. Their faces have been badly damaged, but the attendants in the background retain their clear-cut features; they have beards and long wavy hair and hold military standards on which it is still possible to detect an eagle, a Victory with an olive branch, and a *genius populi Romani*. On the last face, the Emperor is sacrificing at an altar. He is crowned by a small winged Victory and the *genii* of the Senate while Mars looks on from the left and Roma, seated on the right, has the Sun God Invictus hovering behind her. From now on this new Tetrarchic monument would form a permanent backcloth to all the important occasions taking place in the Forum. An extra-ordinary example of such an occasion, as already mentioned, is shown on the *adlocutio* relief on the Arch of Constantine erected 12 years later. Here the

ABOVE: The Forum today. At the top left is the Arch of Septimius Severus. The brick Curia/Senate House is next to the ruins of the Basilica Aemilia. The portico to the right is the Temple of Antoninus and **Fausta and the three columns belong to the Temple of the Dioscuri. In the far distance is the monument to Victor Emmanuel.**
RIGHT: The original marble inlay floor of the Curia, installed by Diocletian.

Emperor Constantine (headless) gives an oration to the Roman people from the Rostrum, behind which is Diocletian's Decennalian Monument showing the five columns, each with a statue on top.

THE CURIA

Restoration of the two adjacent monuments, the Basilica Julia and the Curia or Senate House, was an integral part of this plan. Diocletian had always had a great admiration for Julius Caesar as the man who had adopted Salona, his home town, as a colonia, and perhaps his work in this section of the Forum is an acknowledgement of this early regard. No changes were made to the exterior of the Curia, which is surprisingly simple and unadorned.[123] The present doors are replicas of the originals, which were moved to the Church of St John Lateran by Pope Alexander VII in 1660. The interior is an impressively spacious room: the walls have alternate rectangular and round-headed niches, handsomely framed by columns sitting on carved white marble consoles, all of which date from the Tetrarchy. The floor is also contemporary with Diocletian,

123 Coins minted under Augustus show that the Curia had once had a much more elaborate façade, with a portico at first-floor level and a pediment adorned with statues and crowned by a Victory standing on a globe.

ABOVE: The remains of the surrounding wall of the Baths of Diocletian.

BELOW: Plan of the Baths of Diocletian.

C.   Caldarium
F.   Frigidarium
PAL. Palaestra
T.   Tepidarium
B.   St Bernardo alle Terme

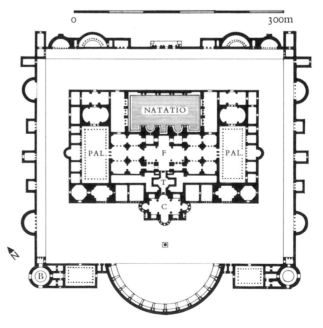

and is one of the finest remaining examples of fourth-century marble inlay, with rosettes, cornucopias, squares and rectangles fitting together to form a patchwork of welcome colour. Red porphyry, purple, green and yellow meld harmoniously together. Along the sides of the room broad, shallow steps held chairs for the 300 or so senators, while a podium at the far end held the chief senator's throne and an altar, together with another statue of Victory. Maxentius, Maximian's son, when redesigning the interior of the Temple of Rome and Venus, was to look back to the Curia for inspiration.

BATHS OF DIOCLETIAN

Baths feature in all Tetrarchic capitals, and Rome was to be no exception. The Emperors intended these baths as a magnanimous gift to the people. Finding a large enough area in which to build such a huge complex, however, meant that countless ordinary citizens had their homes destroyed and were forcibly moved away. (The remnants of some of these buildings were found during a recent reconstruction of the subway.) The story of the Bath's construction is recorded in its dedicatory inscription, which goes into unusual detail.

ABOVE: The interior of St Maria degli Angeli inserted into the original *frigidarium* by Michelangelo in 1563/4. Cross vaults and the eight columns of Aswan granite are original to the Baths.

BELOW: The entrance of the church, originally the *tepidarium*; the *calidarium* has disappeared under today's Piazza della Republica.

Diocletian's baths covered 9 hectares of prime land between the Quirinal and Viminal Hills, and to walk around the perimeter of that ancient precinct takes a good hour even today. Extensive walls enclose the bathing areas of the *tepidarium*, *calidarium* and *frigidarium*; included, too, were the extra facilities required for a grand commission such as the two huge gardens, which acted as *palaestrae*, and the pavilions, libraries and gymnasiums. A small section of the walls still exists together with a broad projecting cornice which played a largely practical role, providing a permanent walkway for workmen to clear the gutters and roofs above.

Little remains of these original baths, as the huge buildings have been adapted, torn down or converted to other uses over the years – the most famous being Michelangelo's conversion of the

124 The baths were active until the sixth century, when the aqueducts were destroyed by barbarian invasions. After the construction of St Maria degli Angeli the outlying halls were used as warehouses until their final destruction following the unification of Italy in the nineteenth century.
125 The Arcus Novus stood next to the Church of St Maria in Via Lata very close to today's Corso. It was destroyed by Pope Innocent VIII in 1491.

ABOVE LEFT: St Bernardo alle Terme, converted in 1598 out of one of the rotundas in the perimeter wall of Diocletian's Baths (see plan).
LEFT: The original coffered roof of the church, which is still in situ.

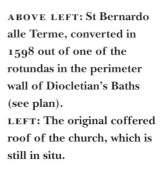

FACING PAGE, LEFT: Column base from the Arcus Novus, depicting Victory holding a palm and military trophy with a kneeling prisoner.
RIGHT: Castor or Pollux holding the bridle of a horse and a banner, depicted on the Arcus Novus.

central section into the Church of St Maria degli Angeli. The *calidarium* has disappeared under the present-day Piazza della Republica in front of the church, the *tepidarium* now forms the church's entrance hall or narthex, and the large *frigidarium* is the main nave. Though the floor level of this nave has been raised, the original cross vaults and the eight huge Composite columns of Aswan granite are still in their original positions, unchanged since antiquity. The large outdoor pool, the *nautatio* – the size of an Olympic pool of today – disappeared as the church buildings were extended, but there are still exciting glimpses beyond the church's sacristy of some of its remaining high walls (once decorated with statues and niches), which originally hid the bathers from public view.

St Maria degli Angeli is the largest and most impressive of the ecclesiastical conversions, but there are two more which also emphasise the scale and extent of these baths. One is the charming small Church of St Bernardo alle Terme, which occupies one of the circular towers which still stand at the corner of its outer walls: it still has its circular shape and original coffering on the ceiling. Another small church has been carved out of the walls along the Via Parigi, of which the façade is the only visible evidence. The baths were built in the record time of eight years, but only dedicated in 306, when six Emperors were listed – the retired Augusti Diocletian and Maximian, the two new Augusti Constantius Chlorus and Galerius, and their new Caesars Severus and Maximinus Daia. As at Felix Romuliana and at Luxor in Egypt, tribute is paid to them all.[124]

ARCUS NOVUS

The third category of building required in any imperial building programme was a triumphal arch. Diocletian chose to place his, the Arcus Novus, also dedicated in 303, in the Via Lata, in close proximity to two existing ones built by Claudius and possibly Aurelian.[125] None of the three has survived. As in the Forum, the Arcus Novus commemorated both the *decennalia* and the *vicennalia*. A fragment of a

LEFT: Column base from the Arcus Novus, depicting a German captive in long trousers and warm cloak.
BELOW LEFT: A Dacian prisoner in a short tunic, depicted on the Arcus Novus. Like the German captive, he has his hands bound behind his back.

sculpted panel, inscribed *votis.x.et.xx* on a shield held by a female figure, is now incorporated into the garden façade of the Villa Medici.[126]

Pope Innocent VIII destroyed the Arcus Novus in 1491. The normal decoration of such arches was a series of free-standing Corinthian or Composite columns standing on carved bases, similar to those on the Arch of Septimius Severus. The reliefs of two such sculpted column bases were discovered in 1523. Fifty years later Cardinal Ferdinando de Medici purchased them for the gardens of his Villa Medici on the Pincian Hill, but subsequently they were removed to Florence to decorate the Boboli Gardens, where they survive today. Copies, however, remain in the gardens of the Villa Medici. The bases were carved on three sides, as the fourth face would have been attached to the wall of the arch; their iconography is appropriately warlike. One face of each column has an illustration of one of the Dioscuri, Castor or Pollux, naked except for a helmet and mantle, holding the bridle of his horse in one hand and a military banner in the other. Two others show captured prisoners, one a Dacian and the other a German, both with their hands tied behind their backs. The German has long trousers tied at the ankles and is draped in a fur mantle to reflect the colder climate of northern Europe, while the Dacian, coming from the south, wears a short tunic; both have haircuts which distinguish them from Roman citizens.

The face of the third column base is carved in deeper relief. It shows two allegorical winged Victories, their elaborate draperies outlining the form of their curvaceous bodies. One, wearing a laurel wreath of victory, holds a palm branch and stands beside a palm tree. Could this symbolise Maximian's successes in North Africa? The other holds a large military trophy made up of a helmet, breastplate,

126 In 1803 Napoleon moved the French Academy from the Palazzo Mancini to the Villa Medici. Doubts have been expressed about the provenance of these panels because their discovery was some distance away from the site of the Arcus Novus. But the custom of reusing earlier sculptures to decorate another later work was widespread.
127 The Praetorian Guard's original role had been to act as personal bodyguards to the ruler of the day. They were finally disbanded by Constantine the Great.

greaves and shields. She stands over a kneeling prisoner, once again with his arms chained behind his back: could this represent Diocletian and his victories in the Balkans and the Far East? The correct order in which to view these sculptures would have been firstly the captives, then the Victories and finally the gods (the Dioscuri). The iconography is a repeat of Galerius's Arch in Thessalonica, for the Persian captives there are paraded before the four Emperors and once again accompanied by divinities, including the Dioscuri.

The Rome that Diocletian left behind was acknowledged as magnificent: 'The first of all cities, home of the Gods, is golden Rome,' wrote Ammanius Marcellinus. But the largesse of Diocletian and Maximian cut little ice with the inhabitants. Both Maximian and Diocletian had already made dangerous enemies of the Praetorian Guard, whom they had distrusted from the outset and whose power they had worked consistently to weaken.[127] They also distrusted the power and influence of the Senate, several members of which were to ally themselves with the same Praetorian Guard for their own personal protection. Maximian had skilfully introduced two loyal Illyrian legions into the city, which undertook many of the duties previously performed by the Praetorian Guard. On the surface the senators remained respectful citizens, but few can have

been left in doubt of Diocletian's displeasure when he left the city 13 days before he was due to appear before the Senate to be invested as a consul.

DIOCLETIAN'S ABDICATION

By the time he left Rome in November 303, Diocletian was both sick and disillusioned. Nineteen years of almost constant travel and the need to be available in any trouble spot in the shortest possible time had begun to take their toll. Tradition has it that he had elicited a promise from Maximian many years earlier that they would both abdicate at some future date of the older man's choosing. He now decided to return to Nicomedia to end his rule. This had been the main centre of his empire in the East since 287, and he had lavished huge resources to modernise it, building a basilica, a mint, an armament factory and two new palaces, one for his wife and one for his daughter. Winter that year was a long and cold one, and it took him nine months, travelling in a closed litter, to reach the city (of which virtually nothing remains today).

The following autumn, in November 304, he dedicated the newly built circus. During the ceremony he collapsed and he did not appear again in public until the next year, by which time it was apparent to all that he was a very sick man. It took a further few months before arrangements could

DEDICATORY INSCRIPTION ON THE BATHS OF DIOCLETIAN

RECONSTRUCTED from four different copies now on display in a large hall of the Museo delle Terme in Rome.

D(omini) N(ostri) Diocletianus et Maximianus invicti seniores Aug(usti) patres Imp(eratorum) et Caes(arum); et d(omini) n(ostri) Constantius et Maximianus invicti Aug(usti), et Severus et Maximinus nobilissimi Caesares thermas felices Diocletianas, quas Maximianis Aug(usts) rediens ex Africa sub praesentia maiestatis disposuit ac fieri iussit et Diuoclatiani Aug(usti) fratris sui nomine consecravit coemptis aedificiis pro tanti operas magnitudine omni cultu perfectas Romanis suis dedicaverunt.

'Our masters Diocletian and Maximian, unconquered senior Augusti, fathers of the Emperors and the Caesars, and our masters Constantius and Maximian (Galerius) unconquered Augusti, and Severus and Maximinus (Daia), most noble Caesars, dedicated to their Romans the auspicious Baths of Diocletian, which Maximian Augustus, returning from Africa, in the presence of his majesty, laid out and ordered to be built and dedicated in the name of Diocletian, his brother, after purchasing a sufficient number of buildings for a work of such magnitude and attending to every detail of its ornamentation.'

MARTYRS OF THE EDICT

MANY CASES of Christian martyrdom under Diocletian's Edict of Persecution are recorded, many of which have been greatly embellished. One of the better documented took place in his own home town of Salona. Four soldiers (like St George, members of his personal bodyguards) and a priest called Asterius were executed together with two eminent churchmen, Domnio and Anastasius. Domnio had travelled from Mesopotamia with a group of his fellow countrymen at the end of the previous century as a missionary. He became the first and much-loved Bishop of Salona. His untimely death caused outrage among his fellow Christians and its date is carefully recorded on his tombstone as 10 April 304.

Anastasius, by contrast, was a simple workman who had arrived from Aquileia in the northern Adriatic. He worked in the cloth trade as a fuller and was thrown into the Bay of Salona with a millstone around his neck. Domnio (or Domnius as he is also known) and Anastasius are still two of the most revered saints in Dalmatia and, by a strange twist of fate, are now buried in the mausoleum Diocletian had created for himself.

Another famous martyrdom in the Balkans is that of the Four Crowned Saints. A revenue officer called Porphyrius, describes how four sculptors working in the Pannonian quarries, north of the River Sava, happily obeyed orders to carve statues of Victories and Cupids, but when asked to produce a sculpture of Aesculapius, the Roman god of healing, they refused. As a result they were condemned to death, put into leaden caskets, and thrown into the River Sava to drown. The infamy of this incident lived far into the future and is recounted in the early guide books to Rome. The four were subsequently adopted by the Christian Church as the patron saints of sculptors, and were represented as such by Nanni di Banco, one of the most renowned of Renaissance artists, outside the Or San Michele in Florence, in about 1420.

ABOVE: The Four Crowned Saints by Nanni di Banco in Florence.

Below the niche is a relief panel of a sculptor's workshop.

be made so that he and Maximian could abdicate simultaneously in their respective capitals of Nicomedia and Milan. This momentous event took place on 1 May 305. Lactantius describes the scene:

> Three miles outside Nicomedia is the hill on which Galerius received the purple. On its summit stood the high pillar with the statue of Jupiter on top. The procession went up to this spot, while a great assembly of the army was drawn up around it. Tearfully Diocletian addressed his soldiers, saying he was now infirm after his years of ceaseless toil and that he had earned a rest from his labours. He was therefore going to resign the Empire into younger and more vigorous hands and at the same time appoint new Caesars.

THE EDICT OF PERSECUTION

It is for another event in 303, however, that Diocletian is generally remembered: the issuing of his Edict of Persecution against the Christian Church. This is both unfortunate and unfair, given that up until this point he had proved himself to be an outstandingly just and able Emperor. Lactantius insists that Galerius, taking advantage of Diocletian's ill-health, put great pressure on the Emperor to take this drastic step. Undoubtedly Galerius disliked the Christians intensely and feared that the refusal of Christian soldiers to worship the traditional pagan gods could destabalise discipline within the army.

The reasons for Diocletian's agreement to the edict remain a mystery to this day, but Diocletian himself was always a supporter of the traditional Roman gods as witnessed by his adoption of the signa, Jovius and Herculius during the very early days of his reign. Lactantius, Diocletian's appointed orator in Nicomedia, writes of lengthy debates between the two rulers. He suggests that Diocletian's reluctant assent was prompted by a positive response from the oracle of Apollo of Didyma.[128] Lactantius, living in Nicomedia, witnessed these events for himself. Diocletian's capital was already home to a flourishing Christian community, which had co-existed harmoniously for many years with that of Rome, building its large church in full view of the Imperial Palace. Nevertheless, immediately following the proclamation of the edict, this church was ruthlessly destroyed, its plate and valuables looted and its scriptures and liturgical books burnt. Lactantius could never forgive Diocletian for such a betrayal. His history, fascinating and immediate as it is, is understandably a prejudiced account of his time and must be understood as such.

The puzzle for historians is that Diocletian's court had, until this moment, been reasonably tolerant. Lactantius himself is an interesting example as he was a recent Christian convert and, in his role of 'rhetor' (teacher of rhetoric), an appointee of Diocletian. Lactantius survived but George, the future patron saint of England, was not so lucky. George was a much-favoured member of Diocletian's imperial guard. Born in Nicomedia of Christian parents, George followed his father into the Roman army, rising to the rank of tribune in his late twenties. Although under great pressure from the Emperor to worship the Roman gods, George refused, turning down gifts of land, money and slaves. He was eventually executed on 23 April 303.[129]

This edict was to prove most contentious, to citizens and Emperors alike. Diocletian's western colleagues, particularly Constantius Chlorus, were reluctant to expedite this new law and fewer incidents are recorded in their half of the Empire. One possible reason for this is that Constantius Chlorus may have been a believer himself. Certainly his son, Constantine, was to pass a new act tolerating Christianity in 313. A few years later he went further and, in 317, adopted Christianity as the state religion, a move that was to have lasting consequences and to revolutionise religious thought throughout the Empire.

---

128 A famous sanctuary on the north-west coast of Turkey.
129 The details of St George's life are much disputed owing to lack of documentary evidence.

Plate XLIX

Pannels of the Arched Cieling of the Temple of Æsculapius

Scale of Feet

Capital and Pilaster in the Angle of the Peristylium

Zucchi sculp.t

CHAPTER X

ADAM'S PRACTICE IN LONDON

Adam sets up his practice and wins his early commissions at Kedleston, Syon, Osterley, Bowood and Saltram.

THE PUBLICATION of the *Ruins of Spalatro* was a seminal moment in Adam's long and successful career. During the seven long years this work had taken to materialise, Adam's rise had been meteoric, and it can be argued that this had done away with any need to publish. The fact that Adam persisted in his determination to do so despite the expense of maintaining Clérisseau and the engravers in Venice – even to the point of sending James out to Italy to take charge – shows how much importance he attached to the whole project. He looked upon it as an essential element in the armoury of any self-respecting architect; his rivals had already published successfully, and he was not to be outdone by them. Adam was ever competitive: 'Greek to the teeth but my God they are not handsome,' he remarked of James Stuart's ceiling in Spencer House.

Was there some truth in this damning opinion, or was Adam simply jealous that Stuart had beaten him to the publishing table? In fact Adam had quite a sense of humour and 'Aiming squibs at Stuart was a favourite sport of Adam and should not be taken too literally.'[130] For Stuart, for all his later shortcomings (he became more indolent as he grew older), was an excellent draughtsman and the engravings he produced for *The Antiquities of Athens* were of a very high standard. From the outset of the project he had been determined to take accurate measured drawings, whatever the obstacles put in his way. In the event the book proved too difficult for the average builder to use as a practical manual, and it largely remained a work of reference used only by scholars – albeit one with great influence and a reputation which endured over many years. Adam, who had waited impatiently for the enthusiasm surrounding *The Antiquities of Athens* to die down before he went ahead with the launch of his own book two years later, would not make the same mistake.

Adam used the success of his *Ruins of Spalatro* to introduce a change of style, using the vocabulary of

FACING PAGE: Three coffers from the Temple of Aesculapius and a capital in the peristyle, which Adam often adapted for his own use. (*Ruins of Spalatro*, Plate XLIX)

130 E. Harris, *The Genius of Robert Adam and His Interiors* (2001).

classical architecture in a completely novel way.[131] After two years studying under Clérisseau's critical eye, he was thoroughly conversant with Roman architecture, its concepts, its plans and its ornaments. He also appreciated, however – when searching and evaluating the architectural fragments he bought to take home – the freer use that some Roman imperial architects had made of these traditional ideas. This allowed him to evolve a relaxed and more light-hearted interpretation of the classical than that in which he had been trained. Clérisseau's picturesque landscape drawing and Piranesi's romantic reconstructions of ancient architecture reinforced this novel approach which was to have such an impact on his return to England. Unlike 'Athenian' Stuart, he allowed himself a freedom from the rules of his predecessors without entirely rejecting everything they had stood for. He himself described his style as: 'Directed but not cramped by antiquity.' His skill was to be able to carry his clients with him: he could work within a framework they too could understand, and his portfolio of drawings was the visible proof they needed to convince them of the originality of these ideas.

While in Rome, Adam had also studied Renaissance ornament, in particular the grotesques of Raphael in the Vatican Palace. 'Grotesques' were the name given to the patterns which Raphael had evolved from frescoes discovered in Nero's Domus Aurea while he was in charge of Rome's ancient monuments in 1505. These could be adapted to fill any shape and created a charming light-hearted decoration, which became hugely popular in the Rome of Raphael's day. A visit to the Vatican to see the Papal apartments was de rigueur for any Grand Tourist and James Adam had made extensive copies of the grotesques in the Vatican Loggia. Robert was to use James's drawings as a guide for the decorative work in the small gazebo he built in his garden. This and the house itself, which was decorated in a similar way, acted as a useful showcase for the type of decoration he was to use in the future.

Such decoration gave a delightfully feminine fin-ish to the overall design he planned for each room and could be adapted to please any taste. It was popular with both his male and female clients and made a pleasant contrast to the heavy ceiling beams of the Palladian era.[132] It was to become part of his most characteristic ornamental vocabulary. Adam chose to stand apart from the passionate debates of his day as the cognoscenti argued the respective merits of Greece and Rome – hence his dismissal of Stuart's ceiling in Spencer House. He saw the antique as source material, to be measured, drawn, cast and (if possible) purchased, and was wide-ranging in the sources he employed. He was as willing to make use of illustrations from other publications, should it suit his purpose, as he was to use his own.

ADAM'S RIVALS
What competition did Adam face? There was plenty of new talent. William Chambers had arrived back three years before him, in 1755, and Robert Mylne,[133] Adam's junior by five years, had returned from his Grand Tour in 1759, having left Rome in a cloud of glory. Mylne had made the same useful contacts there as Adam, but he had also visited Sicily and seen the magnificent Greek temples of Agrigento and Segesta, something Adam always regretted missing. In 1758 Mylne had also won the Silver Medal at St Luke's Academy in Rome, thereby becoming a member of both the academies of Florence and Bologna. On his return to London, he was to win the competition for a new bridge at Blackfriars, defeating 63 other competitors. This was an enormous victory for one so young and inexperienced and immediately set him up in the architectural world.

These were the challengers of Adam's own generation, but what about those of an earlier one? Thomas Hardwick maintained that James Paine and Robert Taylor 'had nearly divided the practice of the profession between them until Mr Robert Adam entered the lists'.[134] This summed up the situation very well, for Adam, who was to become the most fashionable architect in London, seldom built a new country house. Rather, he replaced architects such as James Paine and Matthew Brettingham, following them as the interior architect and often redesigning their original plans.[135] Often the timing of these new commissions worked in Adam's favour: his early clients had recently come into their inheritance, they were young, and open to and excited by his new

---

131 'He substituted a new and elegant repertoire of classical ornament based on a wide variety of classical sources ranging from antiquity to the Cinquecento.' HM Colvin, *A Biographical Dictionary of British Architects 1600–1840* (1954).
132 An unusual use of both themes is the Great Hall at Kedleston, where Adam uses beams on the ceiling and a form of grotesques on the walls.
133 1733–1811.
134 Thomas Hardwick, *Memoir of Sir William Chambers* (whose pupil he was) (1825).
135 James Paine (1716–89); Matthew Brettingham the Elder (1699–1769).

ideas. New ways of entertaining had become fashionable and this too was advantageous, for in addition to the formal rooms required for dining and receptions, smaller, more intimate rooms were also needed for cards, after-dinner conversations and intimate supper parties. Sometimes these pastimes took place simultaneously, which meant that interiors needed to be looked at afresh and required careful planning. Adam had always been fascinated by the need for different room shapes and sizes, so such challenges suited his skills perfectly.

SPALATRO ORDER

Adam's early work is amongst his most successful, and much of it was influenced by his journey to Spalatro. In Diocletian's palace he had found a wealth of architectural ornament, which he was to freely adapt, particularly what he called the 'Spalatro Order'. The source of this idea was in the *peristyle*. Here he found an unusual pilaster capital on which Diocletian's architect had reduced the normal number of acanthus leaves to only three on each face with a row of gadroons or vertical flutes above (p.96). Rather than calling it the 'Corinthian Order' Adam initially called it the 'Doric Order' (on which acanthus leaves would never normally appear).

ABOVE: Entrance front of Kedleston Hall, with external stairs to the hexastyle (six-columned) portico and a pair of one-storey wings. This façade preceded Adam's arrival.

Later it was called the 'Spalatro Order' and his early commissions make use of this feature frequently.

Another adaptation was to put the plan of the *peristyle* and vestibule – the grand imperial approach to the Emperor's private apartments – to a novel use *within* the house. Kedleston Hall in Derbyshire is a particularly good example of this, where the grand entrance of the Marble Hall and Saloon echo that of Diocletian's palace, ie moving from a rectangular space into a circular one. The Marble Hall replaces the open-air *peristyle* and the Saloon the Vestibule.

KEDLESTON

Adam's arrival at Kedleston proved to be the beginning of a long and fruitful partnership with its new young owner, Nathaniel Curzon. Only two years apart in age, Curzon and Adam shared a fascination with classical antiquity – although Curzon had never been to Italy – and they established an immediate rapport.

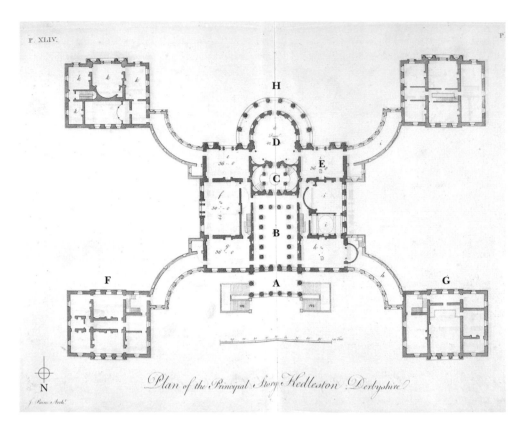

Plan of the Principal Story Kedleston Derbyshire

N

LEFT AND FACING PAGE:
Two plans of Kedleston
Hall, the first (left) by James
Paine in 1759–60 and the
second (right) as adapted
by Adam in 1762–5.

A. Portico
B. The Marble Hall
C. Two sets of stairs
   hidden in shallow
   apses behind columns
D. Saloon
E. Ante-Room
F. Family Wing
G. Kitchen Wing
H. Garden

Such travelling as Curzon had done had been limited to a few months in France some years earlier, during which he had collected paintings and sculptures to furnish the new house that he and his father were already planning. Nathaniel's father (another Nathaniel) had had a very successful career in London as a barrister, and, although the family home was only 50 years old, he was planning ambitious changes. By the time Nathaniel Junior succeeded in 1758, three architects had already submitted plans in quick succession.[136] Young Nathaniel instantly scrapped all these plans and decided to start afresh. He commissioned Matthew Brettingham (the Elder), with whom he and his father had already had extensive discussions, to build an entirely new house consisting of a central block with four pavilion wings linked by quadrant corridors. The two northern wings were planned as a family wing and a kitchen and services wing, while the southern ones were to hold the music room and the greenhouse and chapel wings respectively. At the centre, behind the six-columned portico, were the state rooms, beginning with the Great Hall; this led into the south-facing Saloon, while the Dining-room, Library and Drawing-room were disposed to either side along this same axis.

The history of the new house is extremely complicated, as several different architects and designers worked there simultaneously (quite a normal practice at the time). Building began at once, but a dispute led to Brettingham's withdrawal in under a year, and James Paine took his place as chief architect at the beginning of 1760. Meanwhile, Curzon had made Adam's acquaintance in December 1758 and was immediately captivated by his novel interpretation of antiquity. Adam wrote to James, then in Rome, that Curzon had come and inspected his collection in Lower Grosvenor Street, and had been 'struck all of a heap with wonder and amaze. Everything he converted to his own house and every new drawing made him grieve at his previous engagement with Brettingham. He carried me home in his chariot about three and kept me to four... asking my opinion.'

Curzon continued to double-check Paine's ideas with Adam, but it was not until another year had passed that Paine was dismissed and Adam was given overall control. Adam's greatest contribution was to change the sequence leading out of the Great Hall to the Saloon and to redesign the exterior of the south front. The grand columnar hall had been a feature from the start and Paine,

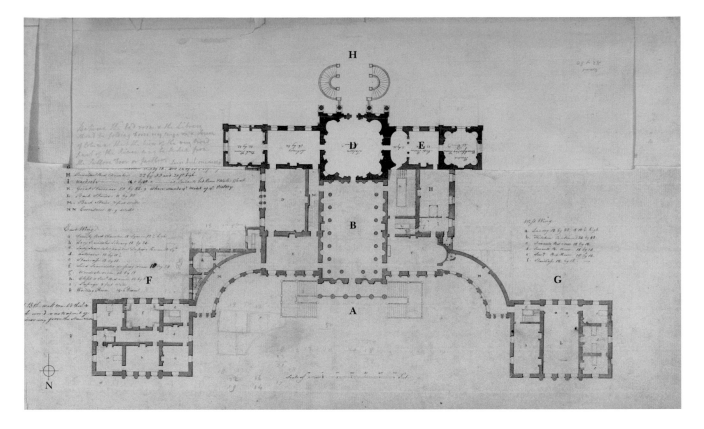

building on that idea, had suggested that the saloon should be designed as a circular rotunda projecting into the garden as a huge bow-shaped façade, in front of which was a row of ten columns. In between these two grandiose rooms he had cleverly inserted the staircase: in fact, he had proposed two separate staircases within this same space, each curved into an apsidal compartment and screened by columns. Paine's design was magnificent, but it was also costly, as it entailed two domes – one to light the stairs and the other the saloon. Adam proposed a cheaper solution: he cleverly maintained the rotunda, but instead of having it push out into the garden, he set it into a square frame, bringing it back in line with the main façade of the house. To make enough room on the inside, the stairs were banished altogether, so that the Hall led directly into the Saloon.

The Marble Hall and Saloon shadowed the *peristyle* and vestibule of Diocletian's palace. The Marble Hall is a double cube and has a row of eight free-standing alabaster columns along each side

to echo the colonnade of the palace. It rises to the full height of the building. The frieze above these columns was continuous, featuring winged lions and putti separated by anthemions[137] – all of which are repeated elsewhere in the house. Sculpture in alcoves and grisaille panels of grotesques complete the wall decoration. Adam would have liked to suggest the open sky of the palace with a coved ceiling and a large top-lit opening of glass, so flooding the place with natural light. In the event, three oval roof lights were substituted instead.

The Great Hall leads into the Saloon, which is intended to echo Diocletian's vestibule. As in Spalatro, it is circular with a dome and an oculus, of which the diameter of the internal circle is the same dimension as Diocletian's. Nathaniel Curzon became the first Lord Scarsdale in 1761, and had a catalogue printed in 1769 which gives the antique sources for what is one of the grandest sequence of rooms in the country: 'The Hall and the Saloon were after the Greek hall and Dome of the Ancients, proportioned chiefly from the Pantheon in Rome and Spalatro.'

The octagonal coffers of the Saloon dome were taken from the Basilica of Maxentius and the Temple of Venus and Roma, which Maxentius had

---

136 The old house, probably by Smith of Warwick, was built in *c*.1700. Of the three architects consulted by Nathaniel Senior, the first is unknown; the second was 'Athenian' Stuart and the third Matthew Brettingham (the Elder).
137 Honeysuckle flowers.

restored with two apses back to back.[138] Adam redesigned the apartments to either side of the Marble Hall to resemble the supposed wings of Diocletian's palace, while, in the Ante-Room, which led out of the Saloon, he introduced the Spalatro Order above a screen of columns.

The climax of this magnificent progression of carefully planned spaces was the descent into the garden. Looking back at the house, Adam contrived a unique design: here the Arch of Constantine in Rome, built by Constantine the Great in 315 to celebrate his victory over Maxentius at the Battle of the Milvian Bridge, is adapted as the southern façade to an English country house. Four free-standing marble Corinthian columns, complete with entablature, break forward to give a sense of movement. Above are statues and an attic storey, complete with an inscription in the central panel which records the completion of the building in 1765 and Lord Scarsdale's dedication: *Amicis et Sibi* ('For his friends and himself').

Had the original Brettingham plan been carried

ABOVE: The Saloon at Kedleston has four diamond coffered apses similar to those in the Temple of Venus and Roma.
BELOW: The Saloon, looking up at both the apsidal coffers and the octagonal coffers in the dome, which are similar to those in the Basilica of Maxentius.

FACING PAGE: The Marble Hall, Kedleston, with fluted Corinthian columns and frieze.

138 Discussed in Chapter 11.

out, two further quadrant wings and pavilions would have flanked this south entrance, matching those on the north front. Such a balanced composition would have proved more satisfactory than the present one, but it was not to be. Adam was very faithful to Spalatro at Kedleston, even to the point of setting this southern entrance over a lower hall resembling a crypt and possibly recalling the simple harbour entrance to Diocletian's palace. Suitably called the 'Caesar Hall', it is the normal family entrance to the house. Visitors, such as the Reverend Stebbing Shaw, would visit and record their impressions, spreading the word of Adam's work at Kedleston: 'Lord Scarsdale's noble palace at Kedleston which for magnificence and elegance eclipses every other seat in England... The Egyptian Hall is thought to be one of the finest rooms in England.'[139]

Throughout his life Adam showed an extraordinary capacity for work and was to prove very skilful at dealing with several commissions simultaneously. Clients could be very fickle, but he remained consistently charming and patient, willing to produce many different versions of his previous ideas. His output was prodigious. The family practice he and James had set up in London formed a perfect background to their operations, particularly after their youngest brother, William, took on the administration of its everyday affairs. The same craftsmen and artificers continued to work for the firm for most of its life, and self-employed artists, plasterers and painters

– many of whom Robert had met in Rome – were happy to contribute to the overall Adam success. Domestic life was efficiently handled for the brothers by the Adam sisters, Jenny and Betty, and this settled background proved invaluable, enabling them to cope with their huge workload.

1760–1 proved a particularly busy year, for in addition to Kedleston the owners of both Syon and Osterley – two old Jacobean houses on the outskirts of London – sought Adam's help. Both were typical

FACING PAGE: The Ante-Room, Kedleston, which led out of the Saloon, showing the screen of fluted columns and Spalatro capitals.

TOP: Kedleston garden façade, which is modelled

on the Arch of Constantine in Rome. Curved staircases frame the ground-floor entrance.

ABOVE: The inscription in the attic storey reads: AMICIS ET SIBI (For his friends and himself).

139 Revd Stebbing Shaw, *A Tour in 1787 from London to the Western Highlands of Scotland* (1788).

examples of early seventeenth-century architecture, each of them being built around a square court-yard. As at Kedleston, Adam had once again to work within the constraints of an earlier design, using the already existing buildings as his exterior framework. The limitations he faced in both cases must have been daunting, for the interiors were particularly narrow and neither house allowed him the grandeur and spaciousness he had found at Kedleston. Once again, the work of refurbishment would spread over many years and Adam would not see the completion of his plans, but both houses are among his finest achievements. In each case within a most unpromising carcass he inserted a suite of magnificent rooms 'entirely in the antique style'.[140]

SYON PARK HOUSE

Sir Hugh Smithson, the owner of Syon House, had inherited the vast Percy estates through his wife, Elizabeth Seymour, sole heiress of the 1st Earl of Northumberland, in 1750. Ten years earlier, when they married, there had been no prospect of such an inheritance and it was only through the death of her brother on his Grand Tour in 1744 that she had become the heir to such an immense fortune. On the death of his father-in-law, Sir Hugh Smithson had taken the arms and name of Percy and in 1766 he was made the 1st Duke of Northumberland.

Smithson and his wife proved worthy heirs and were soon making extensive changes to both North-umberland House in the Strand and Alnwick Castle in Northumberland. Smithson's architect for both houses was James Paine. Paine was also engaged to

design two bridges in Syon Park, and might justifi-ably have expected to win the commission for the house itself.

Syon had been neglected for many years; the Percys looked upon it as a summer residence, charmingly situated on the River Thames opposite the Royal Palace at Kew. Perhaps it was the work of the Prince and Princess Frederick of Wales on the refurbishment of this same Kew Palace and Gardens during the 1740s that inspired the Percys to recon-sider their own property on the opposite bank?[141]

Whatever the reason, by 1760 Adam had pro-duced his first design for modernising the house; but the difficulties he faced were huge. He found narrow rooms circumscribed by the level of the interior courtyard, which created different floor levels inside from those of the outside. The hall, for example, was above the outside ground level but below the principal interior level. Adam, although not allowed to change any of the basic layout, evolved a solution which was both masterful and hardly noticeable.

The original entrance hall was rectangular, with the remains of a medieval screens passage at its southern end. Adam swept away the screens passage and the existing stairs at the northern end of the hall. He replaced the original straight, narrow ends of the old hall with two coffered semi-circular apses – one behind a pair of columns. These columns and the semi-circular apse behind them required thoughtful furnishing, as, on entering the room, they made an immediate impact. Adam's solution was to commission two new sculptures direct from Rome. James, now in Italy on his own Grand Tour, was able to acquire two such suitable works of art, each to become a focal point in the new hall. Both were copies of famous ancient sculptures, one the *Dying Gaul* and the other the *Apollo Belvedere*, both of which would have been familiar to any Grand Tourist. They remain there to this day.

Throughout the hall the Doric Order dominates the design, as it was considered the most appropri-ate order for an entrance hall. A Doric entabla-ture of triglyphs and metopes encircles the entire room. Spirally fluted Doric columns supported on scrolled consoles frame the four windows, forming an interesting contrast with the straight flutes of the columns which flank the doors. This entire design

140 Horace Walpole (1717–97).
141 See Chapter 7.

SYON
PARK

The London Home
of the
Dukes of Northumberland,
as in 1847

ABOVE: Axiometric
drawing of Syon in 1847.

A. Entrance Hall
B. Ante-Room
C. Dining Room
D. Drawing Room
E. Long Gallery
F. Courtyard/Rotunda

RIGHT: Projected plan of
the principal storey of Syon
House by Robert Adam,
*c.*1768 (from *The Works in
Architecture of Robert and James
Adam*, vol. 1, 1778)

FACING PAGE: The front of
Syon Park, which dates from
Tudor times and was built
round a courtyard

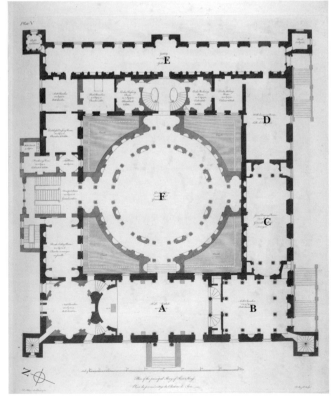

is directly lifted from the frontispiece to the *Ruins of
Spalatro*, which also featured a spiral column rest-
ing on a carved console (p.93). Adam called his
new room the 'Great Apartment' and intended it to
house further casts of antique sculptures.

The Smithsons' idea had been to leave the bulk
of their paintings at Northumberland House but
to bring their sculptures to Syon, where most of
them were to be displayed in the Rotunda. The
Rotunda was an ingenious concept designed to fill
the entire courtyard and – like the courtyard at

LEFT: The Great Hall, Syon, with a copy of the *Dying Gaul* by Valadier in the apse, one of the sculptures acquired by James Adam specifically for this room.

FACING PAGE: The Ante-Room, which leads out of the Hall: note the tripartite theme of a triumphal arch and *verde antique* columns from Rome (sent by James at Robert Adam's request), the gold ionic capitals and statues above.

the British Museum today – would have facilitated traffic through and around the house. It never became a reality. The origin of this idea was probably the huge temporary pavilion created at Syon for the visit of the King of Denmark, George III's son-in-law. An extravagant piece of theatre designed by Adam within the old Jacobean courtyard, it was the successful setting for a magnificent fête lit by thousands of candles with music echoing through the halls. As a permanent fixture, it would have provided access to all four wings of the house, with a useful route through to the grand staircase in the north wing and another to the pair of oval staircases in the east wing. A drawing of such a rotunda appeared in the *Works in Architecture of Robert and James Adam* published in 1778, but it was obviously an afterthought – as was the grand staircase – and after the Duchess's death in 1776 the idea was shelved (Adam finally achieved his dome and Rotunda in the General Register House in Edinburgh, 1774–86).

To complete the progression from Hall to Dining Room and Drawing Room, Adam devised an extraordinarily grand room in the corner of the house within a very small area. Known as the Ante-Room, it cleverly disguises the necessary change of direction, at the same time distracting the visitor by its grandeur. The space to be filled is rectangular but it appears to be square, owing to the positioning of 12 green *verde antique* columns which shorten one side of the room. Nine of these free-standing columns stand along the wall on three sides of the room, while those on the fourth side form a screen and stand two metres away from the wall. Once again James – still in Rome – proved very useful, finding exactly what was needed. Always alert to a good bargain he acquired some genuine old columns recently dragged up from the River Tiber, while any shortfall was made up with specially ordered green scagliola-covered columns. As a prototype for the design of the gold Ionic capitals, which form such a contrast with the deep green of the column shafts, Adam used a mixture of influences, chiefly from the publications of Le Roy and Piranesi. In dividing each side of the room into three, Adam was once again using the Roman triumphal arch as his basic format. The Ante-Room, with its strong colours, forms an exciting contrast to the black and white of the Hall which precedes it, and the gentler colours of the Dining Room which follows.

OSTERLEY

At Osterley, Adam was once again presented with a Tudor courtyard house and commissioned to remodel the rooms within it. Progress was slow, for although the house's owners, the Child family, were immensely wealthy (their forebears had set up Child's Bank at No 1 Fleet Street in 1671)[142] their lives were dogged by tragedy. Two years after Francis Child had commissioned Adam to work on the house in 1761, he died unexpectedly, just a few days before his wedding. He was succeeded by his younger brother, Robert, who was about to get married himself. Fortunately for Adam, the brothers had similar tastes, and a short time later Robert Child confirmed Adam's position.

Adam had arrived in 1761 to find an old Tudor house built in 1577 which had already passed through numerous owners, and left it in 1778 having created a 'palace of palaces'.[143]

Here he produced a different – and perhaps more satisfactory – solution from the one at Syon, as he had a freer hand with the exterior. In this case he managed to create a genuine open-air room or Roman *peristyle* to reflect Diocletian's, by joining the

two wings of the old house with a screen of six classical Ionic columns. This 'see-through' portico gives an exciting glimpse into the opposite side of the courtyard, with an entrance into the hall framed by Prince of Wales capitals.[144] The old Elizabethan towers remained as a frame to the overall composition. Architecturally it is an anomaly but visually it works surprisingly well and was another example of

ABOVE: The entrance portico and screen of 12 Ionic columns at Osterley, closing the fourth side of the courtyard.
LEFT: Osterley Park House, showing the Tudor towers and, to the left, the entrance and stairway to the garden.

Adam's willingness to compromise and work with his clients' wishes.

The Entrance Hall, like that of Syon, has the strongest overtones of Spalatro. The main entrance to the house is in a direct line opposite the portico, with the result that the hall is entered from the centre of its long wall. It was one of the last rooms to be adapted and followed the successful refurbishment of the Drawing and Dining Rooms in the adjoining wings. The result was that the space retained for the hall had difficult proportions, the most noticeable being that it was too wide for its height.

An entrance hall in the eighteenth century did not simply act as a grand assembly point: it also played the role of a gallery in which the owner could display his sculpture collection. As such it was left empty of furniture, so adding to Adam's difficulties, for it was impossible to soften the poor proportions

142 Now part of Royal Bank of Scotland.
143 Horace Walpole.
144 These are again an adaptation of those tall-necked capitals he had found in Spalatro. Adam's favourite decoration on the neck of a capital was leaves or feathers, sometimes called the 'Prince of Wales Order' because he first used it on Marlborough House, next to the Prince of Wales's Royal Pavilion in Brighton.

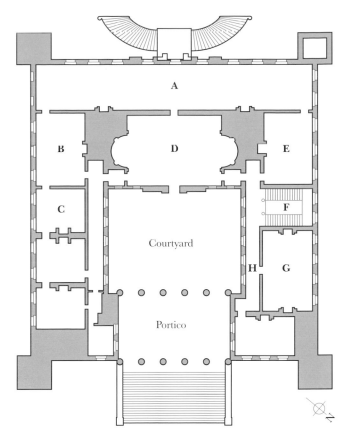

ABOVE: Plan of Osterley.
A. Long Gallery
B. Drawing Room
C. Tapestry Room
D. Entrance Hall
E. Dining Room
F. Great Stair
G. Library
H. North Passage

LEFT: The Entrance Hall, showing the apse and octagonal coffers. The Doric pilasters have capitals of the Spalatro Order and a simple frieze instead of a full entablature, above panels of military regalia.

of the room. The decorative panels on the walls and ceilings stood alone in their purity, there being no clutter to distract the eye, but while the architectural elements could speak for themselves, the size and scale of the room were plain for all to see and criticise. Adam was fully aware of this problem. His solution was to add a shallow semi-domed apse to either end of the room, once again using the coffers of the Basilica of Maxentius as his source, and to surround the room with thin plain pilasters, rather than columns, with capitals of the Spalatro Order. At the same time he reduced the normal entablature – which should consist of three parts – to only one, the frieze.[145] In addition he used a continuous Greek-key pattern as fascia decoration, which allowed him to alter its width as he pleased. He used panels of military trophies alternating with arabesques to decorate the walls, much as he had done at Syon.

ADAM'S RELATIONSHIP WITH THE EARL OF SHELBURNE AND BOWOOD HOUSE

Adam's relationship with most of his clients would appear to have been amicable, and to have survived many years of collaboration. But William Petty, Earl of Shelburne,[146] was to prove the exception, and Adam's work for him was to end in a bitterly public feud. Shelburne was 24 years old, newly returned to England after three years of military service, and had succeeded to his father's title only six months before, in 1761. He needed a house in London and he also wanted to modernise his country seat, Bowood in Wiltshire, purchased by his father eight

years before.[147] He worked fast, and soon the renovation of the interior of Bowood was under way. Then, in 1765, he married and bought the Berkeley Square house of the ex-Prime Minister, the Earl of Bute, as his London base.

Shelburne inherited Robert Adam as his architect on both these sites and he retained him in both cases. At Bowood, the Dowager Lady Shelburne had commissioned Adam to build a mausoleum in memory of her husband in 1761; her son then asked Adam to refurbish the chief reception rooms of the main family home. Delighted with the result, in 1768 Shelburne decided to build a new, free-standing wing to the west of the old house (ie at right angles to it). The idea was that this new wing should conceal the already existing E-shaped service/stable courtyards, which until now had stood apart. This wing was to take the form of an orangery, completely independent of the main house and set well behind

145 An entablature in classical architecture consists of three horizontal members: the architrave, the frieze and the cornice.
146 Prime Minister in 1782–3, when he negotiated the peace with America at the close of the War of Independence, for which he was created 1st Marquis of Lansdowne.
147 Built by Bridgman in 1725 and purchased in 1754.

it. The two buildings eventually became known in the family as the 'Big House' (the original house) and the 'Little House' (the new house). A short time later again, Adam was asked to link these two buildings together by means of a large new drawing room which ran behind the Big House until it reached the corner of the Little House.

The Little House was also known as the 'Diocletian Wing', and when built provided a library and a conservatory/greenhouse to either side of the entrance to the stable yard. The Diocletian Wing had the advantage not only of hiding the 'offices/stables' behind, but also of allowing a better view of Capability Brown's newly landscaped park, which had shifted the focus of its main views appreciably further west. Lord Shelburne had been specific in his desire to have a building which echoed Diocletian's palace, and probably what he had in mind was a freely interpreted version of the Spalatro waterfront. At this point Adam suggested a rotunda as the central point of this new wing, which would have created a magnificent centrepiece when seen from the park and at the same time acted as an 'opera-box' from which to view the landscape beyond.

ABOVE: Façade of Bowood House today and (**BELOW**) detail showing the portico with Spalatro Order. This was the original Diocletian Wing.

FACING PAGE: Bowood: The Mausoleum and its interior by Robert Adam, built as a memorial to the 1st Earl of Shelburne.

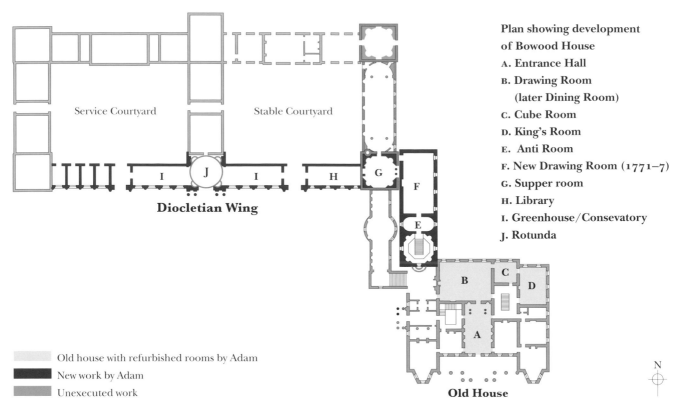

Plan showing development
of Bowood House
A. Entrance Hall
B. Drawing Room
   (later Dining Room)
C. Cube Room
D. King's Room
E. Anti Room
F. New Drawing Room (1771–7)
G. Supper room
H. Library
I. Greenhouse/Consevatory
J. Rotunda

Service Courtyard

Stable Courtyard

Diocletian Wing

N

Old house with refurbished rooms by Adam
New work by Adam
Unexecuted work

Old House

This central domed vestibule shared a similar fate to the rotunda at Syon: it was never built. But the Diocletian Wing survives – ironically, the only section of the house that does. It was undoubtedly inspired by Adam, all its columns are of the Spalatro Order, with long necks and a row of acanthus leaves, but it was completed by others and given no Adam interiors.[148] For with the death of the young Lady Shelburne, who died in 1771 aged only 25, her grief-stricken husband abandoned Bowood and left for a long tour of Italy and France. The relationship between Adam and Lord Shelburne had deteriorated to such an extent that they were no longer on speaking terms. Lord Shelburne had broken off all relations with Adam by opposing the Act of Parliament, passed in May 1771, which authorised the Adam brothers' development of the Thames Embankment at Durham Gate off the Strand in London.

ABOVE: Diagram of the development stages of Bowood House, showing the proposed rotunda at the entrance to the Diocletian Wing.
LEFT: Photograph of Bowood House *c.*1930 before demolition of the 'Big' House to the right. The present house (the Diocletian Wing) sits behind the formal gardens.

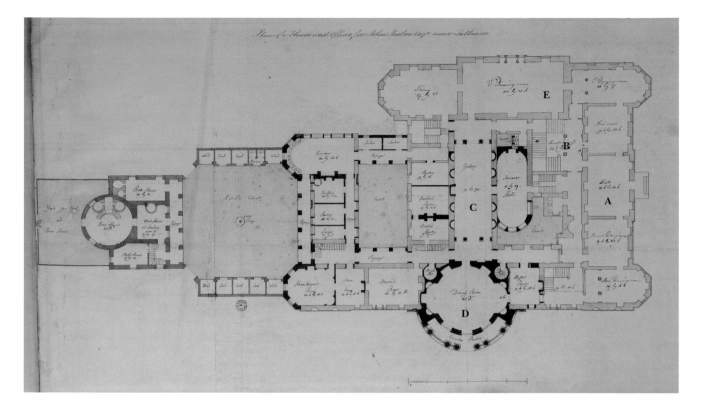

SALTRAM

On occasions Adam had the opportunity to transform the interior of an old-fashioned house by brilliantly refiguring the inconvenient plans of earlier generations. At other times his opportunities were more restricted. It was Lord Shelburne who suggested to his friend John Parker, a fellow student at Oxford University, that he should bring his house up to date by employing Robert Adam. Parker had succeeded to his inheritance, Saltram in Devon, in 1768, but both his father (also John) and his mother, Lady Catherine Parker, had already spent some years modernising the old house, possibly again with the help of Matthew Brettingham. Their initial plans had been very ambitious and, had they been carried out, would have rivalled some of the greatest houses in the land. Although Lady Catherine had been the prime mover in the enlargement of Saltram, John Parker Senior continued to embellish the property after his wife's death in 1758, carefully husbanding his money the while. When he died, ten years later, several bags of cash were found

ABOVE: Proposed plan for Saltram by Adam, 1779.
A. Entrance Hall
B. Staircase Hall
C. Gallery with columnar screen and niches to link the new Dining Room to the Saloon.
D. The circular Dining Room, with a semi-circular portico overlooking the garden
E. Saloon
BELOW: The south front, which predates Adam.

---

148 This is the only section of Bowood to survive today, as after the death of the three sons of the sixth Marquis of Lansdowne in World War II and the subsequent division of the estates, the contents were sold and the original house demolished in 1955. The only Adam room from Bowood to survive in this country is the dining room, now reassembled as the boardroom at Lloyds of London.

hidden around the house: an inventory reads, 'cash in bags placed in the mahogany bookcase £3717; ditto placed in the wainscot toilet £3928'. In all, this hidden money amounted to £32,000 – a sizeable sum. By the time John Junior[149] inherited, the new double-cubed saloon – with a large Venetian window overlooking the park, and a ceiling as high as the main staircase hall – was well under way.

Adam worked at Saltram for six years (1768–74), producing two of his finest designs, one for the Library and one for the Saloon. Once again his contribution was limited to an already existing interior, but in this case he could work within a magnificent setting without any of the disadvantages he had encountered in the past. Skilfully, he imposed order on this huge double-cubed saloon by repeating and

matching all the different decorative elements. The frieze, the double guilloche pilaster panels and the capitals from Diocletian's palace are repeated as surrounds on the doors and the Venetian window. The result is a triumph and was readily acknowledged as such by subsequent visitors – among them King George III and Queen Charlotte, who visited Saltram in 1789.

Thereafter John Parker remained a firm admirer of Robert Adam, and four years later approached him again, this time to redesign the West Wing on the opposite side of the house. A fire earlier that year had destroyed the laundry and brew house, so providing an unrivalled opportunity to rearrange the older parts of this rambling house.

Adam's solution was ingenious. He swept away the old kitchen courtyards, replacing them with a plan which brought the dining-room closer to the kitchens. His designs, had they become a reality, would have revolutionised the house. The new dining-room was to be a grandiose affair: a circular room with an external semi-circular portico overlooking the garden. At the same time it was linked to the saloon by a rectangular columned gallery inserted into the centre of the house, behind the already existing staircase. Perhaps something of this plan might have been salvaged had John's wife, Theresa – always the artistic partner, with links to the Dilettanti Society through her brother Thomas, Lord Graham – still been alive. As it was, like so many of his more elaborate schemes, Adam's ideas remained on the drawing board, proving too expensive to build.

Adam had already begun to make an impact on the architectural fraternity in London before his *Ruins of Spalatro* was published in 1764. But its long list of well-connected subscribers and its handsome bindings confirmed its author as the new and exciting talent and a man whose ideas should be taken seriously. It also provided a very practical proof of his skill as an archaeologist, and the illustrations were invaluable to any future clients. In contrast to James 'Athenian' Stuart, Adam was to build cleverly upon the success of his book and in his own words to create 'a beautiful variety of light mouldings, gracefully formed, delicately enriched and arranged with propriety and skill' with which to ornament his houses.

CAPTION: The Staircase Hall, Saltram, dating from about 1740, before Adam's arrival. The servants' staircase was tucked in behind the far wall.

FACING PAGE: The Saloon, Saltram, a double cubed room, decorated by Adam with repeated and matching elements, while the Venetian window has columns of the Spalatro Order.

149 Created Lord Boringdon in 1784.

BELOW: Head of
Constantine I, one of the
remaining sections of the
statue of Constantine/
Maxentius which
originally stood in the
apse of the Basilica of
Maxentius in Rome.

CHAPTER XI

THE FORMATION OF THE SECOND TETRARCHY

Death of Constantius Chlorus in York; the Second Tetrarchy.
Battle of the Milvian Bridge. Deaths of Galerius and Maximian.
Maxentius's architecture in Rome. Diocletian's death.

DIOCLETIAN'S PLAN that at his abdication the two Caesars – by now men of experience in their own right – should move smoothly up the ladder to become Augusti had been simple enough. Since it also stipulated that each should then choose a new Caesar, Constantine and Maxentius – both sons of ruling Augusti – might have expected to succeed as of right. Both had grown up within the framework of the Tetrarchy but both were to encounter strong opposition on their way to the top.

CONSTANTINE

Flavius Valerius Aurelius Constantius, always known as Constantine, was born in Naissus, Illyria – also the birthplace of his father, Constantius Chlorus – in 272–3. He was 20 when his father became Caesar to Maximian. He grew up, not in Trier as might be expected, but in Diocletian's court in Nicomedia, where he had an excellent education under the

rhetor Lactantius, learning both Greek and Latin, literature and philosophy. The cultural atmosphere at the Imperial Court was openly tolerant, opportunistic and socially mobile, and attracted intellectuals both pagan and Christian.[150] Constantine's military education was equally thorough: he campaigned with Galerius in Mesopotamia, and travelled with Diocletian through Palestine and Egypt. (He was also possibly present during Diocletian's visit to Rome for the imperial *vicennalia.*) The crowds listening to the old Emperor's retirement speech in Nicomedia in May 305 must have fully expected to hear him appoint the young Constantine as Caesar to the new Augustus of the West, Constantius Chlorus.

However, this was not to be.[151] Neither Diocletian nor Galerius (now Augustus of the East) had ever really trusted Constantius Chlorus, so they had made a point of keeping his son under their own strict supervision. According to Lactantius, Constantine, when summoned by his father, had had to escape from Galerius's court at dead of night; and had then marched west at huge speed to join him in Eboracum (York), arriving just in time to see his

---

150 This extraordinary tolerance adds fuel to the theory that Galerius had to apply strong pressure on the ailing Diocletian to agree to the Edict of Persecution in 303 a theory now strongly contested.
151 Instead, Severus and Maximinus Daia were both appointed Caesars.

father before he died in July 306. But Lactantius is not always a completely reliable source and in this instance he spiced up the story. In actual fact, Constantine joined his father in Boulogne in late July 305; they crossed the Channel together and marched north to face the Picts beyond Hadrian's Wall in January 306. Constantius had been in poor health for some time and his son's help was welcome. Constantius died in Eboracum six months later at the age of 56, whereupon his soldiers proclaimed his son Emperor in his father's place.

Eboracum (York) had been an important centre in the north of Britain for many years. It was the headquarters of the local governor, who was also the commander of the Sixth Legion Victrix, and it became an imperial residence whenever the Emperor visited the area. At the centre of the York fortress there are the remains of a large audience hall and hypocaust of the type frequently found in Tetrarchic palaces. Possibly as large as its counterpart in Trier, this *sala regia* was extensively modernised at the time of Constantius Chlorus. Parts of this hall (known as the 'basilica') can still be seen today in the undercroft of York Minster. The rest of the *sala regia* extends beyond the present church

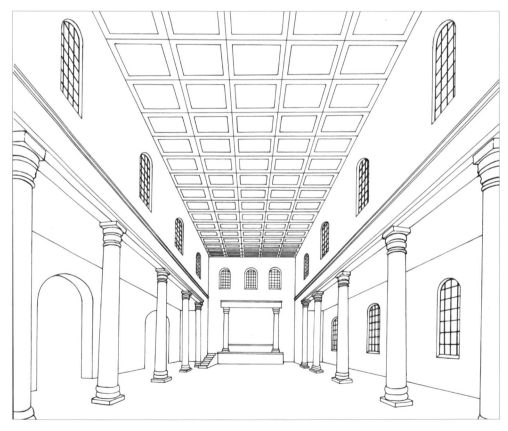

ABOVE: Roman column, 7 metres high, discovered under York Minster and re-erected outside the south door in Deangate.

LEFT: Reconstruction of the *sala regia* (great hall) of the Roman legionary headquarters in York, sections of which are still in the crypt of York Minster. Note that the round-headed windows are similar to those in Trier.

boundary to its south-east. Of the eight pairs of columns discovered in the undercroft, one complete column has been re-erected outside the south door of the Minster. Like the column in the Piazza of St Maria Maggiore in Rome, it gives an idea of the immense scale of these Tetrarchic buildings.[152]

There is still an extensive stretch of the Roman wall which surrounded the perimeter of the military camp in York. A large 14-sided multi-angular tower stands at the south-west corner,[153] constructed of Roman rectangular tiles and stonework. These tiles were inserted into the mortar to reinforce the entire structure and were a common feature of Roman building (they are also seen at Portchester). There are also several other six-sided towers, exceptional for both their size and their elaborate plan, with large internal extensions behind them, the use of which remains a mystery. To find anything of equal complexity one must go to Felix Romuliana, where Galerius had built similar-shaped towers of an even greater sophistication, consisting of 16 sides but attached by only one face and with no internal extensions. Both Constantius Chlorus and his son were familiar with the palace of Felix Romuliana, having lived only a few miles away in Naissus. This might well account for this unusual design here at York. It also gives credence to a date of *c*.296.

With the death of Constantius Chlorus, Galerius became the most senior Augustus, with his own plans for the future of the Tetrarchy. He had already chosen a friend of long standing, Severus, to be the next Augustus in the west to replace Constantius Chlorus, with Maximinus Daia (his sister's son) as his new Caesar. With these appointments Galerius had cleverly established an extensive power base over three-quarters of the Empire, for, like him, both Severus and Maximinus Daia came from Illyria, and both owed their elevation entirely to him. Constantine had little choice but to accept the post of second Caesar under Severus. Wisely, he offered no resistance and took up his residence in Trier, his father's old capital.

RIGHT: Two views of one of the multi-angular towers and curtain wall of the Roman fortress in York.

Note the addition of brick courses as at Portchester. (The arched attic storey was added in the Middle Ages.)

152 The column is 7 metres high and 1 metre in diameter.
153 In the Museum Gardens, York.

MAXENTIUS

Meanwhile the only other contender for the post of Caesar – Maximian's son Maxentius – remained alone in Rome. Marcus Aurelius Valerius Maxentius was born *c.*278 (six years after Constantine) and was 14 years old when his father became an Augustus. Unlike other candidates aspiring to high office, he never held any military position of importance and this was an obvious disadvantage when seeking promotion to the Tetrarchy. As a very young man he had married Valeria Maximilla (Galerius's daughter by his first marriage) with the obvious intention of strengthening his claim to the imperial succession; he also called one of his two sons Romulus in honour of his father-in-law's mother, Romula.

Jealous of Constantine's elevation, and angry at being passed over, Maxentius decided to act independently. But he needed allies, and knowing of the unrest within the Praetorian Guard, he decided to take advantage of their discontent and to enlist their loyalty by restoring their old privileges. Still treading cautiously, but now assured of their support, he proclaimed himself *Princeps Invictus* ('undefeated prince') in Italy and its neighbouring islands of Corsica, Sardinia and Sicily in October 306. Knowing Galerius could never endorse such a move and, needing further military support, he invited his father, Maximian, to come out of retirement and join him as co-ruler. Maxentius was no fool; above all, he was a realist and recognised that his father's rapport with his old Illyrian troops far exceeded that of his own. A military career had never appealed to him, but at this stage a loyal army was essential to his success. Maximian, in his turn, had always resented his enforced abdication and needed no further encouragement. He accepted his son's invitation with alacrity.

In a very short time the new Augustus, Severus, attacked Rome but was defeated by the combined forces of father and son and retreated to Ravenna (Maximian had cunningly bought off many of his soldiers). Rather than have Severus remain in Ravenna where he might have successfully

sustained a long siege, Maximian persuaded him to return to Rome. Initially well treated, Severus was finally persuaded that the only honourable way out of his predicament was to commit suicide. He died in late 306; he had reigned as an Augustus for six months.

After the defeat of Severus, Maxentius assumed the full title of Augustus and extended his rule of northern Italy as far as the Alps. To forestall the impending attack by Galerius, Maxentius used the same tactics that had worked so well against Severus, bribing many of Galerius's soldiers and promising them a secure future in Maximian's army.

At the same time, Maxentius sought to enlist the help of Constantine. Acting as his son's envoy, Maximian set off for Trier to offer his daughter, Fausta,[154] in marriage to Constantine, promising to recognise Constantine's future claim as Augustus on condition that Constantine would accept the status quo in Rome. Constantine was compliant and married Fausta, with whom he was to have six children. However, neither Constantine nor Maxentius trusted Maximian. Events were to prove them justified. Only a few months later, in the spring of 308 Maximian dramatically stripped the purple from Maxentius's shoulders at a public meeting in the Forum. Maxentius appears to have been taken totally by surprise and was preparing to leave the platform when he found himself acclaimed by his soldiers, furious at Maximian's disloyalty. Maximian, by now in total disgrace and completely friendless, fled east to the court of Galerius, where he was forced to acknowledge Licinius (Galerius's replacement for Severus) as the new Augustus.

The entire structure of the Tetrarchy was now in jeopardy, and Galerius in desperation called a meeting at Carnuntum[155] in November 308 to which he invited Diocletian, Maximian and Licinius.[156] Diocletian refused to resume the purple and Maximian was persuaded to abdicate once more. Maximian, nevertheless, made one more attempt to regain power by trying to persuade his daughter to kill her husband, Constantine. This also failed and Maximian, possibly in a very unstable state, fled to Massilia (Marseilles), where Constantine finally captured him. Trusted by no one, he was also persuaded to commit suicide as the only honourable way out of his dilemma, and in July 310 he hanged himself.[157] His erratic behaviour reflected poorly on his son Maxentius, who remained a usurper in the eyes of the other Tetrarchs.

---

154 Also Maxentius's sister (see family tree, p.29).
155 Today Bad Deutsch-Altenburg in Austria.
156 Galerius had been a friend of Licinius's since their youth and had elevated him to the position of Augustus in place of Severus without any service as a Caesar. This is one of the reasons he needed to call the meeting at Carnuntum. Maximinus Daia was so angry at being pushed out that he forced Galerius to elevate him also, so for a short time there six Augusti: Constantine, Maximian and Maxentius in the West and Galerius, Licinius and Maximinus Daia in the East.
157 A medieval chronicle of 1054 refers to the presence of Maximian's sarcophagus in Marseilles.

LEFT: The Temple of Venus and Roma, Rome, built by Hadrian and restored by Maxentius. The two temples lie back to back.

Soon after these dramatic events, Galerius fell seriously ill of a malignant growth, which spread rapidly throughout his body. Fearing this to be the retribution of the Christian God he had been persecuting so vigorously since 303, he withdrew the Edict of Persecution in May 311. Christians were once again allowed to build their churches as long as they prayed for the ailing Emperor; but this was of no avail to Galerius, who was to die an extremely unpleasant death shortly afterwards.

The stage was now left for Constantine to confront Maxentius. Only at this point did Maxentius make a serious tactical error, one that was to cost him both his life and his empire. Instead of sitting out a siege within the walls of his well-fortified city with an army twice the size of his enemy's as he had done so successfully hitherto, he decided to meet Constantine outside Rome near the Milvian Bridge.[158] Part of his preparations for war, however, had been to destroy all existing bridges over the River Tiber. This was to prove his second serious mistake, for after an unsuccessful confrontation when his troops were forced to retreat there was no way back across the river and chaos ensued. The Emperor Maxentius, still fully armed, fell into the river himself and was drowned.

Constantine's victory was complete – a victory he attributed to the sign of the Christian cross which, he said, had appeared to him in a dream on the eve of battle.[159] His retribution on Maxentius's family

was brutal; all were summarily executed and Maxentius's dead body, still in military attire, was paraded throughout the city and then carried to North Africa as proof of his defeat. Meanwhile, the citizens of Rome acclaimed Constantine as the new Augustus and the Senate declared him the first in rank of the three Emperors who then ruled the Empire.[160]

Maxentius had only ruled for six years, but his contribution to the monumental architecture of Rome equalled that of the First Tetrarchy. He introduced ideas that were to influence Roman buildings for many years to come. Like Diocletian and Maximian, he understood the importance Rome's ancient heritage, and his first act was to restore the old and much-venerated temple in the Forum, the Temple of Venus and Roma. This temple had been seriously damaged both in the fire of 283 and again in 306, the year of Maxentius's acclamation. Built by the Emperor Hadrian[161] it had – as its name implies – a dual dedication. Most temples with a dual dedication had either two individual altars (one for each of the two deities) or two *cellae* which ran parallel to each other. Hadrian, with so much space at his disposal, had placed them back to back: a most unusual format.

158 Battle at Saxa Rubra, 9 miles from Rome.
159 This incident has been immortalised in a number of paintings, the most famous being the *Story of the True Cross* by Piero della Francesca in the Church of San Francesco in Arezzo, painted 1452–66.
160 Licinius and Maximinus Daia in the East being the other two.
161 In AD 135.

THE WORK OF MAXENTIUS IN ROME

The entrance to the Temple of Roma[162] faced the Forum, while that of Venus faced the Colosseum. Maxentius chose to retain Hadrian's great terrace and the double colonnade which had survived the fire. The effect was dramatic, with the temples appearing through a forest of columns. Within the temple Maxentius adopted the same new wall decoration which Diocletian had used in the Curia, adding new floors and two new coffered apses (still back to back as before.) Much of Maxentius's work in the temple survives to this day.

His other equally remarkable building is the huge Basilica which bears his name, standing just behind the Temple of Venus and Roma. Dispensing with the normal basilican pattern of a single chamber surrounded by a colonnade, Maxentius introduced a huge central nave, 85 metres long and 25 metres wide, flanked by two side aisles each divided into three bays, each of which flowed seamlessly into the other.[163] The two aisles had coffered barrel

ABOVE: The Temple of Venus and Roma viewed through the remains of the double colonnade which surrounded the huge temple complex. Originally built by Hadrian, it was substantially restored by Maxentius. The Campanile belongs to the Church of St Francesca Romana.

FACING PAGE: The remains of one aisle of the Basilica of Maxentius, which is reconstructed in the illustration below. Note the massive columns supporting the vault and the coffering which was to be so influential to subsequent generations.

vaults, still visible today in the northern aisle (the only one to survive). Such a building must have taken Rome by storm, for nothing like it had been seen before. Robert Adam must have been equally impressed, because he was to use these coffers and those in the Temple of Venus and Roma as his inspiration for the dome in the Saloon at Kedleston and the apses in the hall at Osterley.

The scale and design of this Basilica were unprecedented and both were to be immensely influential. Only one of the eight huge fluted columns which supported the roof survives today. It stands in the centre of the Piazza St Maria Maggiore, holding its own comfortably with both the

162 Today the Church of St Francesca Romana is built into the vestibule of the Roma side.
163 This same plan was to be adapted by the Jesuits in their mother church, the Church of the Gesu, in Rome. Consecrated in 1584, the nave became the dominant feature, with interconnecting side-chapels.

ABOVE: Painting by Giovanni Paolo Pannini (1692–1765) of the Piazza and Church of Santa Maria Maggiore, including the only surviving column from the Basilica of Maxentius, as seen BELOW.

piazza and the church of St Maria Maggiore itself. In order to support the roof, the walls of the Basilica were 1.5 metres thick and were additionally reinforced at either end with an apse and a porch. Any furnishings had to be on the same enormous scale. One remarkable clue as to the size of the original Basilica is the remains of a statue, once in the apse, which now stands forlornly in the courtyard of the Palazzo dei Conservatori at the top of the Capitol Steps. The statue was an acrolith – that is, a statue of which only the head, arms and legs were of marble and the rest (including the throne) of gilded bronze. None of the metal sections have survived, but the marble fragments give an idea of its original size. Travellers through the ages have always marvelled at this; the foot alone is two metres in length, and the hand and the head are on a similar scale. Charles Burney wrote that: 'The head, arm, knee, calf, and feet were attributed to different gods or emperors. Their size was considered proof of their importance.'[164]

Today the statue represents Constantine, but recent research shows that it has been reworked and that originally it portrayed Maxentius. (Such adaptations were common all through the history of the Roman Empire.) Maxentius began to build his Basilica in 306 and Constantine finished it after 313, adding a second apse on the north side. Since then, both Basilica and statue have often been attributed to Constantine, on the grounds that the statue has his features.

The Basilica was the last great building to be constructed in Ancient Rome. It was a very public building for use by an appointed official as a court of law, in recognition of the independence of this ancient city. On his coins Maxentius proclaims himself 'Conservator Urbis Suae'. Here was the building to prove it.

CIRCUS OF MAXENTIUS

In contrast to the confident public face that Maxentius presented to the city, his personal life was riven with tragedy. He lost his son and heir, Romulus, at the age of 14 in 309. Away from the public eye in the grounds of his country villa on the Via Appia, Maxentius built a mausoleum and a circus to commemorate him. Still remote and seldom visited by the general public, it remains one of the most

164 1712–1814.

interesting sites in Rome. As on other Tetrarchic sites the mausoleum was built as a rotunda and was to have an enormous influence.

Whether this enormous mausoleum was intended solely as a burial place for his son or as a dynastic memorial is unknown. Like Diocletian's Mausoleum in Spalatro it had a rectangular porch, similar to that of the Pantheon today, and so followed a pattern of fourth-century sepulchral monuments. Adjacent to it he constructed a circus, which remains a most evocative place. Escaping any subsequent development, it gives a vivid impression of the size and extent of such a stadium. Although the tiered seating has disappeared, great sections of wall outline the perimeter of the track, and the 12 *carceres*, the starting gates, are easily identifiable. Entrance for the competitors was through an arch set in the middle of the *carceres*, while the grandstand for the Emperor and his family was a short way down the northern side, just a few metres below his villa, to which it probably had private access. Reconstructions of this grandstand show an elevated platform approached by two flights of steps, up which the winners would have walked to receive their trophies from the Emperor. The whole composition was topped by a row of temple-like columns.

Traces of the axis or *spina* around which the charioteers raced survive, together with the two *metae* (turning posts) which marked either end. At the centre of the *spina* Maxentius placed the large Egyptian obelisk which had been brought to Rome by Domitian. Today this same obelisk stands at the centre of Bernini's Fountain of the Four Rivers in the Piazza Navona, moved there, this time, by Pope Innocent X in 1651. An inscription on the arch at the far end of the circus reads, 'To the deified Romulus, man of most noble memory, consul ordinary for the second time, son of our lord Maxentius, the unconquered and perpetual Augustus.'

TEMPLE OF ROMULUS

Maxentius had Romulus deified and erected a small temple in the shape of a rotunda in the Forum to commemorate him. Known as the Temple of Romulus, this is a little gem of fourth-century architecture and directly fronts the Via Sacra. The rectangular hall behind it was later converted into the Church of St Cosmas and Damian; the two buildings are now contiguous and a great picture window at the

ABOVE: An imagined acrolithic statue of Constantine, reconstituted from the sections remaining in the courtyard of the Palazzo dei Conservatori (BELOW), of which a head, hand, arm, shin and foot survive. (In an acrolithic statue the head, arms, feet etc made of marble, and the rest, including the throne, of gilded bronze.)

back of the church's nave gives an excellent view into the rotunda. Initially the entire façade of the temple was decorated with columns and richly decorated cornices. Contemporary coins depict a dome on the top, on which there was probably an eagle personifying the spirit of the Emperor's dead son – a similar device to that seen on Galerius's mausoleum at Felix Romuliana.[165]

Constantine's Arch, built to mark his triumph over Maxentius, stands to the south of the Forum. A long inscription on both sides of the attic storey identifies his victory, while six sculpted reliefs illustrate his successful march towards Rome, starting with his departure from Milan and culminating in the Battle of the Milvian Bridge, with the enemy falling from their horses to their deaths in the River Tiber. This military victory is augmented by another relief which illustrates Constantine's imperial discourse as Emperor. As already mentioned, the setting is Diocletian's new Rostrum in the Forum; the five honorary columns commissioned to celebrate Diocletian's *vicennalia* are visible in the background.

Following the Battle of the Milvian Bridge, Constantine was finally secure in his position as the Western Emperor, but as yet in no position to challenge his co-Emperor, Licinius, in the East. Aware that he needed a loyal ally, he approached Licinius, suggesting that they should continue the Tetrarchic tradition of uniting their two families through marriage. Licinius, with similar difficulties of his own in the East, agreed and made a hasty visit to Milan in the winter of 313 to marry Constantine's half-sister Constantia. At the same time the two Emperors issued the Edict of Milan confirming religious toleration throughout the Roman Empire.

The days of the Tetrarchy, however, were numbered. Licinius's stay in Milan was short. In his

---

165 A small inscription on the top of the Arch of Constantine, found only recently, talks of a Colossus dedicated to Romulus. It is possible that this was the Colossus of Nero, which – like the statue of Constantine – is known to have had several name changes over the years.
166 Near Mersin, in today's southern Turkey.

absence, Maximinus Daia had successfully laid siege to Byzantium, an important staging post on any march to the eastern provinces. The final clash between the two Emperors of the East came in a hard-fought battle narrowly won by Licinius. Maximinus Daia fled to Nicomedia, Diocletian's old capital, where he is reputed to have appeared pale and trembling without his imperial insignia. Two months later he was reported dead in Tarsus,[166] having died a slow, painful death ascribed to poison.

With Maximinus Daia's death Constantine and Licinius reigned supreme within their own spheres, but, as in the early days of the First Tetrarchy, the Empire was too large for two men to handle alone. Had Licinius been prepared to accept Constantine as the senior Augustus the system might have continued during their lifetimes. But infringements of territory and continued attacks along the Danubian frontiers encouraged both Emperors to undertake campaigns outside their respective territories. A series of different Caesars appointed by each in turn and disliked and distrusted by the other was an added aggravation. But Constantine did little to improve the situation as he set out to deliberately blacken Licinius's reputation, implying that he was reneging on the directives of the Edict of Milan. Eusebius in his history picks up on this, accusing Licinius of apostasy despite the Edict.

ABOVE RIGHT: The obelisk of the Four Rivers Fountain by Bernini, which was originally on the *spina* of Maxentius's Circus.
RIGHT: The Temple of Romulus with its original bronze door, porphyry columns and marble cornice. The Church of St Cosmas and Damian stands behind it.

FACING PAGE: The Circus of Maxentius on the Via Appia showing the towers which supported the *carceres* (starting gates), of which only the bases survive today.

ABOVE: Two tondo panels from the Arch of Constantine: a lion hunt to the left and a sacrifice to Hercules to the right.

BELOW: Detail of Licinius (main figure) and Severus in the sacrifice scene.

Finally, in September 324, Constantine attacked Licinius at the Battle of Chrysopolis.[167] Constantine fought under the sign of the Christian Cross, whereas Licinius, according to Eusebius, paraded banners of the Roman pagan deities. Defeated on both land and sea, Licinius took refuge once again in Nicomedia. Constantia pleaded with her brother for the lives of her husband and son, and initially Constantine showed clemency and merely imprisoned his brother-in-law. Further alleged scheming, however, gave Constantine the excuse to hang him the following year and his son two years later. Collateral rule was over, the Tetrarchy dispensed with, and Constantine – 18 years after his proclamation as Emperor in Eboracum – reigned supreme. He died in 337.

The first Tetrarchy, which had existed peaceably for nearly 22 years, had been followed by a long period of confusion with seven different Emperors claiming the purple at different times. Finally, Constantine I – always known in history as Constantine the Great – ended any form of power-sharing by proclaiming himself sole ruler in 324. Diocletian's system of Caesars and Augusti, designed to reward merit and foster wisdom, had failed to overcome the stronger ties of family and ambition for power.

167 On the Asian shore of the Sea of Marmara near present-day Scutari.

DIOCLETIAN'S RETIREMENT

OF ALL THE EMPERORS who held office under
the Tetrarchy, the only one to abdicate peacefully
and abide by this decision was the man who had
set it up, Diocletian. His last public appearance
was at Carnuntum in 308. Facts about his retirement are sparse, so completely did he disappear
from the public eye. After retirement his health
improved and it is said that he enjoyed his garden,
growing cabbages and breeding fish on a nearby
island. The most probable date for his death,
either from suicide or illness, is December 312.

While Galerius lived, Diocletian's life was not
in danger. After Galerius's death in 311, this once
all-powerful man could no longer protect even the
closest members of his family. Diocletian's daughter Valeria – Galerius's widow, and now a wealthy
woman in her own right – had been entrusted to
the care of Licinius. However, finding herself no
longer welcome at Licinius's court, she appealed
for protection to Maximinus Daia. Maximinus Daia
laid down unacceptable conditions and on refusing
Maximinus Daia's proposal of marriage[168] Valeria
and her mother Prisca were banished from Nicomedia. Valeria's palaces and estates were confis-
cated, her eunuchs and domestics tortured, and
her loyal friends put under false arrest.

Mother and daughter were pursued from place
to place until they finally found refuge in a small village in the middle of the Syrian desert, where they
remained under guard. Here they appealed
for help to Diocletian. He asked that they
should be allowed to return to Salona, but
his request was ignored. Following Maximinus Daia's death in 313, they were forced
to escape once again and managed to survive
wandering through the provinces in disguise for
another 15 months until they were finally discovered in Thessalonica. Already under sentence of
death by Licinius, they were summarily beheaded in
315 and their bodies thrown into the sea.

ABOVE: Altar to Mithras
in Carnuntum inscribed:
D(eo) S(oli) I(nvicto)
M(ithrae) fautori imperii sui
Iovii et Herculii
felscissimi Augusti et Caesares
sacrarium restituerunt

(To the invincible
sun-god Mithras,
Protector of their reign
The lucky Iovii and Herculii,
Augusti and Caesars,
have reconstructed
the sanctuary).

---

168 Was Maximinus Daia sexually obnoxious? Lactantius recounts how
eunuchs were ordered to examine any woman in whom the Emperor
showed interest in the nude, to establish whether she had any bodily defect.
A custom grew up that no woman should be given leave to marry without the
personal permission of the Emperor.

BELOW: The London
riverfront at the Adelphi
(with York waterworks
tower in the distance) by
William Marlow, *c.*1771.

Note the wide terrace
in front of the houses
which sat over the
arched entrances to
the warehouses.

CHAPTER XII

THE ADELPHI AND ADAM'S DEATH

Adam is excluded from the new Royal Academy.
The development of the Adelphi. Death of all four brothers
and dissolution of the practice.

DIOCLETIAN'S LIFE ended in disappointment, his early success forgotten in the turmoil which followed his abdication. Adam, too, was to suffer deep disappointment as he grew older. For all his success with the young aristocracy, Adam was never fully admitted to the heart of the English establishment – to the government and the circle which surrounded the young King George III and his family.

Initially, the outlook had appeared promising, particularly once he had been appointed joint Architect of the King's Works and engaged by Lord Bute to work on his house in Berkeley Square. But he remained on the outer fringe while many of the friends he had made in Italy were given permanent jobs within the Royal Household. Joseph Wilton, who had guided him around Florence while on his way south and who was to work on many of his later projects, became Sculptor in Ordinary to His Majesty. Six months later, Allan Ramsay, who with his wife had accompanied Adam on many of their youthful expeditions around Rome, was given the title of Principal Painter in Ordinary to His Majesty.

Inspired by the close bond he had formed with his tutor William Chambers, architecture had become one of the King's greatest interests. Unfortunately Chambers had little sympathy with the picturesque style which had developed among the French Academy *pensionnaires* in Rome, of which Clérisseau was such a strong advocate and which Adam was to make his trademark. Both Adam and Chambers had submitted designs to the newly married King and Queen in 1762, when they purchased Buckingham House as their new family home. But the King found Adam's extensive plans for three new ranges set around a colonnaded courtyard too elaborate, and rejected his designs as over-fussy. This must have set an unfortunate precedent and Adam's regret is evident in the following letter written sometime later: 'My own situation at court, or rather my own situation not at court, prevents me from having it within my power to do what would have been very pleasing to me on this occasion.' Chambers remained the King's favourite architect throughout his life and could always count on royal support, often to Adam's disadvantage.

Adam's career was at its peak in 1768, but in spite of this he was not invited to join England's newest and most prestigious art society, inaugurated by the King himself in December of that year: the Royal Academy of Arts. This was not only a severe blow to Adam's pride, but also a calculated insult to his professionalism – and undoubtedly the result of Chambers's intervention with the King. The formation of such a society had been under discussion over a long period, for exhibition space for contemporary art in London was almost non-existent. There was still no publicly recognised body in London to compare with the Académie in Paris established almost 100 years before. Artists in the past had tried to fill the gap with their own privately run classes. The best known was Hogarth and his St Martin's Lane Academy, which he had set up in 1735. The Society of Artists, established in 1760 in Spring Gardens, might have filled this gap, but it lacked any teaching facilities and was beset with internal rivalry. Its first exhibition had been a huge success with 1,000 visitors each day, but the management of the society continued to divide its members. Such was the difficulty of reaching an agreement and so strong was the subsequent feeling of animosity among members that eight artists resigned simultaneously in 1768.

THE ADELPHI

This proved to be the catalyst for a new society. Encouraged by Robert Wood, of Palmyra fame, the eight artists asked William Chambers to approach the King for his support. The new society, which was to be self-regulating and open to all artists, was to provide teaching opportunities and hold a yearly exhibition, but its greatest selling point was that it was a royal foundation in which the King was personally involved. Amateurs and connoisseurs were banned from joining, as their presence both in the Society of Arts and the Dilettanti Society had led to serious disagreements. Joshua Reynolds became the Academy's first president and Chambers, by personal appointment of the King, its treasurer. Chambers thereafter held an unassailable position, and anyone he vetoed stood no chance of joining. The 34 founding members included some of Adam's

closest friends, but neither Robert nor James ever became members.[169]

At the same time Adam began to suffer from the rivalry of younger architects – chief among them James Wyatt, who was beginning to win prestigious new commissions. At only 26, Wyatt had won enthusiastic plaudits for his daring design for the Pantheon in Oxford Street. His remit had been to design a 'Winter Ranelagh', supplying brand-new assembly rooms in the heart of London where fashionable society could gather to enjoy themselves during the winter months. By now Adam had reigned supreme for ten years, but fashion is fickle and clients, particularly younger ones, search out new ideas: Adam himself had benefited from similar enthusiasm during his own early days in London. Work for him remained plentiful, but much of it was humdrum and a continuation of what was already in the pipeline. He was now 40, wealthy enough to maintain the impressive 'equipage' he had always felt was necessary to his position, while at the same time running a very successful partnership with his brothers. But the fact that he had neither won a large governmental commission nor gained admission to one of the most prestigious societies in London was a challenge he could not ignore. He began to look outside the normal boundaries of an architectural practice, searching for an area which he could develop privately and in doing so change the face of London. He found it in a shabby, long-despised section of the city alongside the River Thames.

In 1768 he and his three brothers signed a 99-year lease with the trustees of the Duke of St Albans for an area just south of the Strand known as Durham's Yard. This had once been a very popular stretch of river on which the aristocracy and leading clerics had bought sites. Here they had built their large, fashionable London houses, well away from the dirt and disease of the city on the one hand and safe from the endless intrigues of the Court on the other. This particular site, Durham's Yard, situated halfway between the City of London and the Palace of Westminster, had originally belonged to one of the greatest princes of the Church, the Bishop of Durham. However, after the abolition of the Episcopacy under Cromwell and the subsequent political unrest during the Commonwealth, many of these houses had disappeared. At the Restoration Charles II reaffirmed the Bishops in their local diocese but the

169 Zoffany's famous group portrait of the Academicians, painted in 1771–2, is now in the Royal Collection.
170 York House was demolished in 1672, Salisbury House in 1673 and Arundel House in 1678. All three dated from Tudor times.
171 The stables were extremely spacious, some able to accommodate as many as 16 horses.
172 By the terms of the lease, the brothers had had to retain the public passageways down to the river.

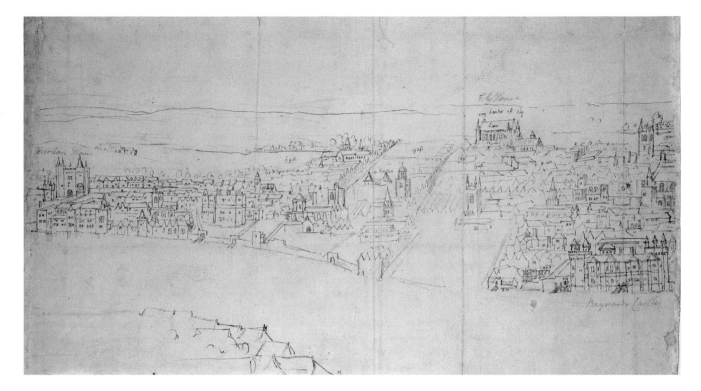

valuable freeholds they had once owned in London now became private property. Durham House, complete with its grand hall, chapel, riverside apartments and an extensive garden, was one of the first to go in 1661.[170] By the mid-eighteenth century, the river had lost its attraction and Durham's Yard consisted of a series of small derelict properties leased out at miserable prices.

Here, Adam felt, was an original and exciting project which would perpetuate his name, and he decided to underwrite it as a private development. It was a massive task and speculative in the extreme – particularly for a private company. The brothers were in a hurry and even before the final agreement had been signed they began demolition. As word of this enormous project spread it aroused jealousy; objections began to be heard, and opinions ran high through all sections of society.

Adam's plan was to build a series of houses on a network of different streets, which extended over the whole 1.4 hectare site. One of the difficulties was the steep gradient between the existing Strand and the river's edge, the difference in level being about 12 metres. The riverside wharfs themselves would disappear to be replaced by a series of graduated brick arches, which would in turn form the foundations of these new houses. These arches would increase from one to three tiers as the streets

ABOVE: **Durham House to the left, with guest apartments on the river and chapel and gardens behind,** **and Barnard's Castle on the extreme right. Taken from the** *Panorama of London* **by Antonius Wyngaerde, *c*.1544.**

approached the river; the upper range of arches could usefully accommodate living quarters for the new residents' coachmen and stabling for their horses.[171] Building this network of arches was by far the most difficult and expensive part of the project. To offset the huge costs, the brothers planned to rent out the new vaults to the government as ordnance stores – a scheme which, if successful, would bring in much-needed income.

Three entrances from the river bank led under the arches into a second network of six streets below ground. Entrance to these same lower streets from the Strand was through the old Durham Gate and a covered path led down to the river as a public right of way.[172]

As the work progressed, the Adam brothers realised that they would also need to build a small embankment to prevent the new vaults being flooded at high tide. By now there was a large body of opinion objecting to any interference with the river bank, claiming the brothers had no ownership of this area. Only an Enabling Bill passed through the Houses of Parliament would solve the problem.

169

Adam had become the Member of Parliament for Kinross in 1769 thereby becoming familiar with parliamentary procedure.[173] Parliament finally approved the Bill in 1773, but its passage through the House galvanised considerable opposition and brought much unwanted publicity. One of Adam's most loyal patrons, Lord Shelburne, and two of his fellow peers had made their objections very clear in open debate. Shelburne felt so strongly that he dismissed Adam from all further work at Bowood. Having employed Adam for over ten years and with many projects still unfinished, this was a very public sign of his displeasure.

At the other end of the social scale, the dockers who worked on the wharves along this stretch of the Thames objected to the development of the riverside and the subsequent loss of their jobs. In eighteenth-century London few people considered the Thames an asset: most thought of it as an occasional form of transport, but even that was questionable owing to the unpleasant stench, especially at low tide. Its usefulness was largely commercial. The Adam family were mocked and the following ditty became a popular jingle:

Four Scotsmen by the name of Adam,
Who keep their Coaches and their Madams,
Quoth John in sulky mood to Thomas,
Have stole the very River from us.

Prejudice against the Scots, many of whom had held important positions in the previous ten years from the Prime Minister downwards, was widespread. The Adam brothers had done themselves no favours by beginning demolition on the site before the lease was signed and dumping the debris into the river. The legal niceties had taken 17 months to settle:

O Scotland, long has it been said
Thy teeth are sharp for English bread.
What, seize our bread and water too,
And use us worse than jailers do?

In addition to objections raised by the Parliamentarians and the dockers, the Corporation of the City of London now entered the lists of battle. The bed of the river itself was deemed to be the ancient property of the City and therefore could not be considered part of the Adam's purchase – hence

'Have stole the very River from us'. Mr Lee, councillor of the City, acknowledged at the bar of the House of Lords that 'The Messrs Adam were very able and experienced architects; but although he admired the elegance of their buildings, he never could allow that from thence alone arose a right of building on that ground.' However, in the event, the brothers – with the backing of Lord North and the King – were successful in gaining the necessary licence for their project. For no improvement to the riverfront, which would replace the existing filth and squalor, could ultimately be rejected by Parliament.

What was the germ of this unusual scheme? Had the brothers found inspiration in the recent redevelopments in Edinburgh, a city they would have known since childhood? Many of the old, narrow wynds in Edinburgh had once been bordered by tall seven-storey houses, but in 1752, 20 years before work began on the Adelphi development, the Burgh authorities in Edinburgh had embarked on a wholesale rearrangement of the old town. They had knocked down the upper storeys of old houses and left the lower sections to act as foundations for new buildings above. In doing so, they had

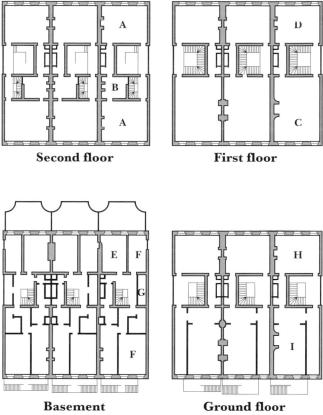

Second floor

First floor

Basement

Ground floor

FACING PAGE: House in the Adelphi on today's Robert Street, overlooking the river.

ABOVE: Detail showing the cornice, with the honeysuckle in both flower and bud.

RIGHT: Plan of the Adelphi
A. Bed Chamber
B. Dressing Room
C. First Drawing Room
D. Second Drawing Room
E. Upper Part Kitchen
F. Servants Bedroom
G. Closet
H. Parlour
I. Dining Room

created the dark underground streets which still exist today.[174]

Another source of inspiration was, of course, Diocletian's palace. Adam certainly adapted the idea of the arcaded *cryptoporticus* to form the basement levels and river façade of his Royal Terrace and the subterranean streets that led off it. As has been noted, the palace's basement levels were not as accessible at the time of his visit as they are today, but he appears to have worked out their design fairly accurately

The Adelphi, a name which in Greek means 'brothers', is for ever part of London, and although only sections of it still exist, it was in many senses way ahead of its time. Indeed, the idea of building identical attached houses in a row and calling them a 'terrace', repeated today all over London, originated here.

The Adams' plan to redevelop the site was both practical and imaginative. The major houses were designed around a rectangle, their backs forming the border of the rectangle and their façades facing outwards onto the three main streets, all of which were given family names: Adam Street, John Street and Robert Street. The fourth street facing the river was the finest and consisted of a terrace of the 14 houses known as the Royal Terrace. Special attention was given to the two end houses of the Royal Terrace, both of which stood slightly apart, being set forward with a road's width between them and the other houses.

The individual houses were spacious, with two basement storeys, reception rooms spread over the two main floors, and bedrooms above. Most were built of plain brick with decorative iron balconies, area railings and graceful lamp standards. A few façades were richly decorated. One of these in Robert Street has survived, allowing us a tantalising glimpse of the original concept. A simple brick façade, set over a rusticated basement, is decorated with stucco pilasters of the Giant Order which rises through two floors to a pediment. It has a typical Adam frieze of anthemions, those in bud alternating with those in flower. The design is simple and dignified.

---

173 In doing so he had had to relinquish his post as Joint Architect to the King's Works, but such was his stature that James was readily accepted as his successor.
174 One such building was the Royal Exchange in Edinburgh (known today as the City Chambers), built in 1753; and Mary Kings Close which lies beneath it. John Adam had won the competition and designed vaults as its foundation.

ROYAL SOCIETY OF ARTS

'From the river, the Royal Terrace had the appearance of a brilliant new palace, a worthy successor to the Episcopal, royal and noble residences of the past.'[175] The finest surviving house today is that of the Royal Society of Arts in John Adam Street, purpose-built between 1771 and 1774. It was an addendum suggested by James in answer to the Society's advertisement for a new venue. Founded 20 years earlier, the Society had aroused an enthusiastic response, its aim being to encourage innovation in commerce and manufacturing by awarding

prizes or premiums for new ideas and inventions. The new inventions covered a wide variety of different products ranging from dyes to large agricultural machinery; it also provided money for the teaching of draughtsmanship to young apprentices. Even today the Society's official letter paper contains the following statement: 'The RSA moved to its current home in 1774. The House has remained a hub for enlightened thought and social activism ever since, with many of the greatest minds of the past two centuries passing through its doors.'

All three Adam brothers were already members of the Society, but it was James who suggested they incorporate it into their scheme. He allocated it

175 D.G.C. Allan, *The Adelphi, Past and Present* (2001).

LEFT: 'The London riverfront of the new buildings called the Adelphi, formerly Durham's Yard', by B. Pastorini, 1768–70. This view, looking towards Blackfriars Bridge and St Paul's, includes the openings of streets leading to the Strand, together with wharfs, arcade and the entrance to the subterranean streets and warehouses of the Adelphi. The house on Robert Street is on the extreme left.

an area of three houses, two in depth (one behind the other) and another alongside to the east as accommodation for the Society's secretary. The depth was needed to provide space for the large meeting room on the first floor required for the presentation of the Society's yearly awards. Another large room below the meeting room was the Model Room, necessary for the exhibition of the award-winning artefacts themselves. The Society accepted the Adams' proposal on condition that the embellishments remained simple. Members felt they

could not justify subscribers' money being spent on unnecessary decoration. The result was that the roundels and statues on the façade today were only added in the twentieth century.

Thomas Malton mentions that the Adelphi façades came in for some criticism as the pilaster projections and string courses were considered too shallow, but his opinion of the RSA overall is high: 'I cannot close my description of this work without the bestowing of praise upon the front of the building… I know of no fabric in London of similar dimensions, that can rival this structure in these characteristics. It is beautifully simple without meanness and grand without exaggeration.'[176]

176 Thomas Malton, *A Picturesque Tour through the Cities of London and Westminster*, Vol. 1 (1792).

The Adelphi became one of the most sought-after addresses in London, appealing to a range of widely different tenants. By 1772 it was almost complete and David Garrick[177] moved into a new house on the Royal Terrace. Another tenant was Dr Graham, a quack doctor and well-known eccentric who had his 'Temple of Health' there, claiming universal cures for most ailments and hiring out his 'celestial bed' (on which perfect children could be conceived) at £100 a night. Topham Beauclerk – described as a wit, politician and friend of Dr Johnson – also took a lease. Robert and James lived at No. 4 John Street and had their offices behind at No. 13. These names are commemorated today on a large plaque on the site of the terrace above Victoria Embankment Gardens.

FINANCIAL PROBLEMS

How could the Adam brothers have ever considered such an expensive and risky venture? To date they had been very successful and between them ran the largest building enterprise in London; in today's terms it was a true conglomerate. Known as William Adam & Co, it employed some 2,000 to 3,000 men. It had diversified into timber yards and brickworks, and held the contract for providing paving stones for eight parishes within London. It was in the happy position of being able to supply most of the necessary raw materials for the Adams' architectural partnership, which remained financially separate. The development might have made a lot of money but for two events, which caused a financial crisis. The first was their speculative investment in a new method of making stucco: the product proved unsatisfactory and led to an expensive court case and further poor publicity.[178] The second, and far more serious, was the bankruptcy of the Scottish Bank of Neale, Fordyce and Downe in 1772. No longer able to honour its bills, the bank's failure had the domino effect of bringing down

ten London banking houses and another nine in Edinburgh. Panic reigned. The Adam brothers had bought heavily into the convenience of paper money and credit notes which the bank could no longer honour. Work on the Adelphi stopped. An article in the *Scots Magazine* for June included the following quotation: 'The Messrs Adam of the Adelphi Buildings in the Strand being unfortunately involved by the failure of some capital houses; upwards of some two thousand valuable artificers and workmen, supported by their undertakings in different parts of the kingdom, were thrown out of employment and their families deprived of subsistence.'

The result was frighteningly sudden, but the next few lines tell of the workmen's dilemma, torn between alarm at their own impending predicament and sympathy for their long-standing employers: 'The poor men had begun their work in the morning before the melancholy news of their masters' misfortunes were communicated to them: when informed of it they came down from the walls in silence and stood for some time in the street in

---

177 Garrick died there seven years later in 1779 and his widow stayed there until her death in 1822.

178 The Adam brothers used stucco throughout. They had recently obtained the patents of two new manufacturers, the Revd John Liardet and Revd David Wark, and manufactured the stucco on site in the vaults below. In the building trade it became known as 'Adam's cement'.

179 Lotteries were a popular method of raising money in the eighteenth century. State lotteries had originated in 1693–4 as an adjunct to the newly established Bank of England. They proved immensely valuable, providing finance for projects of all different types, ranging from capitalisation of a war to building new monuments within the city itself.

180 *Survey of London*, Vol. 18 (1937).

181 'Particulars composing the Prizes in the Adelphi Lottery, the Property of Messrs John, Robert, James and William Adam.'

a body and at last went off one by one, with every mark of regret for the fate of their masters whose business had supported them and their families for several years.'

Perhaps this was putting a gloss on a potentially explosive situation, because other sources claim that to keep their wage bill down the Adam brothers had imported workmen from Scotland who sought less pay than those in London, and whose spirits they sought to keep up by having them serenaded each day by Scottish pipers. In the event the brothers managed to salvage the company and within a few weeks the workforce was back in action. How did they achieve this so quickly? Their solution was to hold a lottery, but before this could take effect another Act of Parliament was needed, prolonging any financial resolution by several months.[179]

THE LOTTERY

To provide immediate funds, the brothers held a five-day sale of their own personal belongings the following February (1773). It attracted a huge crowd, for their art collections were widely known, and the proceeds of the sale eased their immediate cash flow. The lottery itself was held a year later, in March 1774, with 4,370 tickets for 108 prizes going on sale at 50 guineas each. Among the prizes were the houses, shops, warehouses and vaults not already sold. The allocated houses were scat-tered all over the site and were graded according to their value. The 12 most expensive were priced at £50,080. One of the prizes, valued at £9,960, consisted of four houses and a coffee shop.[180] The brothers published a detailed prospectus.[181] The total prize money raised was to be the same as the actual sum laid out by the promoters, plus a 5 per cent commission and a further £1,500 towards the expense of the lottery. In other words the Adam brothers were prepared to build the Adelphi at cost: they wrote, 'They will be perfectly satisfied if they should only draw from this lottery, the money laid out by them on a work they readily confess they have found to be too great for their private fortunes.'

They pointed out, too, that the odds they were offering were far more favourable than those of the normal state lottery, giving a better ratio of blanks to numbered tickets. In the prospectus the houses are described as having several advantages which set them apart from the norm. This was particularly true apropos of fire, which remained one of the major dangers within any large city. Not only did the houses have water laid on to all floors, including the attics, they also had their own fire engines within the complex. In addition there were two new water towers, each of which communicated directly to the river, from which water could be supplied to any house at one minute's notice. Other anti-fire measures listed included lightning conductors on these towers, and the fact that any house could be reached without delay as all the roofs were inter-connected.

The administration of the lottery was strictly controlled to ensure public confidence and the preliminaries were carefully enforced. Tickets were available every day except Sunday from the Adams' offices in the Adelphi and at specifically chosen sites across London. Adam had petitioned the Lord Mayor to allow the draw to take place in the Guildhall, which was the normal venue for these occasions, but owing to the City's early animosity this was refused. Jonathan's Coffee House in the Strand proved a suitable alternative. Two 'wheels' or 'boxes', each closed by seven separate locks, contained the tickets, and both 'boxes' were in turn enclosed in an outer larger box. Accompanied by cheering crowds, banners, 20 constables and a dozen grenadiers, the 'wheels' were taken on ceremonial sledges to the place of the draw. The

FACING PAGE: The Royal Society of Arts building in John Adam Street.

ABOVE: A plaque to the left of the front door.

The Adam brothers' attempts to restore their fortunes led them to undertake four other development schemes in London, the best-preserved being Fitzroy Square in Bloomsbury. Having learnt their lesson from the Adelphi project, they now took out leases on the building land, erected the houses, and then sold them off to recoup their investment. Unfortunately the outbreak of the American War of Independence in 1775 was to unsettle the construction market further, leading to the collapse of their projects in Portland Place and Mansfield Street.

Robert's later work was largely in Scotland, where he developed a picturesque castle style. His health had always been fragile and his workload prodigious; even as a young man in Rome he had had to pace himself, suffering from occasional bouts of what is now thought to have been rheumatic fever. He died unexpectedly at his home in 11 Albemarle Street from a burst ulcer in March 1792, at the age of 63, and was buried in Westminster Abbey. He was given a magnificent funeral, his pall bearers being chosen from among the notable friends who had supported him throughout: the Duke of Buccleuch, the Earl of Coventry, the Earl of Lauderdale, Viscount Stormont, Lord Frederick Campbell and William Pulteney. He is commemorated with a plaque in the northern transept of the Abbey, but there is no monument to him.

His older brother, John, died a short time later in Scotland, resentful of what he considered his younger brothers' ambition and excessive speculation. James and William struggled on until James's death two years later. William was left to cope alone, and by 1801 was declared bankrupt.[183] He sold the remainder of the brothers' pictures, furniture and antiquities in two sales in 1818 and 1821, and with the help of his niece and her husband, John Clerk of Penicuik, assembled the major part of their remaining drawings into albums.

These drawings, nearly 9,000 of them, were eventually sold to Sir John Soane in 1833. Soane was then Professor of Architecture at the Royal Academy, and well known for his meticulously prepared lectures. Among the many illustrations he used in his teaching at the Royal Academy was a plate of the Mausoleum from Adam's *Ruins of Spalatro*, brought up to date with figures of Regency bucks sketching and sightseeing. With this acknowledgement of Adam's great achievement, Diocletian's palace passed into the academic lore of British architecture.

wheel turned out the first ticket on 3 March 1774: it happened to be a blank, but because it was the first drawn it won the seventh prize of £5,000, which happened to be a single property of five flats in Robert Street.

The lottery raised £218,500, thereby easing the company's financial situation and enabling the brothers to pay off their debts and complete their building works. However, many of the purchasers were speculators. Either they did not require a house in the Adelphi or they were not prepared to wait until their allocated house was built, so they put their prize-winning tickets up for auction again, selling them at a considerable discount. The brothers retained any unsold tickets for themselves, which left the ownership of a large part of the Adelphi still in their hands – an enormously valuable asset.[182]

182 It also allowed them to buy back much of their art collection sold the previous February at Christie's.
183 William died in 1822 at the age of 84.

THE ADELPHI IN LATER YEARS

THE EMBANKMENT of the Thames by Joseph Bazalgette took place a century after the building of the Adelphi, between 1864 and 1870, finally solving the problem of flooding in the lower basements of the surviving houses. In spite of all their efforts, this had remained a recurring difficulty for the Adam brothers, as the underground warehouses had been built two feet (0.6 metres) lower than intended, and even after Adam's local embankment of the river they were never guaranteed free of water at high tide.

A new lease of the site was successfully negotiated in 1927, but by then the vault arches which supported the houses above had required reinforcement on several different occasions. In 1936 the entire river block was demolished and the New Adelphi, a monumental Art Deco building designed by Colcutt and Hamp, was erected in its place. During World War II the arches which still survive under today's Adelphi Building were used as an enormous air raid shelter.

Only with the building of the New Adelphi in 1936 was the right of way from the old Durham Gate discontinued. Remnants of the covered path which led down to the river can still be seen beneath the Royal Society of Arts: one can walk, by way of its basement, through underground passages to the Embankment alongside the Savoy Hotel.

ABOVE: Entrance to the Royal Society of Arts in Durham House Street, where the route down to the river started.

FACING PAGE: The vaults of the RSA, which follow the old route down to the river.

EPILOGUE

Brief history of Diocletian's palace in the eighteenth and nineteenth centuries, recounted by contemporary travellers to the Balkans.

WHAT HAPPENED TO DIOCLETIAN'S PALACE after Adam's death? Adam had brought it to the attention of the scholars and academics of his day and, as the first detailed study of this ancient site, his *Ruins of Spalatro* remained the classic guide to British travellers who followed in his footsteps. The Balkans, however, remained a little-known area; only intrepid travellers were willing to explore a place about which so little had been written. Roads into the interior were few, passes through the Dinaric Alps were rare, and where they did exist were little better than rough tracks. Any traveller faced difficult choices. To ride a pack mule through the mountains or to row up the rivers in small boats were often the only methods of gaining access to the interior. Both required considerable stamina and reasonably good health.

John Gardner Wilkinson was one of the most enterprising travellers of the following century. The Balkans fascinated him, and in 1846 he became one of the few to make the journey up the Krka River from Spalatro to Knin and Senj and to return via Salona. He did the round trip by any means available to him: by boat, on horseback and on foot.[184] Already a respected Egyptologist with a volume of academic work to his name, and a Fellow of the Royal Society, Gardner Wilkinson took extensive notes and made numerous sketches, all of which are now stored in the Bodleian Library in Oxford. Like many Englishmen of his day he had no time for the Turks who had dominated the area for so long: his sympathies lay entirely with the Slavs, and the reason for his visit was to see for himself how such a small minority populace had been able to withstand such a large force for so long.

On his way up the Krka river, Gardner Wilkinson was venturing into what had, until very recently, been Turkish territory. He wished to visit two monasteries: one a Franciscan monastery on a small island in the river and the other an Orthodox monastery a few miles further north on a lake. With no road to connect them, the only route possible was by water, and letters had to be sent requesting both the visit and a boat. It was the first time there had been any communication between the two groups of monks. The gamble paid off, and Gardner Wilkinson recounts his delight at his reception.

Gardner Wilkinson used Split as a base to explore the surrounding countryside. He describes Diocletian's palace, remarking that Robert Adam a hundred years before had probably seen much more.[185] Such was the political uncertainty of the time that the palace continued to offer security to its inhabitants 1,500 years after its construction. Travellers seem to agree that the city was very congested, choked by small streets and medieval buildings built among the ruins. This is true even today, particularly of the *cryptoporticus* facing the harbour, with shops built up against it and houses towering over the wall.

A.A. Paton,[186] a geographer and a contemporary of Gardner Wilkinson, was interested in the commercial resources of the country. He gives us his own version of this 'inhabited ruin':

> The grand gallery or cryptoporticus was built all over, with here a Venetian blind and there a pole on which clothes were drying, here vaults and columns obliterated by middle-age battlements or modern house building. It had once had two floors, now in places there were three or even four floors.

The peristyle, by contrast, strikes everyone as spacious, open to the air and bustling with contem-

---

184 Sir John Gardner Wilkinson (1797–1875), *Dalmatia and Montenegro* (1848).
185 Gardner Wilkinson mentions various historical figures, among them two Roman Emperors, Diocletian and Claudius Gothicus (the somewhat dubious ancestor of Constantius Chlorus).
186 A.A. Paton (1811–74), *Highlands and Islands of the Adriatic* (1862).

porary life. The Revd John Mason Neale,[187] writing an ecclesiastical history in 1861 with the express purpose of supplementing the accounts of Adam and Wilkinson, is, however, extremely critical. He writes of the northern section of the city being 'blocked with mean alleyways, staircase streets and huddled lanes' and has no time for the Cathedral (Mausoleum):

the darkest plainest church I ever saw, an opening or two for light and that is all the changes made. The interior entablatures are in the worst and heaviest taste, the sculptures of the frieze; cupids riding or in chariots, lions, bears, stags are equally barbarous. Still the dome which is brickwork is ingenious.

He is rather more tolerant of the Baptistery – once the Temple of Aesculapius – and quotes Gardner Wilkinson word for word. He is delighted that it has been saved by its conversion to Christianity and, perhaps surprisingly, also approves of the destruction of the pre-Romanesque steeple which had been attached to the temple's roof.

One of the most discerning travellers of the nineteenth century was Sir Thomas Graham Jackson – scholar, antiquarian and architect – who visited Dalmatia no fewer than four times, starting in 1882. Viewing the Balkan Peninsula from across the Adriatic, on a hill high above Ancona, Jackson had dreamed of exploring it for some years, and the dream seems to have survived despite the depredations and difficulties he and his wife experienced when actually travelling there. He kept detailed journals of each visit and finally published his experiences in a three-volume book in 1887, which still remains one of the best sources on nineteenth-century Croatia.[188] One of the reasons for his repeated visits was his commission to design and complete

the campanile of the Cathedral of Zadar, which had been left unfinished since 1452. It was built to his plans and completed by 1892, when Jackson and his wife attended its unveiling.

Jackson sailed down the coast stopping at all the small ports en route including Spalatro. His views echo those of other visitors:

Arrived in Spalato about 6 o'clock and walked about a bit before dinner, but the narrow streets and wretched population of Spalato always made me feel creepy in the dark and I was glad to get back to the Piazza where there was a great gathering of people walking up and down.

At the same time he gives an informed description of the city: as an architect and an antiquarian, he could rise above the immediate squalor. 'Even in its present state, ruined and defaced and overgrown with the mean accretions of late centuries, its vast proportions and solid construction excite our astonishment. So much of it remains that it is easy, in imagination, to recover what is lost.'

His comparisons with other cities he had seen along the coast are also enlightening: 'Spalato strikes the visitor as the busiest and most thriving place in Dalmatia, its streets and squares are lit by gas while those of Zara and other cities are still dependent on oil lanterns.'

Like Adam he was intrigued with the way the city obtained its water. He explains how the water originated near Fort Klis (six miles away), winding its way through cuttings – sometimes 12 metres deep – across the valley, and was supported on arches as it approached the city as an aqueduct. In Adam's day Fort Klis had still belonged to the Turks, which explains the suspicions he aroused when he and Clérisseau tried to explore the countryside. By the time of Jackson's visit a new canal had been constructed, but it still used part of the ancient watercourse across the aqueduct and supplied the city with water of great purity.

Jackson, like Gardner Wilkinson, was fascinated

187 J.M. Neale (1818–66), *Notes, Ecclesiological and Picturesque on Dalmatia, Croatia, Istria and Syria* (1861).
188 Sir Thomas Graham Jackson (1835–1924), *Dalmatia, the Quarnero and Istira with Cettinge in Montenegro and the Island of Grado* (1887).

by the rivers. When travelling to Knin along a dry river-bed past several inactive water mills, he describes how these river-beds can run for several miles underground. At certain times of year when the river is about to reappear a 'rumbling and grumbling are heard from the interior and then suddenly out comes the river filling the whole cave and bursting out with a mighty volume which not only supplies the mill races but overflows and occupies the width of the valley with a roaring torrent'.[189] This is a typical description of the karst[190] landscape and is repeated frequently by travellers through the ages.

Jackson was aware of the difficulties of conservation and mentions the clearing of alluvial deposits outside the Porta Aurea of Diocletian's palace earlier in the century. He could also analyse its architecture and, like Adam, appreciate the unusual use of accepted classical norms.

Here we see the first relaxation of the strict rules of ancient classical art; the proportions of the different members of the order are varied, arbitrary. Some members are omitted entirely; new forms of ornament such as the zigzag which was to play such a large part in Norman architecture make their first appearance and the arches are made to spring immediately from the capitals without an intervening entablature.

It was not until 1910 and 1912 that Adam's monograph was professionally updated. An Austrian architect, Georg Niemann[191] from Vienna, and two Frenchmen – one an architect, Ernest Hébrard, and the other an archaeologist, Jacques Zeiller[192] –

all undertook further serious research, producing detailed plans, drawings and convincing reconstructions of its original appearance. Their conclusions differed very little from those of Adam 150 years earlier. By now the city was known as Split; it had expanded enormously, becoming a significant port and commercial centre, but the palace remained the core of the old town along the waterfront. The first Croatian monograph by Bulić and Karaman dates from 1929, with further extensive research continued by Tomaslav Marasović and subsequent scholars who have published extensively since World War II.

Discussion as to what to retain and what to remove remained a central issue between the two wars, but clearing up, excavating and conserving the palace has been a continuing operation – so much so that in 1979 it was declared a World Heritage site, which should protect it for the future and confirm its standing as 'something unique and unusually rare'.[193]

DIOCLETIAN AND ROBERT ADAM

To compare two such different men as a Roman Emperor and a Scottish architect living 13 centuries apart is a challenge. However, there are similarities, and not simply because Adam – as he himself says in his preface to *Ruins of Spalatro* – drew much of his inspiration from antiquity in general and Diocletian's palace in particular. Both men worked with great freedom, and neither feared breaking away from earlier traditions. Diocletian introduced elements from the East which were completely new to Roman architecture: the colonnaded streets from Palmyra, the grid pattern of streets from Miletus, and the combination of an arch and architrave from Ephesus. The very idea of a palace designated solely for the use of an emperor was a new idea introduced by the Tetrarchy, as was the sculptural iconography which reflected the 'Rule of Four'. This is seen at its best in the architecture of Galerius in Felix Romuliana and Thessalonica.

Adam, too, adapted motifs of classical architecture to his own use, giving them new functions

189 Engineers when trying to generate electricity from these rivers after World War II put coloured plastic pellets into these underground channels in an attempt to chart their route. Some emerged as springs under the sea, others in island bays along the coast.
190 See Chapter 4.
191 G. Niemann, *Der Palast Diokletians in Spalato* (1910).
192 E. Hébrard and J. Zeiller, *Spalato, le Palais de Dioclétian* (1912).
193 World Cultural Heritage Register.
194 David Watkin, *Sir John Soane: Enlightenment Thought and the Royal Academy Lectures* (1996).
195 John Summerson, *Architecture in Britain 1530–1830* (1953).

and thereby adding a new splendour to the English country house. Kedleston is one of the best examples. Here the plan of Diocletian's palace is converted into a sequence of rooms. He introduces a new classical order which he calls the 'Spalatro Order', and a garden façade inspired by a triumphal arch. Such originality and daring accounted for Adam's initial success. Sir John Soane, when lecturing to his students as President of the Royal Academy, wrote:

> In this superb structure he has united in no considerable degree the taste and magnificence of a Roman villa with all the comforts and conveniences of an Englishman's noble residence.'[194]

It is also explains why Adam's architecture grew steadily in popularity, becoming a byword for fashion in his own lifetime. Sir John Summerson, one of the finest architectural historians of the twentieth century, summed up his appeal in the following words:

> The freedom of these designs and the feeling that the artist was designing 'out of his head' the occasional introduction of Romanesque or Gothic themes is very remarkable and something entirely new for English Architecture… Adam was probably the first English architect to break with the spirit of servitude to antiquity in this arrogant way.[195]

PHOTOGRAPHIC CREDITS

Bodleian Library, University of Oxford: pp.70, 71, 103
Bowood Estates: pp.146–9
Bridgeman Art Library: pp.19, 119, 169
British Library: pp.89, 134
British Museum: pp.36, 56, 98, 100, 117.
Canoscan.com (Morphari Creations Inc.): p.43
Deutsches Archäologisches Institut Rom: pp.38, 164
Istanbul: Museum of Archaeology: p.22
Milan:
 Museum of Archaeology: p.115
 Duomo Archives: p.115
Museum of London: pp.166, 172, 173
National Portrait Gallery: p.14
National Library of Scotland: pp.32, 33, 36, 45, 84, 93–7, 130, 134
National Trust: pp.133, 135–9, 144, 145, 149–51
Northumberland Estates: pp.140–3
Royal Collection Trust, © Her Majesty Queen Elizabeth II 2013: p.112
Shutterstock.com: p.20 arenaphoto.UK; p.30 Poszlos; p.42 Ilisan Gercelman, Keith Levitt; p.59 Krzysztof Slusarczyk; p.60 Goran Bogicevic; p.66 Waj; p.72 Elenarts; p.77 Kuvona; p.116 Claudio Divizia; p.121 eclipse78; p.128 Conde; p.152 Vladislav Gurfinkel; p.157 Chris Hill; p.159 Claudio Zaccherius; p.163 Brian Kinney, Phoenix79
Sir John Soane's Museum: p.149
Split:
 Museum of Archaeology: pp.27, 43
 Palace of Diocletian: pp.35, 38
Trier:
 Museum of Archaeology: p.111
 Tourist Information: p.106
 Evangelische, Kirchenreis: p.108
Vatican Museums: p.49
Vienna:
 Austrian National Library: p.52
 Kunsthistorisches Museum: p.165
Wikimedia Commons.com: p.123 Giovanni Dall'Orto, Panairjdde; p.124 Jastrow
Yale Publications: pp.37, 110, 122, 159
York Museums and Gallery Trust: p.154
Zaječar, National Museum: pp.58, 78, 81, 82, 83
Other photographs © Alicia Salter
Maps by Russell Birkett: pp.24–5, 64, 105 (© Historical Atlas of Ancient Rome), 50 (© Thames & Hudson)

ACKNOWLEDGEMENTS

This book has had a long gestation and would never have seen the light of day without the generous help of so many friends and colleagues. Emails have proved invaluable and all the institutions I have had to contact, both here and in Europe, have responded with unfailing swiftness and charm. Scholars in the Balkans have been particularly helpful and I am very grateful to Goran Nikšić in Split for all his time and patience over the last five years. Opinions have been sought and skills called upon; all given with great generosity. Jonathan Pegg's input was such that I rethought the entire order of the book, Rosemary Andreae's cool experience proved invaluable as did that of Dr Alexander Marr. Dr Iain Gordon Brown agreed to cast his discerning and helpful eye over the Adam content, while Dr Barbara Levick, Emeritus Fellow of St Hilda's College, Oxford, and Dr Neil McLynn, Fellow of Corpus Christi College, Oxford, did the same on behalf of Diocletian and the Tetrarchs.

I could never have believed the length of time it would take to get such a manuscript ready for publication, and for this I have to thank Anthony Gardner for his editing skill and Derek Westwood for his expertise in the layout and design of the finished product and for being such a support through difficult times. Katy Carter was meticulous in her proof reading; Clemens von Bechtelsheim, Luciana Moretti and John Penney all helped with translations while Donald Payne helped sort out the geological conundrums of Croatia. John Julius Norwich agreed to write an engaging foreword. Finally, it was entirely due to Tim and Susie Sainsbury that I was able to visit Split in the first place, so becoming captivated by its story. Everyone has been unfailingly patient and kind, not least my beloved husband, who must have often wished I had never encountered the Tetrarchs!

January 2013

BIBLIOGRAPHY
FOR ADAM

Adam, R. *Ruins of the Palace of the Emperor Diocletian at Spalatro.* 1764

Allan, D.G.C. *The Adelphi, Past & Present.* 2001

Aurenhammer, H. *J Fischer von Erlach.* 1973

Belozerskaya, M. *To Wake the Dead. Cyrius of Ancona.* 2009

Bićanić, S. *British Travellers in Dalmatia 1757–1935.* 2006

Brown, I.G. *Monumental Reputation. Robert Adam and the Emperor's Palace.* 1992

Browning, I. *Palmyra.* 1949

Bryant, J. *Robert Adam, Architect of Genius.* 1992

Colvin, H. *A Biographical Dictionary of British Architects 1600–1840.* 1995

Edwards, J. *Idealism not Ostentation: The Society of Arts in the Adelphi.* 2006

Fleming, J. *Robert Adam and his Circle.* 1962

Graham, R. *Arbiter of Elegance.* 2009

Guidebooks to: *Bowood House and Gardens, Kedleston Hall, Kenwood, Osterley House and Park* and *Syon, London Home of the Duke of Northumberland*

Harris, E. *The Genius of Robert Adam: his interiors.* 2001

Harris, J and Snodin, M. *Sir William Chambers, Architect to George III.* (Exhibition, Courtauld Gallery.) 1997

King, D. *The Complete Works of Robert & James Adam.* 1991

Lees-Milne, J. *The Age of Adam.* 1947

Mark Millard Architectural Collection of British Books. 1998 [including 'Works of Robert and James Adam' and 'The Society of the Dilettanti']

McCormick, T. *Charles-Louis Clérisseau & the Genesis of Neo-Classicism.* 1990

Pendrill, C. *The Adelphi.* 1934

Redford, B. *Dilettanti. The Antic and the Antique in 18th Century England.* 2008

Rowan, A. *Robert Adam: Catalogue of Architectural Drawings in the Victoria & Albert Museum.* 1988

Rowan, A. *Vaulting Ambition, The Adam Brothers: Contractors to the Metropolis in the Reign of George III.* 2008

Rykwert, J. and A. *The Brothers Adam.* 1985

Survey of London, Vol 18: *St Martin in the Fields II: The Strand.* 1937

Tait, A.A. *The Adam Brothers in Rome.* 2008

Watkin, D. *George III, The Architect King.* 2004

Watkin, D. *James Athenian Stuart.* 1982

BIBLIOGRAPHY FOR THE TETRARCHY

PRIMARY SOURCES

Notitia Dignitatum: *A list of civil and military officers and their staffs together with a list of commanding officers and the names of the units in garrisons at various forts and military establishments*

Lactantius: *De mortibus persecutorum (On the Deaths of the Persecutors.)* Rhetor appointed by Diocletian to his court. Written after the defeat of Maxentius by Constantine from Christian viewpoint.

Eusebius: *Church History Book VIII*

Zosimus: *Historia Nova*

SECONDARY SOURCES

Barnes, T. *The New Empire of Diocletian and Constantine.* 1982

Cambridge Ancient History, 2nd edn, Vol XII: *The Crisis of Empire, AD 193–337.* 2005

Cameron, A. *Later Roman Empire, AD 284–430.* 1993

Cannadine, D. and Price, S. (eds) *Rituals of Royalty.* 1987

Claridge, Amanda. *Rome: Oxford Archaeological Guide.* 1998

Coarelli, Filippo. *Rome and the Environs: An Archaeological Guide.* 2007

Curran, John. *Pagan City and Christian Capital.* 2000

Davison, David, Gaffney, Vince and Marin, Emilio (eds) *Dalmatia: Research in the Roman Province (Papers in Honour of J. Wilkes).* 2006

Gibbon, Edward. *The Decline and Fall of the Roman Empire.* 1776–88.

Hartley, Elizabeth et al. (eds) *Catalogue of Constantine the Great, York's Roman Emperor.* 2006

Johnson, Stephen. *Late Roman Fortifications.* 1983

Haarhoff, T.J. (ed. Galletier, E.) *Schools of Gaul. A Study of Pagan and Christian Education in the Last Century of the Western Empire.* 1920; reprinted 1958

Kleiner, Diana. *Roman Sculpture.* 1992

Krautheimer, Richard. *Three Christian Capitals: Rome, Constantinople & Milan.* 1982

Leadbetter, B. *Galerius and the Will of Diocletian.* 2009

Lepelley, C. *Rome et l'intégration de l'Empire,* Vol 2. 1998

McKay A.G. *Houses, Villas and Palaces in the Roman World.* 1975

McNally, S. *Architectural Ornament of Diocletian's Palace in Split.* 1996

Marasović, T. *Diocletian's Palace.* 1995

O'Sullivan, A.F. *The Egnatian Way.* 1972

Parker, Philip. *The Empire Stops Here.* 2009

Rees, R. *Diocletian and the Tetrarchy.* 2004

Rees, R. *Latin Panegyrics.* 2002

Southern, P. and Dixon, K. *The Late Roman Army.* 1996

Srejović, Dragoslav. *Roman Imperial Towns and Palaces in Serbia.* 1993.

Taylor, R. *Roman Builders: A Study in Architectural Process.* 2003

Ward-Perkins, J.B. *Roman Imperial Architecture.* 1981

Whittaker, C.R. *Frontiers of the Roman Empire.* 1994

Williams, S. *Diocletian and the Roman Recovery.* 1985

Vickers, M. *The Octagon at Thessaloniki.* JRS 63, 1973

Wightman, E.M. *Roman Trier and the Treveri.* 1970

Wightman, E.M. *Roman Gaul.* 1973

Wightman, E.M. *Gallia Belgica.* 1985

Williams, H.P.G. *Carausius.* BAR British Series. 2004

Wilkes, J.J. *Les Provinces Danubiennes.* 1998

Wilkes, J.J. *The Illyrians.* 1992

Wilkes, J.J. *Dalmatia.* 1969

Wilkes, J.J. *Diocletian's Palace, Split.* 1993

Zivic, M. *Felix Romuliana* (guidebook)

INDEX

ΛLICIA SALTER M.A (Oxon) M.Phil. (Bath)
Alicia read history at St. Hilda's College,
Oxford. She graduated to Art History,
specialising in the history of Architecture –
her great love. For seventeen years, together
with two friends she ran her own small
business – Art Circle – concentrating on the
great wealth of art to be found in a city such as
London. Some years later, research into the
work of Sir Robert Taylor led to an interest
in Robert Adam and his archaeological
survey of Diocletian's palace in Split. She
has lectured extensively for NADFAS – The
National Society for the Decorative and Fine
Arts – and taken clients to all the major cities
of Western Europe, while working for Swan
Hellenic Cruises and Martin Randall Travel.
Lecture tours to major museums in the USA
and Australia were followed by exciting new
discoveries in Eastern Europe made accessible
by the fall of communism, among which were
Croatia and Serbia – the inspiration for this
book. She is married with three children.